CANADIAN PRIMAL

CANADIAN

PRIMAL

Poets, Places, and the
Music of Meaning

Mark Dickinson

McGill-Queen's University Press
Montreal & Kingston • London • Chicago

ISBN 978-0-2280-0534-6 (cloth)
ISBN 978-0-2280-0535-3 (paper)
ISBN 978-0-2280-0536-0 (ePDF)
ISBN 978-0-2280-0537-7 (ePUB)

Legal deposit first quarter 2021
Bibliothèque nationale du Québec

Printed in Canada on acid-free paper that is 100% ancient forest free
(100% post-consumer recycled), processed chlorine free

This book has been published with the help of a grant from the Canadian Federation
for the Humanities and Social Sciences, through the Awards to Scholarly Publications
Program, using funds provided by the Social Sciences and Humanities Research
Council of Canada. Funding was also received from the Symons Trust Fund for
Canadian Studies at Trent University.

We acknowledge the support of the Canada Council for the Arts.
Nous remercions le Conseil des arts du Canada de son soutien.

Library and Archives Canada Cataloguing in Publication

Title: Canadian primal : poets, places, and the music of meaning / Mark Dickinson.
Names: Dickinson, Mark, 1973– author.
Description: Includes bibliographical references and index.
Identifiers: Canadiana (print) 20200340336 | Canadiana (ebook) 20200340506
   | ISBN 9780228005346 (cloth) | ISBN 9780228005353 (paper) | ISBN
   9780228005360 (ePDF) | ISBN 9780228005377 (ePUB)
Subjects: CSH: Poets, Canadian (English)—20th century—Biography. | CSH:
   Canadian poetry (English)—20th century—History and criticism. | LCSH:
   Meaning (Philosophy) in literature. | LCGFT: Biographies.
Classification: LCC PS8081.D53 2021 | DDC C811/.5409—dc23

This book was typeset in 10.5/13 Sabon.

Amy, Fern, Clover, and Leelah

It was true. They lived in a world they could
not possibly comprehend. The belief that they *did*
understand was illusion, vanity.

Guy Gavriel Kay

No. There is no need to tear apart anything. The enigma
is hidden in plain sight. The depth of life shows itself at
the surface.

Andreas Weber

I think the land knows we are here,
I think the land knows we are strangers.

Al Purdy

Contents

Preface

Some years ago, a small press in Toronto published a tiny book that became one of the unsolved mysteries of English-language poetry in Canada. *Thinking and Singing: Poetry and the Practice of Philosophy* (2002) consisted of essays by five contemporary poets – Robert Bringhurst, Dennis Lee, Tim Lilburn, Don McKay, and Jan Zwicky – who were all decades into their life's work and had made foundational contributions to literature and culture in Canada. They were the recipients of numerous awards, prizes, and honours, including the Governor General's Literary Award, the Griffin Poetry Prize, and the Order of Canada. They were also all friends, their conversations and collaborative efforts dating back to the mid-1970s. It was not clear, though, what brought them together. There was no mention in the book of a manifesto, program, shared aesthetic stance, chief ideologue, or overarching theory. No one poet surrendered so much as a fraction of their autonomy to any of the others. Their essays touched on a diversity of topics and made recourse to a number of philosophical and spiritual traditions largely forgotten in the West, including shamanism, pre-Socratic Greek philosophy, Taoism, Buddhism, and Christian mysticism. "Each of these poets is a labyrinth," their colleague Stan Dragland noted.[1] If so, then *Thinking and Singing* was like five labyrinths stacked on top of one another, a multi-dimensional structure lacking guides or signposts that few readers or critics dared to enter. Sales were poor, reviews almost non-existent, and the book quietly sank out of sight. It all amounted to a noteworthy omission. Five top practitioners of their craft had come together to collaborate on some sort of super-project, and no one could say what they were doing. Or, perhaps more appropriately, what they were hearing.

This was not the first time in Canadian history a group of artist-thinkers had found common cause in a summons issuing from outside the modern mindset. A century earlier, the Group of Seven and outriding members like Tom Thomson and Emily Carr had returned to the site of encounter between non-Indigenous people and the land, looking to reset a relationship that after centuries had never graduated beyond colonialism, tourism, and a one-dimensional extraction of natural resources. "Every lake and mountain river has a living presence, different from all the others, demanding fresh perspective and an expression peculiar to itself," wrote Lawren Harris, the group's primary catalyst and benefactor.[2] A similar call was heard by a number of writers who came of age in the famous CanLit explosion of the 1960s and '70s. The literary wing of the back-to-the-land movement, if we can call it that, was made up of some of the most gifted creative thinkers of the day, including Margaret Atwood, Ken Belford, Matt Cohen, Wayland Drew, Graeme Gibson, D.G. Jones, Robert Kroetsch, Gwendolyn MacEwen, John Newlove, Al Purdy, and others. Wooed by something they could only dimly intuit, many of them bought farms, started homesteads, joined communes, and moved as far away as they could from towns, cities, and the patterns of thought that flourished in such places. They sensed that new tools – even a new grammar of thinking and speaking – was needed to respond to that which had been shut out of modern society. As Atwood writes in *Survival* (1972): "Part of the delight of reading Canadian poetry chronologically is watching the gradual emergence of a language appropriate to its objects."[3] By the mid-seventies, the back-to-the-land literary movement was something of a spent force. The publication of Marian Engel's novella *Bear* in 1976, with its erotic perspective on human to non-human relationships, suggested that the movement had crystallized around a wilderness ideology that identified meaning with a nature that was strictly "out there," beyond settler culture. As the cultural nationalism of the era gave way to neo-liberalism and free trade, a different set of concerns moved to the forefront of CanLit. Before long, it was something of an anachronism for non-Indigenous writers to speak of the land as a living being, or to suggest that lakes and mountain rivers were presences in their own right.

Yet this call and response between non-Indigenous people and the land continued to evolve and mature away from the Canadian cultural mainstream. Born between 1939 and 1955, the poets of *Thinking and*

Singing were adrift in their formative years, lacking the right resources and guiding traditions, aware that something was missing from their lives but unable to articulate exactly what. In early adulthood, they began discovering voices from the past that taught them the world was much larger and far more mysterious than anyone had suggested in school. By the time they came to creative maturity in their late twenties and early thirties – for none of them had an early lyric flowering – their work was already diverging from that of their peers in the back-to-the-land movement. Meaning is all around us, they said, but because of the way we live as moderns – "distracted, insecure, ill, battered by urban noise and electronic media," writes Zwicky – we are mostly unable to perceive it.[4] What poetry offered was a space *within* modernity where that meaning could be apprehended, and without ever necessarily having to get into a canoe. Beginning with *Civil Elegies* in 1972, their poems served as beacons of intelligence, allowing them to find their way to one another. Throughout the 1980s, they exchanged letters, sharpened their ideas, edited one another's books, dedicated poems to each other, and met in person whenever circumstances allowed. In at least two instances they completely reinvented the medium of print and re-imagined the act of reading to accommodate what they heard. In the 1990s, Lilburn sensed something important happening and organized *Poetry and Knowing*, the first of two anthologies that introduced them as a group. There were also a pair of large gatherings, at Trent University in 1994 and 1996, and a number of smaller workshops, symposia, and even a short-lived field school. Individual awards and accolades continued to pile up in the new millennium. When Lee's *Yesno* was nominated for a Governor General's Literary Award in 2007, it was their *fourteenth* nomination as a group. They continue to visit, correspond, and collaborate with one another to this day, as is evident in books like *Learning to Die: Wisdom in the Age of Climate Crisis* (2018), co-authored by Bringhurst and Zwicky.

Now between the ages of sixty-six and eighty-one, these poets are still, for the most part, unknown. Their core achievement as a group – the recovery of a mode of musical thinking open to ancestors, non-human beings, natural processes, and the genius of specific places – remains unacknowledged and unexplored. It is my conviction, though, that this mode of thinking is of relevance far beyond the field of Canadian literature, and may in fact constitute an achievement of global importance. They offer the rarest of gifts: a cure for the sense of rootlessness and the inability to perceive meaning in the world around us that drives so much of our predatory behaviour as a modern civilization. That they have re-imagined how human beings might dwell on earth – a feat with implications for everything from reconciliation with Indigenous peoples to how we think about the climate emergency – is a signal achievement that *at the very least* warrants further discussion. Yet new ways of being are exceedingly difficult to talk about, which is why I clothe the accomplishments of the *Thinking and Singing* poets with their life stories. I do so with one eye on Maurice Merleau-Ponty's dictum that while the life does not explain the work, "this work to be done called for a certain kind of life."[5]

The title of this book bends in at least two different ways. In *Technology and Empire* (1969), which Lee edited for House of Anansi, George Grant used the term "primal" to refer to those events that shape the soul of a civilization – modern Europe and its engagement with the wisdom of Athens and Jerusalem, or, in the context of English-speaking Canada, the encounter between settlers and "the alien and yet conquerable land."[6] He writes of the Canadian primal as a disaster on every conceivable level, and one that doomed the country to cultural homogeneity, political tyranny, and ecological collapse. While Grant saw no way around this epoch-making failure, I would suggest that the task is to understand the colonial mindset on a deep level so that we can learn from it, correct against it, and possibly even transmute it into its opposite. Hence Lee, who in one of many reversals characteristic of his work, recovers the primal and redefines it in personal and intimate terms. In the essays of *Body Music* (1998), he writes of the primal as an experience that changes the shape of someone's soul. Something in the world reaches out and touches us – a beautiful face, a work of art, a place, an atrocity – and in that moment we realize that we do not belong to ourselves alone. It is possible, in other words, to cultivate in ourselves an openness and an availability that Grant argued the country's first European settlers lacked. We might share our primals with one another, Lee goes on to suggest, and in so doing recover the ability to engage in many-sided conversations made up of a number of different perspectives. Out of these conversations we might arrive at a new consensus about reality, or what the speaker of Lee's *Civil Elegies* calls "the early years of a better civilization."[7] This is precisely what the poets of *Thinking and Singing* have been up to. Each chapter in *Canadian Primal* is organized around significant moments in their lives. While

the details and circumstances differ from poet to poet, the underlying story is essentially the same: encounters with a larger, richer
world followed by painstaking attempts to translate the meaning of
those encounters into words.

For my part, I place even more emphasis than Lee on the world's
ability to actively and purposefully intercede in our lives. Those
conversations and testimonials mentioned above must ultimately
circle around to the fact that we live in specific places that have been
around for far longer than we have, and possess far more agency and
personhood than we have been willing to acknowledge. Among my
influences in this regard is David Abram, whose book *The Spell of
the Sensuous* (1996) has occupied an important place in my thinking since I first read it twenty years ago. Abram's notion of "the
body's silent conversation with things" identifies phenomenology,
or the study of direct experience, as a fruitful angle of approach to
the work of the *Thinking and Singing* poets.[8] In *Plant Intelligence
and the Imaginal Realm* (2014), Stephen Harrod Buhner reminds
me that the ancient Athenians had their own word for primal experiences, and when he describes the impact of such experiences on
the trajectory of one's life he could be talking about the poets of this
book. Also in this book's intellectual family tree is Gregory Bateson
(1904–1980), one of the twentieth century's most original and
unclassifiable thinkers – in large part because he disputed the nature
of thought itself. Thinking was not the private possession of human
beings but a property of reality, he argued, and to remove ourselves
from mental reciprocity with our surroundings was to court disaster
as a species. "The major problems in the world are the result of the
difference between how nature works and the way people think,"
he wrote.[9] There is no better introduction to Bateson's ideas than
the film *An Ecology of Mind* (2010), directed by Nora Bateson. The
younger Bateson does more than maintain her father's legacy, but
actively expands its intellectual footprint. I wish I had known about
her concept of "warm data" at the outset of this project so that I
could have more clearly articulated why I felt I had to go and meet
these poets in person. I will happily settle for the term she coins in
Small Arcs of Larger Circles (2016) that aptly describes what they
are doing as a group: "learning together" to form a *symmathesy*.[10]
And speaking of learning communities, this book is very much the
product of a particular time and place. Among the elders in the territory in which I am guest is Gidigaa Migizi or Doug Williams, fierce

critic of colonial Canada, former Chief of Curve Lake First Nation, co-director of the Indigenous Studies PhD program at Trent, and, according to his student Leanne Betasamosake Simpson, "one of the most important Michi Saagiig Nishnaabeg intellectuals my nation has."[11] It was my good fortune to spend time with Doug inside and outside the classroom, and to glimpse the beauty, genius, and incredible generosity of the Nishnaabeg intelligence system as it expressed itself through one man. I elaborate – discretely – on some of the ways in which Doug and other Indigenous cultural authorities influenced this project in this book's coda.

It needs to be said that the biographical model I use across the five chapters of this book does not allow for on-the-fly critical disputations of their work. Interrupting a life narrative to critique the artistic and intellectual products of that life strikes me as ungenerous, especially in the context of the eighteen years of edifying conversation and correspondence with these poets that went into the writing of this book. My overall intention with this book is to complement their work, not replace it, and in a way that I hope is analogous to the remarks a poet might make about a poem before reading it in public. "Let's go," McKay urges us. "For we shall be changed."[12]

CANADIAN PRIMAL

Dennis Lee

Polyphonic Soul

The Archer, Nathan Phillips Square, Toronto, Ontario.
Courtesy of Christopher Malcolm.

For almost two decades beginning in 1967, Dennis Lee was the best known of the poets featured in this book. He helped launch Rochdale College, co-founded House of Anansi Press, edited some of the biggest names in CanLit, won a Governor General's Literary Award for his long poem *Civil Elegies* (1972), and wrote the children's classic *Alligator Pie* (1974) – all before his thirty-fifth birthday. More books followed. So did a Festschrift at mid-career and a high-profile collaboration with master Muppeteer Jim Henson that resulted in the films *The Dark Crystal* (1982) and *Labyrinth* (1986), and the television series *Fraggle Rock* (1983–87).

Then Lee vanished. In the mid-1980s, he resigned from an important position at McClelland & Stewart, stepped back from children's poetry, and walked away from a number of other commitments. There were rumours of a spiritual quest that involved the paleolithic cave complexes of Europe, Christian mysticism, and a Quaker community in Costa Rica. By the time new work began appearing in the early 1990s, Lee had morphed into "friendly old Uncle Dennis," as his colleague Margaret Atwood calls him – an elder deserving of respect yet one whose relevance had passed.[1] Echoing his retreat into private life, not a single scholar wrote anything about him for a period of seventeen years ending in 2001, a remarkable omission given his contributions to Canadian literature and culture. A definitive biography has yet to be written. Was there really nothing left to say about one of the hardest-working, many-sided, and influential artist-thinkers Canada had ever produced? Or had Lee gone someplace beyond the categories of critical discourse?

Lee has always been drawn to wordlessness. As a young child, he began experiencing spell-states and reveries that felt both strange and completely normal, so much so that he did not talk about them until they came up in our conversations when he was nearly seventy. Those "brown-study fugue states," as he called them, anticipate some of his later fascinations, discoveries, and innovations. These include the descriptions of Einsteinian space-time and the accounts of mystics that captivated him as an undergraduate, the creative source he calls "cadence" that he located in his twenties, and the ruminations on literary polyphony and cosmology he made in his forties.

As much as the spell-state qualifies as one of Lee's primals, it is the *collision* between those states and a modern mindset predisposed to reject them as fanciful or pathological that lies at the core of his work. This conflict is embodied in his poetry in a profound disconnect between content and form. *What* the speakers of his poems are saying and *how* they are saying it diverge dramatically. This complicates any strictly thematic reading of his work. *Civil Elegies*, which takes as its subject matter the spiritual death of modern Canada, is carried along by powerful surges of rhythmic energy as to suggest it is both lament and birth pang. *The Death of Harold Ladoo* (1976) advocates for a cautious and distanced relationship to gods and spirit beings while enacting on the page its own kind of creative mediumship. The poems of *Testament* (2012), which look unflinchingly into cultural and ecological collapse, are tiny eruptions of aliveness. We may find ourselves trapped in the structures of a dying civilization, the split-level nature of Lee's work suggests, yet the energies that could renew us are as close as the white space of the page, waiting for someone brave enough to let them in.

Dennis Lee's ancestors came from Northern Ireland and England. Both of his grandfathers were Methodist ministers who relocated their families every few years from one "charge" or group of three or four churches to the next across southern Ontario. This way of life, Lee gathered from the stories he heard from his parents, Louise and Walter, was "very sturdy, very hardworking, very narrow."[2] Louise's household was especially strict. Card games, like Fish and Rummy, were forbidden on Sundays, and her mother always addressed her husband formally, as "Mr Garbutt," whenever anyone else was around, including her own children. Lee's parents left that world behind to attend university in the 1920s and met in Lindsay, Ontario, during the Depression, where they both worked at the collegiate (he taught commercial subjects, like accounting, typing, and business law, while she taught French and German). After they were married, Walter accepted a position at Runnymede Collegiate Institute in Toronto. They scraped together enough money to buy a house on a new street in Etobicoke, west of the city, and decided to start a family. Dennis Beynon Lee, the second of four children, was born on 31 August 1939, the day before Hitler invaded Poland.

Lee stumbled into the first of his primals before the age of five. One wintry afternoon, Walter and Louise happened to glance out the front window when they saw something strange: their son, in his snowsuit, standing stock-still, leaning forward with one arm over his head, staring off into space: "Apparently I'd gotten part way through some gesture of movement, and gone into a brown-study fugue state in mid-move. And there I stood, for half a minute or a minute or three minutes or whatever it was, frozen in time, occupied with whatever wordless process was going on. My parents were both looking at me idly, and then their looks got more concentrated, and eventually they turned to each other and just looked at one another, as if to ask 'What on earth have we got on our hands here?' Then they turned back, and the moment outside un-froze, and whatever gesture I'd been engaged in completed itself, and on I went."[3] Lee, it seemed, had "been caught out / having an inner life," to borrow from Don McKay, and from that point on, his parents suspected he was different.[4] In conversation, Lee was at a considerable loss to describe where his younger self went and what he experienced while away. These brown-study fugue states were hard to talk about, he said, because they didn't have words or images associated with them. In fact, he didn't remember anything about them other than they felt as natural as breathing and imparted a vague sense of welcome and affirmation. He went on to say that he has continued to have brown-study fugue states on a near-daily basis all his life, and directed me toward some of the poems for children that refer to them. Here is "The Secret Place":

There's a place I go, inside myself,
    Where nobody else can be,
And none of my friends can tell it's there –
    Nobody knows but me.

It's hard to explain the way it feels,
    Or even where I go,
It isn't a place in time or space,
    But once I'm there, I *know*.

It's tiny, it's shiny, it can't be seen,
    But it's as big as the sky at night...
I try to explain and it hurts my brain,
    But once I'm there, it's *right*.

There's a place I know inside myself,
    And it's neither big nor small,
And whenever I go, it feels as though
    I never left at all.[5]

While Lee dreamed, suburbia was taking shape around him. Local contractors were putting up new houses in twos and threes, eating into the fields and vacant lots, presaging the larger post-war developments to come. He remembers there being no trees of mature size on newly created Dunedin Drive, no local idiosyncrasies or landmarks, "no sense of roots going back through the generations."[6] The United Church the family attended, bleached of the narrow intensity of Methodism, was as bland and formless as the suburban landscape around him. "Several ministers seemed embarrassed to introduce the word 'God' in anything but a generic way," he said.[7] The closest thing to a sacred site in the suburbs was the shopping mall – he could ride his bicycle in any direction and reach one. If this was the wondrous new way of life trumpeted over the airwaves and in the advertisements in American magazines that washed up at home, why did he feel so suffocated by it?

Lee found breathing room in two seemingly antithetical locales. The first was a house on Sparrow Lake in the Muskoka region north of Toronto. His father had inherited the place from a bachelor uncle in 1943, and the family began spending summers there after that time. There were bats in the second storey, no indoor plumbing, and an outhouse so far away the children called it "Kapus" (short for "Kapuskasing"). It was, in short, glorious. "We explored, learned to swim, and performed incredible feats of derring-do in our imaginations," Lee said.[8] The second of his lifesavers was downtown Toronto. As soon as he was old enough, he would take the bus to Jane Street, get on the Bloor streetcar, ride down to Bay or Bloor Street, then get out and walk around to get a hit of the city's wild energies. Sidewalks! Restaurants! Movie theatres! Some kind of shared public space! "It was pretty pokey and provincial," he said, "but compared to Etobicoke, it was Manhattan."[9]

As he got older, Lee was increasingly unable to reconcile his brown-study fugue states with other parts of his life. A powerful pattern began to assert itself. Time spent in some kind of trance state would give way to hyperactive, whirling-dervish activity, as if he was overcompensating for how he thought he was supposed to live a normal life but without any sense of appropriate scale. Around the age of ten, he became a "mad devotee" of magic, practising sleight-of-hand tricks, collecting programs from old magic conventions, getting to know the handful of professional magicians in Toronto, and putting on shows at school.[10] When he was accepted on scholarship at

University of Toronto Schools (UTS), a high school for gifted students
at the corner of Bloor and Spadina, he threw himself into his studies
with similar abandon and was told by one teacher that he had a
bright future in mathematics. Then it was the ministry in the United
Church. He carried with him everywhere a copy of *The Practice of
the Presence of God*, a booklet by Brother Lawrence (1611–1691),
and felt compelled to give free and unsolicited spiritual instruction
to his friends ("I was a menace," he said ruefully, "running around
telling other people how I thought they should live").[11] He became
a dancing fiend when he discovered rhythm and blues, submerg-
ing himself in the clandestine world of black music on the eve of
the rock 'n' roll explosion. At sixteen, he worked the first of three
summers with Frontier College, driving railroad spikes by day and
organizing impromptu English lessons in the evenings (according to
his gruff foreman, Lee "worked too hard").[12] In his last year at UTS,
he not only made the senior football team but also earned a reputation for fearlessness for the way he routinely launched himself at
the kicker's foot. "I may be small, but at least I'm slow," he liked
to mock-boast.[13] He finished grade 13 with an exclamation point,
winning the Prince of Wales Scholarship for the highest marks in the
province and serving as class valedictorian.

   In the fall of 1957, and after briefly considering a career in psy-
chiatry, Lee enrolled in the English Literature program at Victoria
College (Vic), part of the University of Toronto. Affiliated with
the United Church, Vic was the place where children of devout
Protestant families could be gently introduced to Darwin, Freud, and
at least a rumour of Marx, and still retain the Church's emphasis on
reverence and social justice. "It was, in its own way, a very appeal-
ing accommodation to the realities of modernity," Lee said.[14] He
went on something of an intellectual shopping spree in his first two
years there. Along with his coursework, he read his way through a
number of existentialist writers, including Albert Camus, Jean-Paul
Sartre, and Colin Wilson, but felt more at home with *The Courage
to Be* (1952) by Paul Tillich, who stressed the importance of spiritual
courage in the face of the anxiety and apparent meaninglessness of
the modern age. He encountered the work of Martin Heidegger for the
first time in William Barrett's *Irrational Man* (1958), the start of an
on-again, off-again intellectual engagement that would last nearly
twenty years. He sponged up books about science – "not the fully
technical stuff, but expositions for the intelligent layman" – and took

a particular interest in the revolution in physics that started with James Clerk Maxwell and completed itself in Albert Einstein.[15] Lee said descriptions of Einsteinian space-time or of a space constantly being reconfigured by the action of moving bodies over time "was instantaneously home-turf when I encountered it."[16] He made an equally important discovery when he came across the writings of the mystic and theologian Meister Eckhart (1260–1328) while browsing the shelves of the Student Christian Movement Book Room. Eckhart was unlike any Christian thinker he'd previously encountered – deep, ballsy, funny. Down-to-earth and in love with exuberant paradox and extreme statements, Eckhart filled Lee with a sense of "zingy exhilaration."[17] A representative example from Eckhart's oeuvre: "If a man thinks he will get more of God by meditation, by devotion, by ecstasies or by special infusions of grace than by the fireside or in the stable – that is nothing but taking God, wrapping a cloak round His head, and shoving Him under a bench."[18]

By the spring of 1959, Lee was beginning to burn out from academic overachievement. He took the 1959–60 academic year off and moved to England for six months, where he chanced upon the Religious Society of Friends, or Quakers, and attended several meetings in London and Cambridge. The "unprogrammed" branch of Quakerism did not make use of liturgy, dogma, or priests; worship was carried out as a group activity and in total silence, unless a member was compelled to speak. In the wake of this sustained encounter with Quakerism, Lee began to let go of the formal Christian mindset he'd inherited during his coming of age. "I realized I no longer believed in or even took seriously the various doctrines and creeds that had been taken as *the* crucial tests of religious purity during the last two thousand years in the West," he said.[19] It all started to seem like a charade, and even a blasphemy: Mary in Heaven, the sprinkling of holy water, persecution on religious grounds, and especially the conceit that human beings could arrive at rational formulations of ultimate truth. "Basing religious authenticity on our supposed ability to give a rational definition of what's true and what's not true seemed like a fundamental part of the problem," he said. "I began to say 'Oh, bugger off' to the whole shooting match."[20]

When Lee returned to Canada and resumed his studies in the fall of 1960, the call he'd felt to join the United Church ministry had receded. It was replaced by a renewed commitment to writing. Vic had, after all, been a proving ground for a surprising number of poets, including Marjorie Pickthall, E.J. Pratt, Margaret Avison, Don Coles, George Johnston, Richard Outram, Francis Sparshott, and others. One of his professors, Jay Macpherson, won a Governor General's Literary Award for *The Boatman* the year Lee arrived; Macpherson's book was dedicated to the college's academic star, Northrop Frye, whose *Anatomy of Criticism* (1957) had lifted him into the ranks of internationally recognized scholars. Lee and another student in his tiny cohort, Peggy Atwood, had from the start of their time at Vic collaborated on goofy poems for the college's literary journal, *Acta Victoriana*, under the pseudonym "Shakesbeat Latweed." New work from Lee published in *Acta Victoriana* included a short story and a smattering of poems on subjects as diverse as the *Titanic*, the cycle of the seasons, and the Crucifixion and Resurrection. He wrote the book and lyrics for a musical, *Mushroom Malady*, which borrowed heavily from Shakespeare's *As You Like It* and was mounted at Hart House as Vic's annual Bob Revue in 1961. He started a novel, *The Refugees*, that drew on his experiences working in two post-war refugee camps in Austria and Germany after he left England, but abandoned the project forty pages in when he realized that all his characters sounded the same. He showed more promise as a critic, writing a couple of essays that caught the eye of Northrop Frye by using the methods set out in his *Anatomy of Criticism*. Lee received very high marks for his work, which applied Frye's study of the structure of story to *As You Like It*; he even found a small wrinkle in how the second triad of summer plots overlapped with the first triad of autumn ones. Yet he wasn't sure what this kind of analysis amounted to in the end, and sensed a serious disconnect in its approach. Frye's work, he said, "was a magnificent and dread example of how *not* to use the mind."[21]

While his coursework introduced him to a disparate group of modernist poets, including W.B. Yeats, Rainer Maria Rilke, Ezra Pound, and T.S. Eliot, the two most important exemplars Lee encountered were not of his century. He was riveted by Richmond Lattimore's translation of the Ancient Greek poet Pindar (518–446 BCE), and even more so by Friedrich Hölderlin (1770–1843), whom he read in the original German. Both embraced the "poet-seer," a figure that fascinated him, "much as I hate that kind of lingo."[22] Pindar sang the praises of successful athletes and their wealthy patrons to gods thought to be listening in on human affairs. Hölderlin, spiritually landlocked by the Enlightenment and its account of a universe devoid of intrinsic meaning, sensed that he was surrounded by invisible entities who could still intrude upon the unguarded consciousness with incredible power, even if he couldn't comprehend what they were. "Celebrate – yes, but what?" he wrote.[23] Both poets took wild, almost-haphazard leaps in content that Lee found wrenching and exciting – as though they were struggling to keep up with something too large and too fast for them. "From my twenties on," he writes, "Hölderlin and Pindar were my rhythmic *Lear*."[24]

After graduating from Vic with the Governor General's Gold Medal in English in the spring of 1962, Lee moved back to London, England, with his new wife, fellow Vic graduate Donna Youngblut. There he began writing a complicated and ambitious sequence of sonnets and sonnet variations – not so much a collection of poems as what Robert Bringhurst describes as an "architectural entity" – called *Kingdom of Absence*.[25] The subject of his book was the meaninglessness of modern life and the fracturing of selfhood that occurs as a result of that condition. Lee had long been struck by his own multi-faceted nature – perhaps since the emergence of the discord between the brown-study fugue state and the rest of his life – and considered that multiplicity proof of his own inauthenticity. He was busy with *Kingdom* when he received an offer from Ken Maclean, head of the English department at Vic, to return to the college as a lecturer. The generosity of Maclean's offer reflected Lee's good standing in the department: any other student looking to pursue graduate studies, as he was thinking of doing, would have normally been offered nothing more than a teaching assistantship. When the couple moved back to Canada in the summer of 1963, Youngblut was pregnant with their first daughter; a second daughter would arrive two years later.

Lee took up his teaching duties in the fall of 1963 and started a dizzyingly ambitious master's degree project that grew out of the intellectual shopping spree of his late teens and early twenties. He'd been struck by the separate yet possibly parallel revolutions that took place in the arts and sciences in the early decades of the twentieth century: a fundamentally different set of intuitions about reality and how it cohered were emerging in fields as diverse as music, painting, fiction, poetry, and physics. Did these modernist upheavals suggest the first stirrings of a new cosmology or sense of meaningful order?

Lee proposed to pursue this question by comparing the revolution in physics from Newton to Einstein with the new "model" or "paradigm" of coherence in *The Cantos* by Ezra Pound. He soon realized he had bitten off more than he could chew and decided to focus on *The Cantos*. At first glance, Pound's mega-poem looked like "a rubble-heap of glittering fragments" that ranged from a line or two to several pages in length.[26] These fragments covered a bewilderingly diverse set of topics, with no clues given to the reader as to why any two or more fragments were placed side by side. "*The Cantos* is written with apparently no order," Lee writes, "not because Pound couldn't help himself, but because things happen in history with no apparent order, and because they impinge that way on the mind."[27] Pound's "rubble-heap" was, in fact, highly ordered. The fragments he had set down on the page *rhymed* with one another. They constituted a kind of music of thinking. The reader's task was to learn how to listen to that music, discerning how different fragments sang to each other even when separated by vast leaps in history and geography. The entire underlying strategy of *The Cantos* can be gleaned from an earlier two-line poem Pound had published in 1913, "In a Station of the Metro." He wrote: "The apparition of these faces in the crowd; / Petals on a wet, black bough."[28] The poem, set in a Paris subway station, consists of two images devoid of any interpretative comment – faces in an indiscriminate crowd; petals from a flowering tree, standing out against a dark, rain-soaked branch. By putting these images side by side, Pound invites the reader to recognize how they fit together. Both faces and petals stand out as precious and perishable against the visual noise of their respective backgrounds. There is also difference within the rhyme in the way the urban setting contrasts with the natural one, suggesting that the poem's speaker is being gently realigned. "In the midst of a clogged urban setting, he's transported to a visual parallel in a natural green one, where perhaps his heart is more at home," Lee said.[29] In his master's thesis, defended in May 1965, he christens this strategy "ekstatic form," emphasizing its self-certifying dimension. The reader has to experience for himself how the jumble of seemingly unrelated particulars fits together. "This enacts a way of reading, of parsing the world: by manoeuvring your way through it, with your own alert nerve-ends as your guide," he wrote. "You spot similarities; you register differences. You're not relying on large, generic versions of 'order' from the dim and distant past; you're finding your own way."[30] The landscapes of our lives can be scanned like a poem, allowing us to occasionally apprehend the existence of a deeper set of patterns below the level of conscious awareness that usually go undetected.

Meanwhile, Lee's home city was changing around him, furnishing him with both the setting and theme for the poem that would mark his breakthrough as a poet. In September 1965, New City Hall and its accompanying urban park, Nathan Phillips Square, were officially opened to the public after years of planning and construction. Lee had followed the process closely, riding his bicycle down to Queen Street to watch Viljo Revell's futuristic towers and spaceship-like council chambers take shape inside a beehive of scaffolding. In a city blighted by runaway development, it seemed almost wondrous that a space was being pried open where people might celebrate the simple fact of "communal being," as he would later write.[31] "The beautifully pro-portioned towers, and the amplitude of the square, were a physical token or promise that we could (maybe) create a noble human com-munity here."[32] Hogtown was finally doing something right.

Lee was clearly beginning to grow beyond the academy. He stayed on as a lecturer at Vic for another two years after defending his master's thesis, and was now regarded as one of the English depart-ment's most promising young faculty members. He burnished his credentials by co-editing, with Roberta Charlesworth, *An Anthology of Verse* (1965) for Oxford University Press. The natural course was to enrol in doctoral studies and continue the "let-us-compare-cos-mologies" project he'd imagined as his life's work, building on parallels between Pound and Einstein.[33] Yet he didn't have enough math to follow Einstein's theory of general relativity and wasn't sure he wanted to backtrack to acquire it. He also couldn't help but notice the deep disconnect between the revolutionary cosmologies he was drawn to and the procedures for analyzing those cosmol-ogies on offer in the academy, which were themselves products of an older, value-free approach that stranded the thinker outside the world of relationships they enacted. Lee no longer wanted to analyze cosmology at a safe distance but to experience it from the inside: "I wanted to directly re-enact the torrent, and kafuffle, and down-time of meaning," he said.[34] He was making no headway in his own apprentice work, *Kingdom of Absence*, which remained trapped in a pre-modernist rhythmic universe:

The trumpets of the randy Renaissance
came blowing wind and integers, blew news
high to the good old concert of the spheres:
linear mind is the measure of all things.

Newton played his scrawny masterpiece
upon that single string. René Descartes
heard one vibration twanging through his brain,
intoxicating monotone, until

he cried that only measurement is real
and the measuring mind; and with that declaration
shrunk the universe to three dimensions,
drubbed it down to fit the bed of the mind.

Crumpled through the slot of single vision
van Gogh bleeds his sanity away.[35]

Lee's difficulties with *Kingdom of Absence*, which dragged on for
seven years, can be attributed to the peculiar predicament in which
he found himself. At the level of content, the sequence concerns itself
with a spiritual and societal constriction pressing in on the speaker
from all sides, asphyxiating him. At the level of form, Lee found
himself within a pre-set sonnet structure that was equally suffocating, even though he'd already found a different set of exemplars in
Pindar, Hölderlin, and Pound. What resulted was a kind of double
gridlock in which his movements were inhibited on two planes of
meaning at once.

Yet his ear for classical prosody served Lee well on other fronts
and, in one of the great ironies of his career, allowed him to write
his most famous poem. One day in the spring of 1966, in between
teaching classes at Vic, he got on his bicycle and headed for the corner
store to buy a quart of milk. As the pedals went around the crank,
he began to hear a loopy chant that revolved around the words "alligator pie." Other verses about "alligator stew" and "alligator soup"
quickly followed. Lee couldn't get this strange earworm out of his
head, so he turned around, went home, and scribbled down everything before resuming his errand. "And that was the end of that,
or so I thought at the time," he writes.[36] He was, of course, wrong.
His daughters loved it, and so did their friends, and with its inclusion in the mimeographed and undated version of *Wiggle to the
Laundromat*, published in either 1967 or '68, "Alligator Pie" was on
its way to becoming the most beloved and universally read poem of
all the poets in this book. While this wacky wordplay came easily
enough to him, especially in comparison to his poems for adults, Lee

worried that accumulating a number of nonsensical verses composed in "ye olde poetical forms" would disqualify him from being taken seriously as an adult poet and consign him to "career perdition."[37]

In December 1966, Lee made the bold move of resigning from Vic so that he could concentrate on writing. He had become convinced that the longer he remained an academic, the more his analytic powers would thrive at the expense of his poetic growth, preventing him from breaking through the gridlock he was experiencing with *Kingdom of Absence*. The whirling dervish in Lee, however, would not be so easily appeased, and his resolution to dedicate himself to poetry gave way to a paroxysm of conflicting commitments. These cut deeply into his writing time and snared him in a "spaghetti tangle" of overwork that makes a chronological account difficult.[38]

Lee was still completing his final year of teaching at Vic when he accepted an offer to join Rochdale College, a unique experiment in self-directed education emerging out of the University of Toronto student ghetto. The arrival of the post-war generation had strained the resources of the traditional university to the breaking point: lecture halls overflowing with hundreds of students, seminars tripling or quadrupling in enrolment, and a corresponding shortage of rooms in university residences. As a major player in the "student housing" movement, Campus Co-operative Residence Inc. (Campus Co-op) bought up old homes around the U of T campus and made plans for a new high-rise student residence at the corner of Bloor and Huron. They also added an educational component in the form of Rochdale College, which, in keeping with the '60s dissatisfaction with big institutions, involved a complete, top-to-bottom reconsideration of what might comprise a university education. Rochdale's founders believed that all structures associated with the university, including courses, professors, degrees, and the institutional hierarchy, had to be swept away in order to secure a new start. Students could study whatever they wanted and rediscover what education was supposed to be all about: graduating into a more sophisticated sense of how the world cohered. Lee's role, as one of the college's two "resource persons," was to organize seminars around whatever students felt compelled to study. When the college opened in the fall of 1967, operating out of those old houses Campus Co-op had bought in the U of T student ghetto, his first task was to organize a seminar on phenomenology. There he encountered for a second time the philosophy of Martin Heidegger, which, he said, "stopped me dead in my tracks."[39]

Lee's next institution-building effort also came about by complete surprise. He had published a handful of his sonnet variations in *Canadian Forum* in the spring of 1966, which had caught the ear of Dave Godfrey, a fellow Frontier College alumnus, Trinity College lecturer, and rising literary star (his novel *The New Ancestors* would go on to win a Governor General's Literary Award in 1970). Godfrey had just returned to Canada after two years teaching in Ghana, wanted to try his hand at publishing (he'd later jump to computer programming and winemaking), and thought *Kingdom of Absence* would make an ideal first vehicle.

When the two met for beer in the spring of 1967, Lee and Godfrey quickly realized how aligned their politics were. Lee had experienced something of an awakening at a teach-in about the Vietnam War at Varsity Arena a couple of years earlier. There he'd learned the extent to which the American media had been lying about the war, and how the Canadian media had parroted those lies. He began to suspect that his own patterns of thinking and feeling "seemed to have come north from the States unexamined."[40] It was an extraordinary realization: he was behind enemy lines inside his own head.[41] Godfrey, for his part, had long been bothered by the absence of all things Canadian from the university curriculum. As an undergraduate at Trinity, he had asked a faculty member how long it would take to establish a Canadian Literature program at U of T and had been told ten years – "if the right people die."[42] A decade later, they hadn't yet. Walking into the University of Toronto Book Room, this time as a faculty member, he couldn't help but notice that almost all the books on the shelves were by British and American authors. Lee and Godfrey felt that a country should reflect back to its citizens the central dilemmas and concerns of their lives instead of duping them into thinking that a meaningful existence always took place somewhere else. Over the next few weeks, they shot back and forth "a series of increasingly nutty names" for their publishing house, and eventually settled on "House of Ananse" after the Ashanti spider god and owner of stories (their spelling mistake was corrected six months later).[43] Three hundred copies of *Kingdom of Absence* were printed in the spring of 1967.

Seeing *Kingdom* in print was for Lee a major catalyst. "I was no longer hog-tied to an impossible project," he said.[44] One night that summer, he decided to experiment with automatic writing. This technique, which had been practiced by a number of authors, including W.B. Yeats, André Breton, and William S. Burroughs, involved deliberately marginalizing the conscious mind so that a peculiar, trance-like creative state could manifest completely. The writer simply put pen to paper and, as Lee put it, "let it take off like a bat out of hell."[45] This deceptively simple move aligned his writing with the brown-study fugue state he'd known all his life, and the results were dramatic. Words started whizzing through him, carried by rhythms that pushed his writing in unexpected ways. "A sentence might start in one direction, but soon it would swerve to include another urgent something, and then another," he writes. "There was a 'say-everything-at-once' quality to the pulsing energy, and at times it stretched conventional syntax almost to the breaking point."[46] Lee, it seemed, had discovered *flow*. Ideas and concerns he'd been nursing for years were washed along in the current, each giving rise to the next in a single continuous gesture. For the first time in his life, he actually felt something for what he wrote – not sentimentally but viscerally, especially in his forearms – and likened it to a kind of creative possession. "I remember sitting up each night in a kind of dictation high – both cowed and exhilarated by the rhythms that had taken me over."[47] In the following passage, one of the first to emerge from this writerly version of the brown-study fugue state, the speaker is sitting on a bench off to one side of Nathan Phillips Square, the large concrete expanse attached to New City Hall in downtown Toronto. The sights and sounds of children at play prompt him to think about the mess of a civilization they are inheriting, which in turn leads to a rush of other thoughts. Note how the passage ultimately circles back to its own starting point, closing this micro-movement of musical intelligence:

It would be better maybe if we could stop loving the children
and their delicate brawls, pelting across the square in tandem,
   deking
from cover to cover in raucous celebration and they are never
winded, bemusing us with the rites of our own
gone childhood; if only they stopped
mattering, the children, it might be possible, now
while the square lies stunned by noon.
What is real is fitful, and always the beautiful footholds
crumble the moment I set my mind aside, though the world
   does recur.

Better, I think, to avoid the scandal of being – the headlong
    particulars
which, as they lose their animal purchase
cease to endorse us, though the ignominious hankerings
go on; this induces the ache of things, and the lonesome ego
sets out once again dragging its lethal desires across the world,
which does not regard them. Perhaps we should
bless what doesn't attach us, though I do not know
where we are to find nourishment.
    So, in the square, it is a
blessed humdrum: the kids climb over the Archer, and
the pool reflects the sky, and the people passing by,
who doze, and gently from above the visible pollutants descend,
coating the towers' sheath. Sometimes it
works but once in summer looking up I saw the noxious cloud
    suspended
taut above the city, clenched, as now everywhere it is the
imperial way of life that bestows its fallout. And it did not stay
inert, but across the fabled horizon of Bay Street they came
    riding,
the liberators, the deputies of Jesus, the marines, and had
    released
bacterial missiles over the Golden Horseshoe for love of all
    mankind,
and I saw my people streaming after calling welcome for the
    small change,
and I ran in my mind crying humiliation upon the country, as
    now I do also for it is
hard to stay at the centre when you're losing it one more time,
    though the pool
reflects the placid sky, and the people passing by, and daily
our acquiescence presses down on us from above and we have
    no room to be.
It is the children's fault as they swarm for we cannot stop
    caring.[48]

The transformation from *Kingdom of Absence* to *Civil Elegies*, as Lee
called this new work, is unmistakable. The sonnet structure has been
obliterated. The recurring image of children at play, chunks of philosophical abstraction, and snatches of rhyme all flash by with no time

to process them. The passage's vivaciousness collides head-on with its subject matter, which, as the title suggests, concerns the spiritual collapse of modern Canada. Gridlock at the level of content is countered by the live organic flow of the writing. Each pushes against the other, creating a volatile dynamic in which the poem is constantly in conflict with itself. This dramatic discontinuity between content and form was to become the energetic signature of all Lee's meditative poetry to come. It echoes a deeper split in the colonial condition in North America: while our bodies have grown up here, our minds are so often nurtured by ideas from somewhere else.

In *Civil Elegies*, this deep fracture at the core of who he is drives the speaker to a degree of self-scrutiny he might have otherwise wished to avoid. Triggering his ruthless self-examination is the appearance in the opening lines of the poem of the country's first European settlers, homeless spirits who demand of the living "whether Canada will be."[49] Can we rise above the colonial worldview and learn how to truly inhabit the land? This is the difficult, epoch-defining challenge the settler ancestors put to the speaker. Memorable moments on his journey include an imaginative encounter with Tom Thomson, forerunner to the Group of Seven, whose connection to the non-human world is initially celebrated and ultimately dismissed as antiquated: "Thomson is / done and we cannot / malinger among the bygone acts of grace."[50] Later, the speaker wonders if home might be found through some sort of reconciliation with the emptiness at the centre of the modern Canadian condition, a notion that points directly to Martin Heidegger. In the poem's final lines, alienation and anger give way to a sense of renewed optimism, even if the source of that optimism is unclear: "Now lately I have thought I also could begin my life."[51] Lee, it seemed, had roughed out some of the pieces of a good poem, perhaps even a groundbreaking one, but the ancestors' challenge had not yet been fully answered.

Shortly after House of Anansi published *Civil Elegies* in April 1968, Lee drove to Dundas, Ontario, to meet with George Grant (1918–1988), chair of the Department of Religion at McMaster University, outspoken public intellectual, and the person who would. help him understand why it was so hard to move beyond a colonial apprehension of reality. Lee first came across Grant at the teach-in about the Vietnam War held at Varsity Arena in October 1965. He had read Grant's essays with growing interest, including "Canadian Fate and Imperialism," published in *Canadian Dimension* in the

spring of 1967, and wanted to talk with him about putting together
a book of his writings for Anansi. What Grant had to offer, Lee
wrote him in a letter shortly after their first meeting, would be "of
great service to people who are only beginning to think their way
into a critique of North American society at a deep level."[52]

Grant owed that depth of perspective to a series of formative events
that took place during the Second World War. As an air raid warden in
the south of London, he had witnessed the technological savagery of the
Blitz first-hand, including the incineration of a neighbourhood shelter
under his care. He left the city some months later, physically ill and
spiritually broken, and found work on a farm in the Buckinghamshire
countryside. Early one morning, while walking his bicycle through a
gate, he apprehended what he described in a letter to his mother as
"a different plane of existence" and "mysterious forces within man
that are beyond man's understanding."[53] This intimation of a realm
beyond time and space – a realm that was ineluctably *good* – healed
him and accounts for the optimism of his early writings. Perhaps the
wisdom traditions of ancient peoples, organized as they were around
such primal experiences, could provide direction to a civilization that
had clearly lost its way. "There is an order in the universe," he wrote
in his first book, *Philosophy in the Mass Age* (1959), "that human
reason can discover and according to which the human will must act
so that it can attune itself to the universal harmony."[54]

By the mid-1960s, though, Grant's optimism had curdled. In
Lament for a Nation (1965), the book for which he is best known,
Grant argued that the defeat of the Diefenbaker Conservatives
in the 1963 federal election, and the decision taken by the subsequent Liberal government to allow American nuclear weapons on
Canadian soil, was more than just a betrayal of national sovereignty.
It signalled a shift away from an ethos of reverence – traces of which
were still found among the Red Tories – to one of mastery. Modern
human beings, Grant realized, had not accidently overlooked the
existence of a higher order. They had actively *rejected* it because
it interfered with a decidedly different project: "the conquest of
human and non-human nature." [55] Human beings no longer lived in
a cosmos through which a non-human moral order expressed itself,
but a neutral universe that could be measured objectively, controlled
and tamed for their benefit. Such were the activities that could give
our existence a sense of meaning and purpose – not simple-minded
contemplation of some fatuous impersonal order.

In *Technology and Empire* (1969), the result of his collaboration with Lee, Grant traces the impulse to mastery back to the beginnings of colonization in North America. In the book's first essay, "In Defence of North America," he recounts how settlers were unable to graduate beyond an instrumental relationship to the land because of the ideas and assumptions they carried with them. In one particularly harrowing passage, he describes how settlers had to cauterize themselves of their own sensitivities so that they could disfigure the land. "When one contemplates the conquest of nature by technology, one must remember that that conquest had to include our own bodies," he writes. "The punishment they inflicted on non-human nature, they had first inflicted upon themselves."[56] This failed encounter with the land – the inability on the part of settlers to recognize the land as a *being* in its own right that could take them in and heal them – is the foundational experience for technological civilization in North America. The Canadian primal continues to dictate the course our lives take. "Now when Calvinism and the pioneering moment have both gone, that primal still shapes us. It shapes us above all as the omnipresence of that practicality which trusts in technology to create the rationalized kingdom of man."[57] We carry the Canadian primal around inside us, below the level of conscious awareness. It threatens all our relationships, including the ones we might build with things we might only dimly perceive, dooming us to permanent spiritual exile. "When we go into the Rockies we may have the sense that gods are there," Grant writes. "But if so, they cannot manifest themselves to us as ours. They are the gods of another race, and we cannot know them because of who we are, and what we did. There can be nothing immemorial for us except the environment as object."[58]

The crux of *Technology and Empire* is Grant's claim that the system of thought that grew out of the colonial encounter with the land is closed to everything except its own assumptions about human and non-human nature. It is exceedingly difficult to engage in any sustained criticism about technology, for example, because every corner of our thinking is saturated with the assumptions that made technology possible – even when the fit between those assumptions is inexact (we might ask how technology can be both inherently good and value-neutral at the same time). A claim originating from beyond the modern mindset – like Grant's apprehension of a universal harmony or Lee's brown-study fugue states – can be dismissed on personal grounds, as falling outside of the scope of value-free inquiry, and thus relegated to the ghetto of subjective experience (on university campuses, this ghetto is known as "the humanities"). Modern reason has nothing to say and no validation to offer for some of the most meaningful experiences of our lives because such things are deemed unimportant in what we have taken to be our collective work. To be a modern, then, is to find ourselves trapped in a prison for the soul. We are caught inside our own "hectic subjectivity," alienated from our surroundings, and cut off from the genuine sources of human excellence. The universal harmony has been replaced by the "universal homogenous state," a political reality in which everyone thinks and feels the same.[59] The land is beginning to "show signs of revolt."[60] The only thing left to do, Grant argues at the end of this forgotten little book, is hunker down in the dynamo of technological civilization and listen for hints of the richer life we could be living – those "intimations of deprival which might lead us to see the beautiful as the image, in the world, of the good."[61]

While editing *Technology and Empire* was an electrifying experience for Lee, it is testament to his intellectual and artistic character that he began pushing back against his mentor's pessimism as soon as work on that book was complete. He knew from the composition of *Civil Elegies* that another way of thinking still existed, one that unspooled itself through the gestures of the poem. The empty page was a place where the deep structure of the modern mind could be exposed and its limitations surpassed, allowing something else to reach through and touch us.

Lee articulates one such moment in "Sibelius Park," an important early poem published as a broadsheet in September 1968. The poem opens *in medias res* as the speaker trudges up Walmer Road in mid-town Toronto in a light rain, meditating on a difficult day split between Rochdale and Anansi ("Sibelius Park," like most of Lee's work, relies on biographical flourishes from his life). He does not realize he is caught up in a binary way of thinking. He idealizes certain people and events, turning them into icons of how he wishes the world to be, while consigning everything that contradicts this version of reality to a kind of psychological sewer. When the speaker comes to a public park he has walked past countless times, he is ambushed by its presence. A carefully cropped, otherwise unremarkable green space stands out as alive in its own skin. Lee enacts this moment of ontological encounter (or *aletheia* as Heidegger might have called it) in a gentle arc across the page:

And then Sibelius Park!
            The grass is wet, it
      gleams, across the park's wide
            vista the lanes of ornamental
      shrub come breathing and the sun has filled the
                  rinsed air till the green goes luminous and it does it
                              does, it comes clear![62]

This meeting with the being of the park has a radical impact on the speaker's consciousness. His thought processes are completely reordered by it. Where he was once engaged in denying anything that interfered with his idealized version of life, he now seeks to integrate those shadows into his perception of things. He realizes that neither the "dank manholes of ego" nor his idealized icons are real; he is no longer imprisoned in the warfare of false alternatives, or of "myself against myself."[63] Both halves of the dichotomy are accepted without flinching; he has found the courage, through that moment of epiphany in the park, to bring them together and experience reality in a new way. He has been guided to a way of thinking that is far more subtle, complex, and expansive than the binary mode he had known before. While Grant argued that the modern mindset was essentially wired shut by its own assumptions about reality, Lee asserts in "Sibelius Park" that despite our mental conditioning the world can still reach in and move us if it wants to. If it can find us through a carefully cultivated green space in the country's largest city, then it can find us anywhere.

Rochdale College had enjoyed a somewhat fraught and modestly successful first year operating out of the U of T student ghetto. When the college moved to a high-rise tower with occupancy for more than 800 people in September 1968, the fledgling educational experiment spiralled out of control almost overnight. For a start, there were the physical limitations of the building. The elevators didn't work, and some of the rooms on the upper floors did not have glass in the windows. The sheer number of participants, many of whom were students enrolled elsewhere, choked consensual decision-making. The school's radical agenda was further destabilized by waves of migrants, including hippies displaced by the gentrification of Yorkville, draft dodgers, and street people. George Grant showed up to teach a course in Ancient Greek thought and left almost immediately when he saw that students were more interested in the toxic counterculture at Rochdale than they were in being part of a community of learners. Huge quantities of LSD circulated freely among residents, and before long, the college was known as one of the country's largest drug distribution centres.[64] Here was proof that one couldn't just throw open the barn doors to those energies that had been tamped down in modernity and expect alternative structures to emerge harmoniously. "It would have taken someone comfortable with simultaneous alternative realities to flourish in that brave, indulgent, destructive cacophony," Lee writes. "Someone with an instinct for multidimensional human chess: a delight in watching systems and countersystems tumble through their changes ... I was not that someone."[65] By late fall, he had essentially checked out, "ghosting around the place like a zombie."[66] He hung on until the spring of 1969 before leaving in dismay. When the college finally closed in 1975, the police had to weld the doors shut to keep out the true believers. "For some years," he told me, "I could barely look at the building when I walked by it."[67]

As Rochdale cratered, Anansi flourished. Lee took over as editor-in-chief in the fall of 1968 after Dave Godfrey went to France on sabbatical. He immediately sensed that some sort of literary awakening was underway in Canada. Lee often pictured a street at dawn, writers appearing in every doorway and window, wild-eyed and under-slept. Each one was clutching a manuscript written at tremendous personal cost, all of them part of an enormous cultural upwelling as the polyphonic soul of a nation became aware of itself through the stories it told. Lee gravitated to manuscripts by Canadian authors that larger presses, many of them American-owned, considered too experimental. Some examples include *The Honeyman Festival* by Marian Engel (1970), *Five Legs* by Graeme Gibson (1969), *The Telephone Pole* by Russell Marois (1969), *The Collected Works of Billy the Kid* by Michael Ondaatje (1970), and Ian Young's *Year of the Quiet Sun* (1969), described by John Barton as "the first book of openly gay male poetry to have appeared under the imprint of a recognizably English-Canadian publisher."[68] Lee approached his editorial work with the dedication of a spiritual advisor. He made himself available to his authors twenty-four hours a day, passing on insights whenever they occurred, and conducting editorial conferences wherever possible. "The process was never what you call formal," Margaret Atwood recalls. "Given the choice of a dining-room table or a kitchen full of dirty dishes and chicken carcasses and cat litter boxes, Dennis would go for the kitchen every time."[69]

Lee's literary midwifery also left him with little creative energy for his own work. He composed a handful of poems that were never published, including pieces on Gandhi, St Francis of Assisi, and a soliloquy on light. He had nothing good to say of his writings that did make it into print, including his translations of parts of Rainer Maria Rilke's *Duino Elegies* and the short story "Notes on a WASP Canadian Nationalist" (the latter is not without interest in the way he experiments with the paradoxical reversals that will figure prominently in his next major work). The overall effect in all these efforts, though, was mostly unremarkable. "Twenty words on a page would set me wincing at their palpable stiffness and falsity," he recalls.[70] Gridlock had turned into creative paralysis.

By the spring of 1971, Lee was burning out from seventy-five-hour workweeks at Anansi. Water damage from a nearby fire destroyed a good deal of the press's stock. Interpersonal struggles proliferated to the point someone suggested that Anansi be renamed "House of Atreus" after the mythological Greek family that slaughtered and served up its own members. Lee's marriage to Donna Youngblut, which had been stressed for years, collapsed under the weight of it all, and other relationships at the press soon followed.

When Anansi's budgetary shortfalls forced Lee to cut back on his hours, he decided to devote more time to writing. Instead of setting out in a new direction, though, he embarked on a complete renovation of *Civil Elegies*. To his ear, his 1968 long poem sounded "like a car stuck in high gear" because his speaker was so committed to big civil themes and "boombox" public declarations that he was unable to explore other dimensions of the modern Canadian condition "with any richness or subtlety."[71] He decided to add a second, more private voice – that of a seeker concerned with finding meaning beneath the meaninglessness of modern life. He then brought the two voices into dialogue, allowing for "a fairly simple form of counterpoint" that in fact constitutes Lee's first experiment with literary polyphony.[72] This move, inspired by Yeats's "A Dialogue of Self and Soul" (1933), only added to the speaker's ability to examine himself for those colonial ways of thinking and feeling he internalized during his coming of age.

Such inner work allows the earth to emerge as strongly as it does in the second version of *Civil Elegies*. In a robust new passage, the civic speaker senses in Henry Moore's sculpture The Archer the same primordial energies that were present at the formation of the earth's surface – energies so powerful they render insignificant even "the sterling human achievement of Nathan Phillips Square and New City Hall."[73] In another new passage, the civic speaker identifies the tragic consequences of settler society's inability to acknowledge let alone reconcile with those energies:

> For a people which lays its whiskey and violent machines
> on a land that is primal, and native, which takes that land in greedy
> innocence but will not live it, which is not claimed by its own
> and it sells that land off even before it has owned it,
> traducing the immemorial pacts of men and earth, free and
> beyond them, exempt by miracle from the fate of the race –
> that people will botch its cities, its greatest squares
> will mock its money and stature, and prising wide
> a civil space to live in, by the grace of its own invention it will
> fill that space with the artifacts of death.[74]

In the ninth and final elegy, having come to terms with colonial failures both internal and external, the speaker begins to grope his way toward a different way of being that would allow him to enter "the early years of a better civilization."[75] The end of *Civil Elegies* is nothing if not sweeping. Centuries of human migration, settlement, and struggle collapse into a single perception. Void and everyday life overlap and interpenetrate. Other binaries that structure the colonial mind, including the division between nature and civilization, fold into one another. The settler ancestors who inspired the speaker's journey are nowhere to be found, having been given their proper discharge via the speaker's most important realization. In the poem's closing lines, he recognizes "Earth" as the ultimate arbiter in human affairs. Earth is the living source around which everything must be organized. In Lee's "Earthrise" moment, akin to the first photograph of the planet taken by the *Apollo 8* mission in December 1968, the speaker offers something of a prayer, in a language from somewhere else, asking for permission to come home to where he is:

> Earth, you nearest, allow me.
> Green of the earth and civil grey:
> within me, without me and moment by
> moment allow me for to
> be here is enough and earth you
> strangest, you nearest, be home.[76]

Nick Mount, one of the few literary critics to pay attention to Lee in the new millennium, calls the 1972 version of *Civil Elegies* "the closest that Canadian literature has come to a founding epic – our *Waste Land*, but also our *Aeneid*."[77] It is important to note, though, that Lee's long poem is not a creation story, but identifies what will happen to a civilization that does not have one. Without a creation story – without an account of how the land *birthed* the soul of a people who defer to its genius and who do not look elsewhere for meaning – that people will have neither the guidance nor the interior resources to survive through time. A country founded on the absence of a meaningful dialogue with its surroundings will ultimately collapse in upon its own achievements. Lee articulates the absence of a shared meaningful life in the place we call Canada, and suggests where such a thing might be found. By saying the worst out loud – that Canadian civilization is wrong at the ground floor and doomed to fail – he clears a space for something new to emerge, the intimations of which reverberate through the joints and sinews of his poem.

Lee elaborates on the process of the writing of *Civil Elegies* in "Cadence, Country, Silence," a hugely influential essay that began as a ten-minute talk at an authors' conference in Montreal in 1972. What is so bracing about "Cadence, Country, Silence" is just how openly and unapologetically Lee writes about the creative force that barged into his life in the summer of 1967. Here is how he introduces that force on the first page of his essay: "Most of my time as a poet is spent listening into a luminous tumble, a sort of taut cascade. I call it 'cadence.' If I withdraw from immediate contact with things around me, I can sense it churning, flickering, thrumming, locating things in more shapely relation to one another."[78] According to Lee, cadence is an energy that exists in the world, a life spirit moving through all beings and things, "a presence, both outside and inside myself."[79] Cadence cannot be compelled to appear. It behaves of its own volition. It *chooses* (Lee repeats this point four times in the first three pages of the essay). And to come into contact with that force, to conduct some small trace of it into words, is his vocation as a poet, no matter the seemingly impossible nature of the task. "The rhythm of what I've written is such a small and often mangled fraction of what I sense, it tunes out so many wavelengths of that massive, infinitely fragile polyphony, that I often despair."[80] From these and other passages, it is clear that Lee isn't even trying to win over hardline rationalists. He isn't interested in reconciling with the

ecology of assumptions that structures the colonial mind but bull-
dozes through them to a different way of being in the world, one in
which mind, body, and spirit are not so alienated from one another.
For cadence, above all else, is a physiological phenomenon, a *kinaesthetic* experience, a force we can learn to feel on our nerve-endings
regardless of whether or not we can make sense of it with our minds.

What helped Lee find words to explain cadence was a curious
incident that took place at a restaurant in Yorkville in the early
1970s. He was halfway through a meal with friends when he began
to feel a slow, pulsating vibration in his body – "fairly mild, not
unpleasant, with no accompanying sound."[81] There wasn't a jack-
hammer in the street and no one else in the restaurant seemed to
notice. He asked the waiter about it, who winced and explained
that there was a room below the restaurant where a rock group
practised. The room was fully soundproofed, but the beat of the
over-amplified bass travelled up through the bones of the building and made the whole structure shake. Lee loved the experience
because it crystallized what was happening in his writing. The
buzzing in the building, like cadence, was given freely, without his
foreknowledge or control. "It came out of the blue, and I scrambled
to keep up."[82] He had no explanatory structure for these rhythms;
they convinced him they were real by *being* real.

In the lengthy second section of the essay, Lee describes the existential threat peculiar to anglophone writers in Canada, and one
that silenced him during his creative coming of age. He reminds
us that the English language was imported here from somewhere
else. It is alienated from the earth energies particular to these
landscapes and lacks "native charge."[83] Thus the words that the
English-speaking writer has access to are "drenched with our
nonbelonging."[84] Resonant speech can only come about when we
reconnect our words to the vast reservoir of meaning that has gathered over centuries of human experience but gone unarticulated.
One of the ways we can do this, he goes on to argue, is by making
our non-belonging the subject of our work. The prison of the soul
that Grant had discovered is where we must begin. "But perhaps –
and here was the breakthrough – perhaps our job was not to fake
a space of our own and write it up, but rather to speak the words
of our spacelessness. Perhaps that *was* home."[85] Embracing colonial silence was his new energy source as a writer. "The impasse of
writing that is problematic to itself is transcended only when the

impasse becomes its own subject, when writing accepts and enters and names its own condition as it names the world."[86]

In the third and final section of his essay, Lee describes how this paradoxical reversal allows us to perceive ourselves and our surroundings in a radical new way. When silence and non-being are reintegrated into the fabric of everyday life – not kept at a distance by a dichotomy – we can apprehend how all beings and things are lit up from within by their own inevitable absence. "There is a moment in which I experience other people, situations, things as standing forth with a clarity and a preciousness that make me want to cry and to celebrate physically at the same time," he writes. "We realize that this thing or person, this phrase, this event *need not be*. And at that moment it reveals its vivacious being as though it had just begun to exist."[87] The meaning of the beings and things around us reaches us in a way that is undeniable and irrefutable. The world has touched us through the particulars that comprise it – "*this* friendship, *this* orange tree, *this* street corner" – and one of the ways we can confirm the primacy of such moments is with gestures of our own making.[88] These are the moments that make for good writing, and allow us a glimpse beyond the colonial mind.

In his tribute essay "At Home in the Difficult World," published in *Tasks of Passion: Dennis Lee at Mid-Career* (1982), Robert Bringhurst describes Lee's next major poem, *Not Abstract Harmonies But*, as "the fruit of the decision" made by the speaker at the end of *Civil Elegies* to remain in the world.[89] First published as a chapbook by Bringhurst's Kanchenjunga Press in 1974, *Not Abstract Harmonies But* stands apart from the rest of Lee's oeuvre. Elsewhere in his work, Lee habitually strands his speakers between the modern world they have been conditioned to perceive and the richer reality they can intuit with his body, never letting them fully explore that other place. While this stance has been incredibly productive for him as a writer, we might be left wondering if and when we'll ever be allowed to cross the threshold. In *Not Abstract Harmonies But*, Lee does just this. He lets his speaker off his leash so that he can go on a remarkable walkabout through the world as it actually exists, undigested by the modern condition. There he finds himself in a realm where meaning emanates from all beings and things around him. This is "the vibration of beings simply *being*," regardless of whether they are naturally occurring or human-made.[90] The longer the speaker is able to hold this perception, the more he notices how

the particulars of the world gravitate toward one another, weaving
themselves together into "a field of near-coherence."[91] Here is the
speaker's entry into "the world as jubilee":

How·did I
miss it? that
haltingly, silently,
stubbornly, home,
each mortal being announces the pitch of itself
in a piecemeal world. And
here! it was always here, the living coherence.
Not abstract harmonies but, rather, that
each thing gropes to be itself in time and what is lovely
is how, once brought to a pitch, it holds & presides
in the fragile hum of its own galvanic being.
And more: as it persists it tunes to
every thing that is, neither in outright
concord nor yammer but half alive on
all those jumbled wavelengths,
inciting a field of near-coherence
in the spacey surround.

One luminous deed, amid the daily
gumbo of motives; a well-made
journey, or tree, or
law; a much-loved parent; the fullness of grief –
whatever: let that
flourish in its completeness,
and every nearby thing begins to
quicken, tingle, dispose itself in relation,
till smack in the clobber & flux,
coherence is born...
So each live thing endures,
rife with the itch to pick up
currents that do not mesh and
live their concert – each thing, which makes for a
welter of harmonies, until those
jagged cadenzas of meaning
ripple like simultaneous fields of light.

>   And if a man could stay
>   clear enough, stay near and distanced enough,
>   resonance by resonance it would ease down into itself, coherences
>   cohering till almost he senses
>   the world as jubilee: I mean
>   the hymn of the fullness of being –
>   the ripple of luminous cosmoi, up/down &
>   across the scales of
>   orchestration in many-
>   dimensional play, here good now bad but
>   telling the grace of daily infinite coherence.[92]

From this excerpt, it is clear there has been another transformation in Lee's work at the level of form. His lines have broken free of the left-hand margin and now browse across the blank space of the page. "Here's the $64 question," he asked me in one of our e-mail exchanges. "After any given line-break, what's the reason for choosing one margin over another for the next line? And in larger terms, why adopt this convention at all?"[93] My own sense is that Lee took to "open-field" composition (or "open scoring") as readily as he did because it allowed him to keep up to his evolving perception of the world. His lines flick back and forth like the needle of a seismograph because he is desperately trying to trace the vibrational shapes he senses around him. Rare is the moment in his oeuvre when content and form cohere so smoothly: to enact a world in constant flow, Lee makes use of a form that flows.

With the runaway success of *Alligator Pie*, Lee went from respected poet and accomplished essayist to something of a children's rock star. Demand was so intense when *Alligator Pie* hit the market in 1974 that his publisher had difficulty securing enough paper for a second printing for Christmas. Lee was profiled in numerous newspapers and magazines, given the moniker "Canada's Father Goose," and was even served alligator meat during a live radio interview. What accounted for Lee's incredible success as a children's poet? There was, for a start, his remarkable ability to recreate the singsong textures of childhood ("You can almost hear the skipping rope slapping the sidewalks," wrote Margaret Laurence in a blurb on the back of the book). Then there were the Canadian place names, landmarks, and symbols that located his poems in a world that younger readers would recognize as their own, unlike the "piglets and plum pudding and pease porridge hot" of *Mother Goose*.[94] There was the obvious sincerity with which he honoured and respected the opposite intensities of childhood – the ferocity of its fear, the depth of its delight, the all-absorbing nature of its grief. This is because Lee himself had not lost sight of his own childhood self, or, for that matter, his many childhood *selves*, all of which remained intact inside him "like growth rings on a tree."[95] In order to write for children, his task was to "get in touch with one of those children, and go where his instincts lead me."[96] Here again is Lee's sense of the many-stranded, protean nature of the self, and his reappraisal of that inner multiplicity as a source of strength. "What I want from a book is that it be a birthday party, to which all our selves are invited."[97] No surprise, then, that the atmosphere at readings he gave at schools and libraries across the country was giddy and electric. Children knew instinctively to trust him, this man-child in their midst who still had light in his eyes, who daydreamed on a daily basis, and who was well aware of the central truths of childhood, including the fact that more than one being can occupy the same place at the same time.

Overlooked in the frenzy around *Alligator Pie* was *Nicholas Knock and Other People*, a surprisingly dark and stormy book for older children also published in 1974. Lee described the title poem, "Nicholas Knock," as "a whole little fable about the brown-study fugue state."[98] It tells the story of a little boy who is separated from his imaginary friend by the disbelieving adults around him. On one of his peregrinations around the neighbourhood, Nicholas meets the silver honkabeest, a mysterious creature described in ambiguous terms whose impact on him is anything but:

A trick, a flicker of the light:
The tiny creature, like a flight
Of warblers, seemed to ride the air
And shed a frisky lustre there.
And yet it did not move a hair.

Its eyes were dusky, deep, and clear.
It rose; it flew; it settled near
And Nicholas stood by its delicate side,
Nicholas stood and almost cried.[99]

For a month they meet each other every morning at the corner of Brunswick and Bloor, delighting in one another's company. This is a sustained encounter with what Lee calls "the emissary of larger life," a being whose very existence broadens the little boy's horizons.[100] This may be why Nicholas's parents completely lose it when their son shares with them the good news. They take him to a series of specialists and authority figures, all of whom try to convince Nicholas that the honkabeest is a figment of his imagination. He eventually ends up before a judge of the Supreme Court, who inadvertently reveals one of the crossed wires of the adult mind. The judge orders Nicholas to declare the honkabeest a fiction, yet at the same time threatens him with decapitation and promises to mobilize the army to kill it if he doesn't. Is the honkabeest real or not? Even the adults seem to know it is real even while they insist on it being imaginary. It is the judge's task, though, to protect the narrow boundaries of modern reason, actively beating back the helper spirits who call out to the children growing up within them. The poem's warning is clear: coming of age in this culture involves a spiritual maiming and a diminishment of our childhood selves. In order to enter into the adult world and partake of its privileges, we must denounce our deepest and most heartfelt intuitions about reality. In "Nicholas Knock," Lee is giving his readers, especially the most sensitive and spiritually attuned among them, a serious heads-up. Childhood in modernity is nothing less than an ontological, epistemological, and cosmological battleground. True resistance to the dehumanizing forces of colonialism and technology begins there.

Yet "Nicholas Knock" also suggests that even to affirm our intuitions does not guarantee we will emerge from our confrontation with adult society unscathed. Nicholas is left permanently tainted by his encounter with the grown-ups around him, so much so that the honkabeest seems to deny him the effortless connection they enjoyed earlier. Yet whenever Nicholas starts to lose faith in his friend, the honkabeest would appear again, teasing him with its fleeting appearances, leaving him "sometimes in despair / And sometimes full of joy."[101] Full coherence is no longer possible, but neither is he cut off altogether. The poem's final section gives us Nicholas wandering the streets in search of his friend, tantalized and tormented in equal measure. Is the honkabeest simply playing a different kind of game now that Nicholas is older, regardless of whatever obstacles

modernity throws up in our path? It is the nature of the beautiful to
show itself and then withdraw, making us aware of our own emptiness, imploring us to move beyond the life we are living in order
to become full, which will precipitate another visitation, subsequent
retreat, and renewed pursuit on our part. The deep nature of reality
only reveals itself to us through the equivalent of a child's game of
hide-and-seek.

Yet the quest for that deeper reality can easily go off the rails.
This is the subject of Lee's next major poem for adults, *The Death
of Harold Ladoo* (1976). Robert Bringhurst, who also published
Ladoo through Kanchenjunga Press, told me that the poem was
about "a man who could not control his relationship to spirit
beings."[102] The descendant of indentured Indian immigrants to
Trinidad, Harold Sonny Ladoo was an intensely driven young
writer whose first book, *No Pain Like This Body* (1972), Lee edited
for Anansi. Ladoo was murdered while on a trip back to Trinidad
in 1973, caught up in the same intergenerational feuding he wrote
about. Lee's poem begins in the manner of a traditional elegy,
the speaker seeking to utter "the words of high release" so that
Ladoo's memory no longer weighs so heavily on him.[103] Things
quickly get away from him, though, when the speaker realizes that
he is mythologizing Ladoo, papering over his many faults and giving his own neediness and egotism a free pass. "Why should I tell
it like a poem? Why not speak the truth? / although it cancels /
all those images of chiseled desolation, / the transcendental heroes
I made up / and fastened to the contours of my friends."[104] This
abrupt turn to honesty takes the poem up a level and signals the
struggle to come. Because the writers that rallied around the flag at
House of Anansi were "a tiresome gang of honking egos: / grace-
less, brawling, greedy, each one in love with / style and his darling
career."[105] Because Ladoo "never missed a trick," "soaked up love
like a sponge," and "knew white liberals inside out: how to / guilt
us; which buttons to push; how hard; how long."[106] Because the
speaker used Ladoo as well, "that kindly editor / with his handy
thesaurus & verse – out for the kill, like all the others / taking what
he could get."[107] Yet there are kinder moments and passages of
genuine dismay for a life concluded much too soon, and a growing
awareness of the ephemeral nature of existence. This struggle is
reflected in the poem's wildly innovative structure, which whips
back and forth between open scoring and stanzas flush with the

left-hand margin, "an under-pendulum swing" or "zigzag dialectic" that shapes the speaker's journey from grief to praise to angry recrimination to self-accusation to weary calm.[108] Lee employs all kinds of voices to facilitate this journey, shifting from timbre to timbre in what constitutes his most aggressive use of polyphony to date. "Grieving and raging and celebrating and thinking and remembering – they all have to be orchestrated," he writes.[109] In the following excerpt, the speaker recalls the exciting early days of his professional relationship with Ladoo, a memory that prompts him to a high elegiac voice, printed in italics. This declaration, though, is interrupted by a mordant outburst by another voice that calls out such pretentiousness:

How it all floods back in a rush in my forearms:
those endless sessions together, the
swagger & hard-edge glee.
And as my nerve-ends flicker now, they do they
start up in the dark –
the words I've waited for:
If any be rage,
pure word, you:
not in the mouth   not in the brain, nor the blastoff ambition –
yet pure word still, your
lit up body of rage. As though…

But Harold – Harold, what bullshit! Sitting here making up epitaphs.
You're *dead.*[110]

In the second half of the poem, the speaker looks to examine the deeper forces that made Ladoo who he was. He meditates on the station of the artist, and how in modernity the artist can unconsciously internalize the destructive appetites of the civilization around him, converting other people into sources of creative inspiration. In a fascinating passage, he says that those who devour others for the sake of their work suffer from a kind of demonic possession, inhabited by a monstrous version of all the gods and numinous powers whose existence modern civilization refuses to acknowledge. "A world that denies / the gods, the gods / make mad. And they choose their / instruments with care. / Leaders, artists, rock stars are among their darlings."[111] The tradition of the

poet-seer, which involves co-operating with earth energies to bring
a work of art to life, may now be off limits to us. Anyone fool-
ish enough to open a space for the gods we have denied could be
blown apart by their rampaging energies. Here, Lee acknowledges
the substantial risk that comes with the pursuit of the primal. The
world may be able to reach out and touch us, he suggests, but
that may not necessarily be a good thing if we cannot manage
our end of the connection. More than one being can occupy the
same place at the same time, but that can lead to disaster if we are
unaware that we can be subject to peculiar forms of cohabitation.
In the poem's final lines, the speaker decides to forego a direct-hit
connection with the numinous. He is wary of the archetype of the
"Tragic Artist" who would burn himself up in a creative fireball
and destroy himself as a way of bringing his own myth to life. The
speaker chooses to honour the gods at a distance; he will wait "till
their fury is spent and they call on us again / for passionate awe in
our lives, and a high clean style."[112] Once again, though, the form
of the poem suggests a more complicated relationship.

Lee elaborates on the fraught nature of the modern condition in
Savage Fields: An Essay in Literature and Cosmology (1977). Much
of the book is devoted to close readings of Michael Ondaatje's
The Collected Works of Billy the Kid (1970) and Leonard Cohen's
Beautiful Losers (1965), yet it is his treatment of cosmology that
is of interest. For Lee, cosmology is the coherence (the *logos*) of
what-is (the *cosmos*). By what-is, he means specifically "the fundamental structure of being in our era" or "the nature of things on
our home planet in this stage of modernity."[113] To explore that cosmology, he borrows the terms "world" and "earth" from Martin
Heidegger and bends them to his uses. As Lee defines it, "world"
is reality from the vantage point of modern human understanding.
The affairs, concerns, and appetites of human beings take centre
stage. Nature has no value or meaning apart from what human
beings assign to it; our relationship to it is one of management,
mastery, and control. "Nature becomes a gigantic gasoline station,
an energy source for modern technology and industry," Heidegger
wrote.[114] This places "world" in direct conflict with "earth," which
is equated with natural processes, biology, instinct, and everything
else that falls within the blind spot of modern humankind. World is
on the march, out to conquer earth and absorb its mysteries. Earth,
for its part, antagonizes world simply by existing – by being there

and flowing out of itself and provoking the kind of moment-to-moment control necessary to keep it subdued. "Both fields are in play all the time," Lee said. "But world and earth are murderously at odds. Thus the planet is in the grip of 'savage fields.' And every thing that is is on both sides of the civil war at the same time."[115]

Lee's spin on modern cosmology is radical, novel, and weird. He has adopted a dualistic framework from Heidegger, but gives that framework such a twist that it doesn't resemble any dualism we may be familiar with. Heidegger saw world and earth as akin to two warring armies, each with its own territory, or like the opposing sections of a pie that has been sliced in two. "It's the knife-cut version of dichotomy, so basic to Western thinking, that I was abjuring," Lee said.[116] *Savage Fields* is an attempt to talk about the whole pie as belonging to earth and world simultaneously – how everyone and everything is caught in a jangle of overlapping claims – and then to think through the strange, non-Western-rational dynamics that emerge from this state of strife. If we are to get any purchase on the condition we inhabit, we must learn how to perceive world and earth at the same time, holding them together as a single contorted, tortured, self-opposed entity he calls "planet."

Having articulated this model of fraught coherence, Lee wanted to know if there were forms of earth-knowing that can pass, more or less intact, through the grid of world-knowing. He took up this question in *The Gods*, published as a Kanchenjunga chapbook in 1978 and revised for inclusion in a book-length collection of the same name a year later. He had used the term "gods" in *The Death of Harold Ladoo* only after considerable deliberation, and in *Savage Fields* had attempted a "veiled smackdown" of Heidegger for his assertion that poets enjoyed a privileged relationship with such entities, whatever they were.[117]

> For a man no longer moves
> through coiled ejaculations of meaning;
> we live within
> equations, models, paradigms
> which deaden the world, and now in our
> heads, though less in our inconsistent lives,
> the tickle of cosmos is gone.[118]

Lee's speaker acknowledges that the notion of a world alive with active powers is mostly beyond his abilities to imagine. Part of the difficulty is that we lack "a common syntax" and "a possible language" with which to speak of them. Our minds are cluttered with centuries of caricature and misrepresentation and iconography. Against his own doubts, the speaker tries to summon a bear in his imagination, and the impact of this mental encounter is so intense that the poem risks disintegration:

> And yet
> in the middle of one more day, in a clearing maybe   sheer
> godforce
> calm on the lope of its pads
> furred   hot-breathing   erect, at ease, catastrophic
> harsh waves of stink, the
> dense air clogged with its roaring and
> ripples of power fork through us:
> hair gone electric   quick
> pricklish glissando, the
> skin   mind skidding, balking is
> HAIL
> and it rears foursquare and we are jerked and owned and
> forgive us[119]

Here, Lee uses an unusually large number of margins – twelve altogether – in a desperate attempt to keep up to the undomesticated and uncontrollable energies of earth as they force their way into the poem and threaten to blow it apart. Earth, it seems, has not lost the ability to pass through and make a mess of the modern mindset regardless of the categories that structure and protect it. This scene also constitutes something of a spiritual dare on the part of the speaker – an attempt to see how close he can come to raw meaning without courting the kind of "hot lobotomy" that destroyed Harold Ladoo.[120] The vocation of the poet-seer has not been completely rejected nor is it being fully embraced; rather, the speaker is learning how to control the size of the opening, however cautiously. We don't necessarily have to stick our finger in the light socket of the sacred to experience the meaning of the world. Thus the gentle apprehension of lake and sky as a single indivisible whole that points back to Lee's boyhood summers on Sparrow Lake. The speaker tells of a "dimen-

sion of otherness" that can "come clear / in each familiar thing –
in / outcrop, harvest, hammer, beast."[121] At the end of the poem,
he wisely claims no knowledge of the gods, even though the poem
itself is shot through with their comings and goings. They remain all
around us, and we can still engage with them on a daily basis, even
if we cannot make sense of these encounters on the plane of rational
understanding.

Lee's star continued to rise throughout the late 1970s. He
appeared on television to talk with Peter Gzowski about the success of his children's poetry, which now included *Garbage Delight*
(1977), *The Ordinary Bath* (1979), and sales surpassing 200,000
copies. He threw the first pitch at a Toronto Blue Jays baseball game
at CNE Stadium to celebrate Book Night in July 1979, a confluence
of poetry and professional sports likely never to be repeated. He collaborated with Marc Lebel and legendary Québécois poet, publisher,
and public thinker Gaston Miron on a French translation of *Civil
Elegies* (1980), a project that transcended the two solitudes in their
mutual desire to intuit a homeland through well-chosen words.

Then, trouble. Lee went to Edinburgh on the Canada-Scotland
writer's exchange in the fall of 1980, and, over Christmas, he and his
partner of six years, Linda Scott, broke up. He stayed on in Edinburgh
for another six months, where he embarked on a love affair, drank
too much, nearly went mad, and started a sequence of poems about
a love affair featuring a speaker who drinks too much and nearly
goes mad. He made an unlikely – and enduring – contribution to
Scottish politics when his friend the Glaswegian novelist, painter,
and nationalist Alasdair Gray proposed that a modified line from
Civil Elegies be engraved on the Canongate Wall of the Scottish
Parliament. "Work as if you live in the early days of a better nation"
went on to become an enduring motif in Scottish politics, showing
up in blogs, Twitter profiles, and even an art print commemorating
the first referendum on Scottish independence in 2014.

The most important thing Lee completed in Scotland was
"Polyphony: Enacting a Meditation," an essay that builds on
some of the hunches that came out of the writing of *The Death of
Harold Ladoo*. He begins with the seemingly commonplace observation that the human voice is wide-ranging. It shifts from timbre
to timbre as we move through our day, changing itself from one
situation to the next according to who and what we encounter. Yet
it is the "monophonic" or singular voice that dominates the medium

of print, including much contemporary poetry. This is a voice that remains trapped within a single timbre – whether lyrical, liturgical, amorous, analytical, jocular, stentorian. It never includes more than a single facet of the speaker's makeup. There is no reason why a poem has to conform to the monophonic voice, Lee argues, for it has the resources and the versatility to express a whole range of timbres. "A poem can change the inflection of its voice five times in thirty lines," he writes. "It can rage, state, noodle, cavort, then shudder with grief."[122] Moreover, it doesn't shuttle between these timbres like fixed points on a map; rather, each must be fully inhabited, or, to introduce another of Lee's keywords, *enacted*, before moving on to the next (Al Purdy, his most important exemplar when it comes to literary polyphony, goes unmentioned here). He goes on to describe how the trek from voice to voice offers him a more satisfactory way of apprehending reality as opposed to value-free analysis. The essay begins to edge into abstraction when he introduces the term "cadential space," an energy field that expands and contracts as it moves, shifting from two to three dimensions without warning, its texture continually changing from one moment to the next. Cadential space, he writes, is "a field of luminous force, knotted and folding and stalling and skittering back, perpetual live energy."[123] Such passages demonstrate the degree to which Lee had taken to the language of Einsteinian space-time, perhaps because he saw in it something that accorded with his first-hand experience. "When I go into a zone-out in the course of working on a poem, the experience of polyphonic energies is unmistakable," he told me. "I sense a dance of simultaneous, kinesthetic energies, operating both outside and inside my body, with one of them having ascendancy for a few seconds or longer, and then another, and then another. And they're distinguished by coming from different directions, and having very different wavelengths and tonalities."[124] In the essay's final lines, he voices his own hunch that cadence may in fact be "the process of be-ing" or the unfolding of life energies through time and space that he has tuned into somehow, "like a fluke of reception on a shortwave radio."[125]

Back in Canada, his personal life a shambles, Lee couldn't resist the impulse to lose himself in another spaghetti tangle of overwork. In 1981, he received an invitation from Jack McClelland to take over both the poetry program and the fiction program at McClelland & Stewart (M&S). When he saw just how rundown the former was, he opted to concentrate on poetry alone and developed a publishing program with three streams that would re-establish M&S as "*the* go-to place to discover our best poets."[126] He published new collections by poets already affiliated with M&S and scouted out the best of the younger poets, including Robert Bringhurst and Don McKay, putting together what were essentially mid-career Selected volumes. He initiated the Modern Canadian Poets project, a series of Selected or Collected volumes by the very best among living Canadian poets who were not contractually committed to an existing publisher. He also edited *The New Canadian Poets 1970–1985* (1985), a comprehensive survey of the eclectic generation of poets who came to maturity – in huge numbers and from a diversity of backgrounds – after the CanLit boom of the late 1960s.

In the midst of his work with M&S and his ongoing wrestle with the sequence of poems he'd started in Scotland, Lee embarked on three major projects with Jim Henson, creator of *The Muppet Show* and one of the most influential figures in the entertainment industry. Henson's company had settled on a new show called *Fraggle Rock* that was to be shot in Toronto in co-production with the CBC. Lee and a friend, musician Phil Balsam, had been writing songs for some time, with Lee as lyricist. They were chosen as songwriters for *Fraggle*, and from 1982 to 1986 they wrote one to three new songs a week for each of the show's ninety-six episodes. Impressed with the first set of songs, Henson then asked Lee for help on *The Dark Crystal* (1982), a fantasy film shot in two fictitious languages that proved incomprehensible to preview audiences even after it was dubbed into English. With the release date quickly approaching, Lee was given a copy of the film and spent more than a month shuttling from scene to scene, looking for tiny openings in which to insert voice-over or a new line of dialogue to help clarify the film's plot. Lee's script work on *The Dark Crystal* having proved helpful, Henson invited him to write the script for his next feature-length film, *Labyrinth* (1986). In June 1983, Lee submitted a short treatment that he described as "one of the unmistakable failures of my writing life."[127] Yet even with numerous revisions by other screenwriters, many of his characters and ideas survived intact into the final film. His conception of the labyrinth as "a school for the soul," or a kinetic, responsive environment that constantly reconfigures itself in relation to the seeker's internal state, is a brilliant mid-career cosmological hunch.[128] Despite Lee's misgivings about his contributions to the film, *Labyrinth* went on to become a cult classic and, more than three decades after its release, was hailed in *The National Post* as "the ultimate puppet masterpiece."[129]

By the mid-1980s, Lee was beginning to feel "seriously overextended as a human being" and was getting clear signals that it was time to either "get out, or get ready for a heart attack."[130] He decided to step back from children's poetry for a while after the publication of *Jelly Belly* in 1983, resigned from M&S a year later, scaled back his other editorial commitments (all undertaken pro bono), and got his drinking under control. He renewed his friendship with radio journalist and producer Susan Perly, whom he'd first met at Rochdale, and proposed to her while on a whale-watching trip in Tadoussac in the summer of 1985. After they were married, he settled into a writerly practice he'd keep for the rest of his working life. In the past, he'd written wherever circumstances allowed. *The Death of Harold Ladoo*, for instance, had been written on a folding card table in the basement of a house on Summerhill Avenue. Now he rose before dawn and installed himself on a love seat on his front porch, writing in longhand on a pad of paper in his lap and retreating to his study from time to time to type up the results. He kept a pile of crossword puzzles nearby to keep his vocabulary from atrophying, dropped the blinds when the sun got too hot in summer, and dressed in extra layers in winter.

Lee also began seeing more of the world after his marriage to Perly. The newlyweds made a memorable visit to the paleolithic cave complex at Lascaux in France, which had been a site of lifelong fascination for him. Lee had petitioned to visit the original cave complex, which had been officially closed to tourists for more than twenty years, while still allowing a handful of people into the caves every day, but his letters went unanswered. When he and Perly showed up at Lascaux II, the elaborate simulacrum of the complex built only steps from the original, he asked again, and to his surprise, the clerk behind the ledger simply looked up and asked him when he would like to go. Their elderly guide happened to be one of the teenagers who had discovered the cave complex with his friends in 1940 after their dog fell through a patch of juniper concealing the entrance. "One of the things I love about Lascaux," Lee told me, "is that it is alien and yet recognizably human at the same time."[131] Next, Lee went to Saddam Hussein's Baghdad for a "completely sham International Poetry Festival," an experience he described as "scary" and "not something that activated my writing reflexes."[132] Two years after that, he and Perly bought a small house on a couple of acres of land in Monteverde, Costa Rica, to use as a writing retreat. There, Lee reconnected with the Quakers, a group of whom had established the tiny mountain town in 1950. Lee and Perly joined their weekly gatherings as "attenders," or non-Quakers active in their "meetings for worship." His hosts were lively and engaging, and their meetings were exhilarating – even if Lee had no words to describe what went on there. "The real thing is content-free as it's taking place," he said.[133] After a few years of dividing their time between Toronto and Monteverde, though, Lee and Perly found themselves increasingly drawn into the various conflicts and controversies breaking out between their Quaker friends, the international scientific community, and the tourism industry. They became more activist-oriented in their "place of dreamland escape" than they'd been in Toronto and decided to leave Monteverde for their own "psychic survival."[134] Once back in Toronto, Lee became disenchanted with the Quakers owing to the fractious nature of the Meeting and the fanaticism of a few of its members, and his involvement petered out for good.

Around his fiftieth birthday, Lee was growing increasingly frustrated with the dilettante approach to spirituality he felt he had taken in his teens and twenties, and how that approach had failed to provide him with an enduring spiritual foundation. "Forget whatever I'd read in Heidegger and Grant; screw the Buddha and Jesus," he wrote. "I was *hungry*, and I wanted real food. Specifically, I wanted two things. To simplify my life. And to find a devotional practice – or else to discover, by looking, that I couldn't find one."[135] Lee was, in a sense, looking to bring some structure to the brown-study fugue state he had experienced all his life – to live it in a more disciplined way. He devised for himself a modest daily practice that involved sitting quietly for fifteen minutes or so, accepting whatever came into his mind and then letting it go.

During this time, Lee also returned to the classical mystics whose pull he had felt decades earlier, including the mysterious sixth-century figure Pseudo-Dionysius, the anonymous author of *The Cloud of Unknowing*, and Meister Eckhart, whom he'd first read at Vic. They shared a stance or disposition known as the *via negativa*, or negative way, an experiential path that involves surrendering material and spiritual attachments, including all our ideas of God and even the expectation of spiritual reward. This is in sharp contrast to the *via positiva*, the "affirmative way" of traditional religious belief, which took as its focus "inspirational scenes from the Bible, revealed theological truths, or some other positive religious content."[136] Lee felt that the *via positiva* was closed off to him, as it was to anyone who had been conditioned to think within the categories of modern reason. "All a person with a modern mind-set is going to do, in devotions of that kind, is argue with the assumptions of the exemplary material," he writes. "It's hypocritical to nod along piously with the old truths if you live in a world in which they're unthinkable."[137] In Lee's view, the *via negativa* steps outside those "old truths" and the entire edifice of religious thinking that endorses them in favour of a patient, discrete love that knows it may not be reciprocated but goes on loving anyway. This felt like home to Lee, "partly because I had no structure of traditional beliefs to rely on."[138] For the classical mystics, belief was a given; for Lee, it was an impossibility. His stance, then, would be one of "worship without belief."[139] The hunger he felt as a modern could be reclaimed as the basis of a spiritual path for someone "blindsided by awe, and barred from belief, and prepared to change his life."[140]

Lee soon found that the demands of a daily spiritual practice, however modest, and those of writing were together too onerous a burden. He thought back to a poem by Yeats called "The Choice," the first four lines of which seemed to speak to this dilemma:

> The intellect of man is forced to choose
> Perfection of the life, or of the work.
> And if it take the second must refuse
> A heavenly mansion raging in the dark.[141]

Yeats had felt on a profound level the call to a life of spiritual development, which led him into a number of esoteric traditions: numerology, the Kabbalah, theosophy, mediumship. Yet he always pulled back from these leadings and returned to poetry, his original vocation. Lee saw in these lines a confirmation that he couldn't have it both ways. "Either I buckled down to a lifework of contemplative living, for which I hadn't found any real-time guide, or else I accepted that I already *had* a vocation," he said. "Getting even a few words that rang true on the page was a tall order. It would be dilettantism to think I could do both."[142]

With that, Lee transferred his spiritual quest back to his writing, where it would remain for the rest of his life. Two new sequences emerged in the early to mid-1990s, *Riffs* (1993) and "Nightwatch" (1996), both of which had been originally conceived as different parts of the same long poem. *Riffs*, which he started in Scotland during that booze-soaked burst of creative energy, traces the arc of a disastrous love affair from hopeful stirrings to ecstatic heights to scorched-earth aftermath. The sequence is built entirely around the jump-cut, leaping from voice to voice (this progression is clearly audible in the recording of *Riffs* on the Brick Books website). This is a wild attempt to honour "the sense of expanded possibility you get when you fall in love" – along with the abrupt emotional contraction we feel when we fall out of it.[143] For the woman in the sequence is married and gets back together with her husband, a creative decision on Lee's part that casts the entire affair in a morally ambiguous light. And even though the relationship ends in "crash and blurn," the speaker is brought back in touch with his deepest hunches about life's possibilities. He is re-sensitized to news of faraway atrocities, and made to question his own attachment to ecstatic experience. "How to sort out the squalid and the sublime in all of that?" Lee asked in conversation. "Nothing is simple."[144]

In the "Nightwatch" sequence, which consists of two long title poems surrounded by a cluster of shorter ones, Lee approaches the subject of the mid-life crisis through what St John of the Cross called "the dark night of the soul." This is a form of spiritual work in which purification comes by way of an intense and relentless self-scouring. The speaker of the two "Nightwatch" poems sits alone in his house, drinking and listening to music, combing through all his mistakes, betrayals, and failures of nerve, and asking himself if he has wasted his life. "It's one of those scary seasons we enter, oh, maybe a handful of times," Lee said in an interview. "Where we have to test ourselves by saying the worst out loud." The sequence makes for a harrowing, deeply personal read, for Lee draws on specifics from his own life to a degree unprecedented in his work: too much booze, workaholism, the dangers of the unpoliced ego, a couple's inability to get past their own differences, and the catastrophic impact of divorce on children. The speaker's journey is not staged in terms of the jump-cut, as in *Riffs*, but by "an incremental bending of the tone."[145] Thus the drunken belligerence of the two "Nightwatch" pieces, for example, gives way to the bilious and sardonic voice of the two hangover poems, "Something About A Train" and "One More Morning." Christian mysticism touches the sequence directly in the five "Blue

Psalms," which were inspired by Lee's reading of the Gnostics during the late 1980s. He was struck by the Gnostic belief that a person had an earlier existence lived in direct contact with divinity yet was fated to go through daily life haunted by a sense of something larger and more real from which he'd been separated since birth. The "Blue Psalms" are concerned with the speaker's sense of being in the wrong place, the shame he feels at having chosen to just go along with it, and his resolve to push his way through the sell-out culture he had previously accepted. In the fourteen "Night Songs" – initially conceived as the third "Nightwatch" poem – the speaker has arrived at a weary reconciliation with his life, humbled by his failures but no longer punishing himself for them. On the other side of the "Night Songs," the speaker of "Hunger" finds home by acknowledging the huge yearning at his core for something beyond words – "a playful itch, a volt of desire which / hankers towards what / God was a blasphemy of."[146] In "Heart Residence," the final poem in Lee's suite, the speaker contemplates, with love, the beings and things with whom he shares a place on earth. In a quiet note of letting-be, he turns his attention to his most intimate familiars – his "principled sprawl of a family," his friends with their "low-rent jokes" and noble lives, his wife and children "who fasten my heart."[147] This is the hard-won reward for his confrontation with himself: the ability to perceive with renewed love the miracles of ordinary life.

How do the structures of the modern mindset interfere with our ability to be emotionally and energetically present in our own lives? What would a different form of reason look like? Such questions are at the centre of Lee's 1998 collection of essays, *Body Music*. In that book's tiny packed preface, Lee returns to the dichotomy between "facts" and "values" that grew out of the discoveries of the Scientific Revolution, and describes how this bifurcated way of making sense of reality strands the most meaningful experiences of our lives outside of mainstream discourse. "What we know by living our lives, and what we can think within the categories of educated discourse, are no longer on speaking terms. We need a more sophisticated form of thinking."[148]

In "Grant's Impasse," the most philosophically accomplished essay in the book, Lee offers a rough sketch of what this new way of thinking might look like, building off of one of his teacher's intuitions. Our starting point, he proposes, should be our own personal primals, or things that we know to be true from our own first-hand experience. "We would do well to begin, not from general doctrines or theories, but from our experience of non-provisory claiming in the everyday world."[149] Lee is calling for some sort of larger conversation, one in which we are willing to talk honestly and openly with one another about the most meaningful experiences of our lives. The basic categories for a new way of thinking would grow out of such conversations, evolving organically through a sharing of our different truths. "Many kinds of witnesses are needed."[150] As for the warring fields of facts and values, Lee suggests that we do away with the knife-cut dichotomy between them altogether. We shouldn't dismiss these categories, though, but reintegrate them. "I'm calling for a new model of how they're related in the first place," he told me, "and one that cuts the cake in a different way. Or rather, one that refuses to cut the cake at all."[151] What we must learn to recognize and honour is the existence of simultaneous, overlapping truths. We would be capable of both observing the world objectively and participating in it subjectively, blurring but not erasing the distinctions between the two. "The world is factual; the world is meaningful; both truths are true."[152] The basic categories of "polyphonic reason," if we can call it that, would be drawn from both scientific truth and our personal primals. These two orders of truth are each co-extensive with everything that is; they are not separated into separate corners, "snarling across a Great Divide."[153] Everything is objective, and factual, and can be analyzed as such, including the elements of our own subjectivity. At the same time, everything participates in the realm of meaning, and must be recognized as such. In this regard, Lee's desideratum for new cosmology looks very much like the overlap between gridlock and flow, the union of nature and civilization, and the interpenetration of world and earth that he had been reaching for since almost the beginning.

What would polyphonic reason look like? Lee doesn't say so explicitly, but the whole project of *Body Music* – and of his lifelong wrestle with words – suggests at least a partial answer. One form it could take is the searching voice of his own poetry, where the tension between gridlocked subject matter and flowing form leads to a kind of reasoning that doesn't turn its back on traditional rationality, but situates it in a much richer and more complex matrix. Considered from this angle, Lee's major poems are attempts to exemplify the kind of musical thinking he found missing in the academy, and from modernity in general. "Kinaesthetic polyrhythm is one alternative to the impasse of modern reason – to the inability of technical thought to know the world, except by shrinking it to its own value-free categories," he writes in the book's titular essay. "Polyrhythm thinks beneath the impasse, within the impasse, beyond the impasse."[154] And if polyphonic reason seeks to address the Canadian primal, or our collective inability to recognize the deeper dimensions of the land around us, it would do well to remind itself again and again of the hard-won insight at the end of *Civil Elegies*: the earth is the ultimate arbiter in all human affairs.

Lee's most important poetic undertaking of the new millennium began on a three-week working holiday in Barcelona in 2000. Lee and Susan Perly were holed up in the city's old quarter – a place that gave him the protective camouflage he needed to write – when he made a first pass at a meditative poem about cultural and ecological collapse. What kind of planet was modern humankind handing on to its descendants? He thought he might write a long sequence in the manner of *Civil Elegies* or "Nightwatch," in which he could shift from voice to voice over several hundred lines. He produced a handful of pages of elegiac verse, but the draft felt like an opinion piece, the earth "out there," the poet poised to lament its passing. "The poem was earnest, and worthy, and it bored the pants off me," he writes.[155] He threw everything out and started again from ground zero.

> Scribblescript portents unfurl, world-
> to, worldfro.
> And to comb the signs, to
> stammer the uterine painscape
> in pidgin apocalypse – how now not
> gag on the unward, the once-upon, us-
> proud planet?[156]

Lee wasn't sure at first if such writing qualified as poetry. "It spooked me, to tell the truth."[157] He realized that in order to speak about the double-barrelled collapse of both human civilization and ecosystems worldwide, language itself had to fall apart. "Language was no longer situated at a safe remove from the planetary crisis – able to hold it at arm's length, issuing objective pronouncements *about* it. The crisis had invaded language itself; words were already part of the global disaster. Which meant that, to give true testimony, they had to undergo the very disintegration they were trying to articulate."[158] This constituted the third time in his life a new way of writing had reached out and grabbed hold of him. "It's something you dream of – a whole new way of moving on the page barging through and grabbing you by the root hairs," he told me. "But you can't make it happen just by willing it, and it's a kind of thunderbolt grace if it *does* happen."[159] Three wildly experimental books resulted from this Barcelona thunderbolt: *Un*, published in 2003; *Yesno* in 2007; and *Testament* (2012), which combines the earlier books into a single sequence with numerous revisions and additions.

The polyphonic gestures of *Testament*, while at first glance hard to spot, are right in the language itself as words slide around, decompose, and reassemble themselves into unfamiliar portmanteau contraptions. This is a polyphony of meaning, not of voice – in that regard, "polyvalence" or "polysemy" might be more accurate terms – and one that Lee doesn't appear to recognize as a possibility in his various discussions of poetics. The most common form of polyphony in these poems is simultaneous, when antithetical meanings are compressed into the same word. A single word or phrase is now capable of conveying a particular meaning as well as its diametrical opposite at the same time. "Yesno," for example, puts both "yes" and "no" into our heads at once, however difficult it is to hold them together. Some other examples include "fewful," "wreckabye," "quotidi-aeonic," "bountyzip," "stumblebum gandhis," "cacahosanna," "gracemare," and "cosmochaos." Lee is attempting to collapse the separation between apparent opposites at the granular level of individual words, holding them together to form a fraught coherence. This is in keeping with other attempts on his part to rethink the figure of the dichotomy that go all the way back to *Civil Elegies*, "Cadence, Country, Silence," and *Savage Fields*.

Elsewhere in *Testament* the sequence's underlying logic is not so antithetical in nature. In these instances, meanings rammed together aren't polar opposites. The most spectacular of these, the enormous thunderword at the beginning of "excalibur," encapsulates the civilizational challenge before us now:

Flin-
tinlyexcaliburlockjut.

Tectonic aubade.[160]

The inspiration for this poem came from Lee's recollection of reading about King Arthur when he was a child – both the stories themselves and his own fragmented memories of them. The image at the centre of the poem is of the sword Excalibur embedded in a great stone, *before* Arthur has stepped forward and asserted his leadership over a besieged kingdom. The first two lines are, at first glance, a fused lump of words that convey a sense of gridlock and impasse and paralysis right on the page. "Flin- / tinly," for example, sorts itself into "flint" and "inly," or a gnarled description of the pinioned position of the sword; the line break, after "n" instead of "t," temporarily transforms "flint" into "tin," compounding the complexity of the gesture. On the other side of the sword, "lockjut" repeats the predicament – the sword is locked in the rock with its handle jutting out (the echo with "lockjaw" increases the sense of imprisonment). "That grotesque, single-word first stanza is itself an embodiment of what it is talking about," Lee told me, referring to one of the only concrete poetry moves in the sequence. "The redemptive sword is imprisoned; we have to free it. And deciphering the stanza is the way to set it free – at least in terms of reading the poem."[161] The second stanza, for its part, offers a wildly hopeful commentary on the test that modern civilization currently faces. If we can learn how to engage in a different mode of thinking, or so to speak, free the sword from the stone, our efforts would be worthy of an aubade or dawn-song announcing our emergence into a different way of being in the world. "Might we-as-Arthur someday step up and release the logjam?"[162]

While Lee never won another major prize after *Civil Elegies*, he received a number of accolades over the long third act of his writing life. He was named an Officer of the Order of Canada in 1994, the same year Trent University gave him an honorary Doctor of Literature. In the fall of 1996, his contributions to the craft of literary polyphony were recognized at a lively gathering held in his name at Trent University. In 2001, he was appointed by unanimous decision to the position of first Poet Laureate of the City of Toronto. Instead of writing poems commemorating sidewalks and sewage plants, he wanted to add something to the city that had figured so prominently in his own work. He brought together a group of volunteers, The Friends of the Poet Laureate, and together they generated a wish list of projects that included the creation of a poetry park and an interactive poets' wall. They also started the Toronto Legacy Project, active to this day, which weaves into the city's fabric the names of the most important cultural figures who lived there at one point or another. Lee became friends with Scott Griffin, who in 2001, and with Lee's assistance, established the Griffin Trust For Excellence In Poetry and its signature vehicle, the lucrative Griffin Poetry Prize. Lee was one of the judges for that prize in its inaugural year (Robert Bringhurst and Don McKay were among the nominees; Anne Carson won for *Men in the Off Hours*). Griffin also approached Lee about getting a statue to Al Purdy erected in Queen's Park, a process that took eight years and a significant amount of bureaucratic wrangling to complete. Lee joined the Toronto-based theatre company Soulpepper as a mentor-in-residence in 2008; acclaimed adaptations of *Civil Elegies*, *Alligator Pie*, and a third Lee-themed show called *Lost Songs of Toronto* followed.

Lee's most recent book is *Heart Residence: Collected Poems 1967–2017*, published in the spring of 2017 by the press he started, House of Anansi. *Heart Residence* is a wild sprawling birthday party of a book, for all the voices in his oeuvre are present: the small child, the older child, the pre-teen, the young adult, the middle-aged adult, the old man. Lee tolerated for the first time the inclusion of a short selection of sonnets from *Kingdom of Absence* as well as a sampling of his little-seen translations of George Faludy (one notable omission are his translations of Rilke's first two *Duino Elegies*, published in *Quarry* in 1969). *Heart Residence* includes a new sequence, "Autumnal," that offers a jazzy, funny, and insightful perspective on ageing. The speaker is an old rocker out of rehab, hungry "for one last kick at karma on the road again, / one more banged-up *bitte* at the brink of eden."[163] In "The God in Autumn," the former "guitar god" awakens in "a place beyond / acclaim, beyond fast fame, beyond / fond honorific irrelevance."[164] He knows he is yesterday's man and everything he's done amounts to "chickenfeed," but he also knows that the energies he'd lucked his way into are forever.[165] Even just to feel their touch is to be marked for life, come what may. The last time I met with Lee, in October 2018, he'd just given a brilliant, high-octane reading at Trent University that went on for an hour and a half. He summoned all his voices, answered questions for another half-hour, and then went on mingling with audience members over drinks and snacks until well past my bedtime. He was only months away from his eightieth birthday. "You have to keep responding," Lee told me the next morning over coffee, "even when you no longer have the resources *to* respond."[166]

2

Don McKay

Shapeshifter

Cabin in Glengarry County, Ontario. Courtesy of Don McKay.

The shapeshifting poet (*Mutantur figura poeta*), also known as the shape-changer, is an extremely rare member of the shapeshifter family. Members of this species once inhabited cultural landscapes around the world, yet are now critically endangered according to criteria set out by the International Union for Conservation of Nature. These include habitat fragmentation, severe population decline, and at least a fifty per cent chance of going extinct in the wild within ten years. Efforts to preserve the species through captive breeding programs in university English departments have mostly failed. Their numbers, though, remain difficult to determine because they are shy and solitary creatures widely scattered across their range. They are characterized by a chameleon-like ability to blend into their surroundings, effortless acquisition of local accents and mannerisms, delight in metaphorical play, deep reading on a wide variety of subjects, and a willingness to share what they know with an enthusiasm some observers find contagious.

A tiny population of shapeshifting poets, numbering exactly one individual, was discovered in Canada in the early twenty-first century after living there undetected for decades. Don McKay had actually come close to outing himself in his first two major works, *Long Sault* (1975) and *Lependu* (1978), both of which featured shapeshifters who goaded the communities that had rejected them, mocking their impulse to master and manage their surroundings by changing from one increasingly outrageous physical form to the next. By 1980, it appeared as though McKay had broken decisively with the shapeshifter, announced the error of his ways, and gone cold turkey. It was a brilliant ruse, for the shapeshifter was alive and well in the birding poems that established McKay as a respectable poet and one of national importance. What he had done was take the meta-move of transforming the nature of shapeshifting itself, repurposing it from a physical act to an interior one. No more outward acts of shape-changing but an infinite number of inward ones, hidden behind the guise of the bird nerd, the speakers of his poems constantly being stirred and stretched by what they encounter. Yet as soon as McKay was pigeonholed "the Lord of the Wings" by critic John Oughton, restlessness set in.[1] Another wholesale transformation was imminent. By the early 1990s, poems about musical instruments, utensils, tools, appliances, automobiles, and other artifacts of the domestic world began appearing. A new power had been tapped, but the shapeshifter wasn't done yet. After moving to British

Columbia in 1996, and from there on to Newfoundland a decade later, McKay underwent yet another metamorphosis as he expanded his range of encounters even further outward to include rocks and geological processes.

It should come as no surprise that McKay counts among his exemplars the Taoist sage Zhuangzi, who embraced change as the central fact of mortal existence. Or that he admires the Greek god Hermes, at home in times of transition. Yet the most important of his teachers is the Lithuanian-French philosopher Emmanuel Levinas, who affirmed for him that the central transformation involves going from a preoccupation with ourselves to a preoccupation with, and care for, everyone and everything with whom we come into contact. Long before he picked up Levinas, though, McKay already knew that non-human others hold the key to our humanity. While they might recede from our presence, they can also, in certain moments, look back, and with a transformative power all their own.

Don McKay's parents, Margaret (Fleming) and John, were born in Owen Sound in 1915 and 1916, respectively. They attended Victoria College (Vic) at the University of Toronto, married in 1940, and lived for a short time in Cornwall, a small city on the St Lawrence River. After the Second World War broke out, John joined the Royal Canadian Air Force and completed his training in Clinton, Ontario, but because of poor eyesight was funnelled into a program tasked with the development of radar systems. He was then seconded to Britain's Royal Air Force and dispatched to the Middle East to install radar bases from Egypt to Turkey. He was a flight lieutenant when the war ended, but was never keen on the military mindset because of what his son described as "his own well-developed sense of irony and the absurd."[2] Margaret decamped to Owen Sound for the duration of the war to be closer to family, and Donald Fleming McKay was born on 25 June 1942. He did not meet his father until after the war, and was eventually joined by two brothers and a sister.[3]

The family moved back to Cornwall in 1946, where John took up a number of different editorial positions with the Cornwall *Standard-Freeholder*, including sports and the women's page, before being promoted to the position of editor-in-chief in the early 1950s. Margaret, one of the first graduates of the School of Social Work at Vic, found employment with the Children's Aid Society. They returned to Owen Sound every summer, "with its relatively benign bourgeois values incarnated in doting aunts."[4] According to their son, neither one lost the "relative innocence" of their hometown despite the jobs they held and the rougher, hard-edged life that swirled around them.[5] Cornwall was dominated by heavy industry, including a pulp mill, a rayon mill, and a cotton mill ("my Dad, like probably every father in every paper mill town in the galaxy, always said the chemically enhanced air smelt like paycheques").[6] The city's strategic location at the intersection of many borders with Mohawk reserves on either side of the St Lawrence meant that smuggling was almost a civic pastime and a point of entry into a "bouquet" of other criminal activities.[7] McKay spent most of his teenaged years "in survival mode, including surviving the naïveté of my parents."[8] He was given the gift of a dictionary in grade 8, which opened his mind to the possibilities of language. His godmother, confined to a wheelchair, introduced him to classical music and the arts, and through their conversations, he realized that he was starving. He poured his energies into basketball – "a defensive measure to establish male credibility in a rough neighbourhood" – and won a place on the basketball team as a point guard.[9] For respite from the city, the family bought an old farm near Williamstown in Glengarry County, in the borderlands between Ontario and Quebec. The farm hadn't been operational since the middle of the nineteenth century and its fields were already returning to natural possibilities when Margaret and John made the forward-looking decision to put the whole place back to trees.

McKay was still in his teens when construction started on the St Lawrence Seaway, a bi-national canal-building project designed to facilitate shipping between the Great Lakes and the Atlantic Ocean. Standing in the way was the Long Sault Rapids, a ferocious stretch of whitewater that had impeded river travel for centuries ("A dread encounter of water," wrote one Victorian-era traveller, describing the "voice-like hissing and howling of fierce beasts" that emanated from the rapids).[10] Some 1,500 machines were mobilized against the Long Sault and surrounding landscapes. The Hartshorne House Mover, for example, could pluck houses and other buildings clean off their foundations, carry them overland at six miles per hour, and set them down in some other part of the countryside – famously without disturbing a table setting. Telephone poles were pulled out of the ground, power lines coiled in giant spools, graves exhumed, and entire communities simply rolled up like a giant carpet. Ten villages

that were home to more than 6,000 people, many of whom were the
descendants of Loyalists who had settled the area in the late 1700s,
were relocated. "In the months before, some of us would bicycle
from Cornwall to the doomed villages and walk through deserted
houses, feeling vaguely transgressive," McKay recalled. "We were
in thrall to the spectacle being organized by technology. Since my
father was the editor of the newspaper, I got to tag along on a tour
of the dried-up bottom of the rapids."[11]

The drowning of the rapids was something of a royal ribbon event,
with many of the townspeople and a number of dignitaries seated
in bandstands overlooking the doomed landscape. At eight a.m.
on 1 July 1958 – "Inundation Day" – the cofferdam holding back
part of the river was vaporized in a massive explosion broadcast
nationwide on CBC Radio. Twenty thousand acres of farmland were
drowned, 36,000 acres of forest removed, and newly formed Lake
St Lawrence stretched out for nearly 150 kilometres behind the three
hydroelectric dams that replaced the rapids.

McKay was not in the bandstands for Inundation Day. He was
already spending parts of every summer at Kamp Kanawana, a wilderness camp run by the YMCA in La Vérendrye Park, three hours
north of Cornwall. There he began learning his woodcraft, developing his extraordinary sense of direction, and figuring out how
to use a canoe as a point of contact with the land. At nineteen, he
was hired as a coordinator at Kanawana. He organized haphaz-
ard, long-distance canoe trips without field guides, life jackets, or
safety precautions of any kind. Campers were routinely encouraged
to ride on the backs of moose caught in the water at mid-crossing.
Staff once concocted a plan to kill a nuisance bear by lacing a jar of
jam with glass shards, which the bear delicately picked out and left
in a tidy pile beside the tent it slashed open. On another occasion,
McKay made a nerve-rattling drive more than 200 kilometres south
to the nearest hospital when a young camper had a severe reaction
to blackfly bites, his head swelling: "football, basketball, balloon."[12]
Despite these and countless other calamities, his love of the land
and its waterways was born in southwestern Quebec – a love made
all the more poignant because he was completely oblivious to it the
first time around. He would later write of these times with a sense
of wasted opportunity, of having moved through spectacular landscapes without noticing where he was. "We travelled through this
amazing country in a spirit akin to tourists who do the Louvre in

an afternoon. 'We covered 250 miles in five days': could that have been true?"[13]

McKay's interest in poetry was piqued when he came across the English Romantic poets in an undergraduate course at Bishop's University in the Eastern Townships region of Quebec. He was fascinated by William Blake's creative mythology and memorized "whole swatches" of William Wordsworth's *The Prelude*.[14] For a young man who had grown up among the dark Satanic mills of Cornwall, it was nothing short of revolutionary to come across nature depicted as pure imagination and benevolent teacher.

Inspired by these exemplars, McKay decided to pursue the writing life. He dropped out of Bishop's after two years and moved to Montreal so that he could "become Leonard Cohen," writing bad verse in cafés and bars while waiting for "Marianne-or-Suzanne equivalents to show up whereupon I would commence scribbling excellent verse about said Marianne-or-Suzanne equivalents."[15] He specialized, for a time, in love poems that made use of hockey metaphors. While no Mariannes or Suzannes showed up to inspire his writing, he did learn how to be solitary in public, which he considered a great gift.

To make ends meet, McKay, now twenty-one, took a job with the Warrendale Institute, controversial for its application of therapies in which patients were encouraged to act out their aggressions while being physically restrained. John Brown, the "messianic figure" who ran the place, claimed that they never had a failure because they never gave up.[16] At Warrendale, Rousseau and Freud collided with 1960s idealism, liberation, and a deep suspicion of all government and institutional structures. "People like me – a university drop-out, basically – were doing the work of trained psychiatrists and nurses." The result, he said, was mostly chaos. "Yet I don't doubt it did work for many, since it provided a raw emotional commitment that many of the kids were lacking, however loony the theory supporting it."[17]

After Warrendale, McKay switched to the University of Western Ontario and pursued a double major in literature and philosophy. He was now just down the road from his parents, who had relocated to Sarnia in 1961 after John was hired as publisher of the *Observer*. McKay published his first poems in *Folio*, the student magazine, and met his idol when Leonard Cohen showed up on campus while on a book tour with Irving Layton, Earl Birney, and Phyllis Gottlieb. "The arrival of Apollo himself would have had a less profound effect on the female population," he said.[18] He took his girlfriend at the time, a philosophy major who was seriously into Immanuel Kant, to the reading. He had tried more than once to get her to set aside *The Critique of Pure Reason* for some of the books he was into, including Colin Wilson's *The Outsider* and Albert Camus's *L'Étranger*, but to no avail. "After the reading, we students were invited to mingle, with refreshments, with the poets. As you may imagine, the leather-clad Leonard was surrounded by girls while the others (even Irving Layton, despite his boasts) were not. Leonard asked my quasi-girlfriend what she was studying. 'Philosophy,' she replied. 'Who's your favourite?' he asks, and she, without a moment's pause, responds: 'Albert Camus.' Were the great shear between street-reality and my parents' notions not sufficient to create disillusionment, this act of (understandable) perfidy would have done the job."[19]

After graduating with his bachelor's degree in 1966, McKay wrote a master's thesis on Dylan Thomas, widely considered among the most prominent of Neo-Romantic poets. He then took a job as a course instructor at the University of Saskatchewan in Saskatoon, moving to the Prairies with his wife Jean, whom he had met in London, Ontario. Their daughter was born in Saskatoon in 1967. "The great sweep of the prairies was hugely inspiring, and somewhat scary, to my mid-continental, boreal-forest-inflected eye," he said.[20] He was drawn to the sloughs with all their ducks and wading birds, and couldn't help but notice how they seemed to act as a great nursery, "which, of course, they were."[21]

In the fall of 1969, McKay moved his family across the Atlantic to begin a PhD at Swansea University College in Wales, where his son was born. Dylan Thomas, a Swansea native whose hard-drinking life and tragic early death were already the stuff of literary legend, remained the focus of his academic work. As part of his research, McKay visited all the places the poet loved and wrote about – the cliffs and beaches of the Gower Peninsula, the shoreline at Laugharne where Thomas holed up toward the end of his life. On one occasion, he followed Thomas's lead and walked from Swansea to Rhosilli and the Worm's Head, a natural landform at the Gower's extreme point (according to Thomas, "the very promontory of depression"), getting terrible sunstroke in the process.[22] It was difficult to distinguish the literary landscapes from the actual ones, which, McKay said, were buried under "the shifting layers of sentimentality, mythic resonance and linguistic bravura which makes the poetry so lively and elusive." He also toured the poet's watering holes, "including several failed attempts to down a pint in every pub in the Mumbles in one evening."[23]

McKay's doctoral research picked up on certain problems that had arisen during his master's – "problems that were linguistic and theoretical rather than 'natural' in nature" – and inspired a dissertation, defended in 1971, that he describes as "post-structuralist-before-the-event."[24] As he explained in a letter: "Thomas was, as I came to realize, indulging in a semantic play (often dismissed as willful obscurity), which a post-structuralist reading would easily exploit."[25] McKay admired how the Welsh poet made it so difficult for critics to pin him down, how he was forever dodging and weaving on the page, shifting allegiances and upending expectations, swerving away from the habitual, and keeping the work open to accidents and imaginative possibilities that he was not aware of when starting out. While this anti-procrustean approach resonated profoundly with McKay and would influence his aesthetics in a lasting way, Thomas wasn't the only poet he was absorbing through his pores, or, as it happened, the seat of his pants. "I should probably point out that I was carrying around Ted Hughes and Seamus Heaney in my back pocket as well," McKay added. "Is it just my imagination, or are my copies of *Death of a Naturalist, Lupercal*, and *The Hawk in the Rain* still shaped to the arc of my backside?"[26]

In 1972, after a year teaching at Cambrian College in Sault Ste Marie, McKay joined the Department of English Literature at the University of Western Ontario. He was a modernist by label and was assigned courses in creative writing, contemporary literature, children's literature (a favourite), and modern poetry. His approach to the latter was to bring in whatever happened to be in the air at the time, from the Beats to concrete poetry, and then stand back and see what took hold. Christopher Pannell, who studied with McKay at Western in the late 1970s, described how his teacher would retreat to the back of the classroom to let students take turns reading poems out loud ("probably a desperate measure to get some 'class participation' going," McKay said).[27] He taught his students that a poem exists in the air, on the breath, as an expression of the body. When one of them was reading Allen Ginsberg's *Howl* at the front of the room, for instance, McKay took the text from him ("no, no, no") and proceeded to belt out the lines – a memorable demonstration that Ginsberg's lines were constrained only by the amount of breath a speaker could muster.

There also existed at Western a small group of writers with whom McKay could talk poetry outside of class, including Stan Dragland, Les Arnold, and Marg Yeo. Another colleague and "sometime mentor" was James Reaney, a proponent of Northrop Frye's archetypal criticism and dedicated regionalist who insisted his students know their trees.[28] McKay's position also brought him into contact with a number of well-established Canadian poets, some of whom had a substantive impact on his own development. He prepared for a night of hard drinking with Al Purdy by doctoring a six-pack of beer with apple juice, a tactic that worked flawlessly – until Purdy plowed through all the regular beers then sipped a phony one. McKay joined Robert Kroetsch in a performance of the latter's proto-polyphonic poem "The Ledger," and Kroetsch was so enthralled with his young host's reading that he lost his place in his own poem.

The visiting poet who had the most influence on McKay was Margaret Avison, writer-in-residence at Western the year he arrived. He shared with her the poetry manuscript he was working on, and she in turn offered him crucial early support. Moreover, Avison modelled for him how to be a poet without being boxed in by that label. An ascetic at heart, she was deeply uncomfortable with awards and recognition of any kind, and once commented that publicity should be "deferred until after people are dead."[29] What matters most, and must be considered sacrosanct, is our relationship to reality. She suggested as much in the poem "Snow" from *Winter Sun*, winner of a Governor General's Literary Award in 1960. "Nobody stuffs the world in at your eyes. / The optic heart must venture: a jail-break / And recreation."[30] Avison and McKay remained friends for the rest of her life; after her passing in 2007, she bequeathed to him Ernest Klein's massive *Comprehensive Etymological Dictionary of the English Language*. In her autobiography, *I Am Here and Not Not-There* (2009), Avison also offers a rare public sighting of McKay circa the early 1970s: "Once, after miles on the sidewalks and deep in the working-class area of London, I came upon a movie theatre advertising a re-run of *M. Hulot's Holiday*, a film which enchants me afresh every time I see it. The seats were uncomfortable, the place shabby, but I sat happily through the feature I'd come to see. When the lights came up at the end, I saw only one other person in that matinee audience, long legs sprawled out into a far aisle further forward, and recognized Don McKay, the poet, then professor of English at UWO. (He did not see me.)"[31]

McKay published his first book of poems, *Air Occupies Space*, in 1973, when he was thirty-one years old. His debut is not to be confused with *Moccasins on Concrete* (1972) by one Donald McKay, another poet who spent time in Montreal and the author of immortal lines like "this wine / tastes / real good" (of course McKay would have a doppelgänger). While not every poem in *Air Occupies Space* works, the book contains a number of moments in which McKay stickhandles through language with astonishing ease, orchestrating a brilliant spatial arrangement of words, or recreating on the page the interior texture of a lived moment. One such example is this account of an interminable trudge through the streets of London on the dreariest of days:

> one and two and
> > plunk plunk plop my kid's red boots
> > > through the puddles
> > Jesus jesus jesus
> > snuffle my shoes along the street
> > > under the sky[32]

Note the meandering indents that echo the hop from sidewalk to puddle and back – among the numerous visual moves evocative of concrete poetry in McKay's work – along with the use of plosives ("plunk plunk plop") that conjure the sound of rubber boots. McKay adds to these effects in the assonance of the penultimate line ("snuffle my shoes along the street"). "Reading McKay is often a very physical experience," writes Stan Dragland in his review of *Air Occupies Space*. "Sometimes it's the leaps … that do it, sometimes it's a fracturing of syntax or a manipulation of rhythm, or both, to suggest states of mind, often situations of stress or mental turmoil."[33] In its emotional under-energies, there's something else that readers familiar with McKay's later works will recognize in this book: an overcast emotional palette and a chronic dissatisfaction with the particulars of late twentieth-century life. Other later concerns anticipated in *Air Occupies Space* include the impact of the human presence on how we perceive the land, and the centrality of language and culture to perception. Here is an excerpt from "Down River, Into the Camp," in which the speaker comes upon an old logging camp in the process of being reclaimed by the woods: "Step into this has-just or / something about-to-be place, this / demotic am am am among the trees."[34]

In his scholarly writing of the early 1970s, McKay was increasingly drawn to the figure of the trickster. There are "pre-echoes" of the trickster in his doctoral dissertation on Dylan Thomas, while *Crow* by Ted Hughes and Gary Snyder's coyote poems were other important early influences.[35] He was unafraid of science, finding an element of the trickster in the work of the Nobel Prize–winning physicist and chemist Ilya Prigogine, who described how trickster-like disturbances to a system – or "dissipative structures" – could vault it to higher levels of organization and complexity.[36] McKay would augment his reading in later years with general studies by Karl Kerenyi, Lewis Hyde, and analyses of the role of Hermes in Greco-Roman mythology.

The drowning of the Long Sault Rapids continued to gnaw at McKay through his lengthy poetic apprenticeship. Alongside *Air Occupies Space*, he began work on a manuscript that attempted to think through the events that destroyed the last great non-human feature of his home place. It wasn't long, however, before the manuscript sat up, blinked, and began to move in a number of unanticipated directions: "At first I had in mind something short and tough, left jab, angry elegy. But doing that I found other planes of the subject, realized that the moves and power of the Long Sault weren't really locked up in the dam, began thinking of all the rapids I'd experienced and found them moving in surprising places and pushing the writing into different forms, looked into historical accounts which touched on the Long Sault, like those by Alexander Henry and George Hirot (whose words introduce "At the Long Sault Parkway"), and I guess generally got sucked in, the way my eyes always got sucked into watching the Long Sault during Sunday excursions, and still get mesmerized by that furious stillness."[37] What fascinates me here is the kind of mental reciprocity McKay describes taking place between the Long Sault and other bodies of water he had known. He thought of whitewater he'd paddled while in La Vérendrye Park with Kamp Kanawana, including on the Gens de Terre and the Capitachouane rivers, and how both shared in the dynamic movements of the Long Sault. He heard an echo of those movements in other more unusual places – his young daughter's exuberant dancing, the oral traditions and fiddle music of Glengarry County. These things *rhymed*. They shared an energetic signature. Metaphor, he realized, was not just a figure of speech but also a way of perceiving the warp and weft of the world around him.

McKay's gift for metaphor is evident from the very start of *Long Sault*, published by Applegarth Follies in 1975, complete with a number of charmingly naïve illustrations and maps by the author. Newly created Lake St Lawrence, for example, "nuzzles the muddy shore as a vacuum cleaner / purrs across the carpet."[38] Then it is "a bowl of mushroom soup, / tepid and tumid."[39] The speaker of "At The Long Sault Parkway" marvels over the effort made to transform the new shoreline with beaches and picnic tables, comparing it to another man-made monster:

> No sutures, no Frankenstein bolts through the neck, only
> the dam at the end of the lake, a white wink
> like a distant TV set
> betrays the operation.[40]

Elsewhere in the first part of the sequence, McKay reconsiders images and events from his youth that, at the time, he didn't know how to process or question. The Hartshorne House Mover is here, its shape and cargo hinted at in the placement of words on the page:

> For a time, we were
> amazement –
>   they got
>   this house-moving machine with tires so big I can
>   show you the picture my brother standing up
>   inside the hub he is ten years old that can move
>   a house so gentle they just leave the pictures on the walls –
>
> unfettered, soaring in suspension of feeling[41]

These and other metaphors charge the sequence at every turn, preparing the way for the wild metamorphoses of the fourth and final section of the sequence. There the Long Sault returns in a number of wacko guises to destabilize and overthrow the society that shunned it. Word gets out in "Long Sault Blues" that the rapids have reconstituted themselves as an itinerant musician on the loose in northern Ontario, a randy saxophone player who is "chasing / Every piece of tail around for sale or loan."[42] Next they take the form of a prize-fighter who handily defeats Maalox (the laxative), spouts the usual sports clichés in his post-match interview, and then absconds with his

sparring partner, the poetry of Margaret Avison, "for a holiday at an
unspecified location."[43] In "Long Sault Breakdown," the final poem
of the sequence, the irrepressible energy of the rapids is everywhere,
"looking for a body he can seize and dance through / twitching at
the skirts of the lady at the bus stop / hanging in the talking in
the all-night restaurant."[44] We might try to shut out the trickster,
McKay's speaker suggests, but he will simply respond by dissolv-
ing himself into the pour of life only to re-emerge somewhere else.
There is no punctuation in this final poem, only a torrent of words
that bounces around the page and flows over the name of the rapids
themselves. Here are the last lines:

you can
lock him up constable
shut him out citizen
he'll drink your liquor and he'll steal your woman, hey
catch that motherfucker never letcha pants down
c'mon now kiddies while I spin you a tale
about the thunder and the blood
and the virgin and the purleyman choose
your partners for the

                                    LONG SAULT[45]

When McKay launched *Long Sault* at the University of Western
Ontario (Western) in 1975, he underwent an extraordinary transformation of his own – hands and fingers waving about, the tremendous
concentration in his face, his whole body a conduit for some larger
energy that seemed to come right out of the ground and up through
his legs like the *duende* of Andalusian folk culture he'd later admire.
The sequence's ecstatic arc was unmistakable, building from the
generic voice-over of "See" to the raunchy "Long Sault Blues,"
which followed a traditional structure of two repeated lines and one
breakaway, before culminating in the shamanic chanting of "Long
Sault Breakdown." McKay's colleague Stan Dragland called the evening "an undiluted delight," adding "my head was lifted off by it";
the poet's metamorphosis, he said, was unmistakable: "It wasn't my
friend up there, but some kind of writer."[46]

Shortly after the launch of *Long Sault*, McKay was "cajoled" by
Dragland into joining Brick Books, a new poetry press that emerged
out of a couple of tiny publishing ventures that had been abandoned

by their original founders.[47] Brick Books' publishing program was, in the beginning, modest, consisting of two or three titles a year. Becoming an editor gave McKay the chance to put himself inside of someone else's aesthetic in order to help a poem become its best self. Always unobtrusive with his feedback, his preferred technique was to draw a tiny arrow toward a word. This was a way of applying a bit of pressure to that section of the poem, signalling to the poet that something wasn't really working. Before long, Stan and Don were joined by their wives, Truus and Jean, and Brick Books became a two-family operation based out of McKay's home in Lobo Township, just north of London. *Brick* magazine came along in the spring of 1977, and, when John McKay began contributing book reviews to it, the double-jointed Brick enterprise became an intergenerational affair.

Lependu (1978), McKay's third and most critically neglected work, emerged amidst this flurry of activity. Here it is not a dammed river but a condemned man – London, Ontario's Cornelius Burley – whose rogue energy returns to haunt the community from which it has been excluded. The historical Burley was wrongfully convicted of murdering a constable in the 1830s. He was hanged twice (the rope broke the first time), and his skull toured the continent before the lower half was finally put on display alongside the stuffed heads of wild game in the house of one of London's founding families. In McKay's retelling, Burley returns after death as "le pendu," meaning "the hanged man," who, like the Long Sault, is a trickster-like presence that taunts the citizens of the city who shunned him. Along the way there are non-professional drawings and maps, a number of outrageous transformations, a fiddle tune, and antler-headed figures from pre-colonial Ontario whose appearance in the poem gives it a genuine jolt of strange energy.

After the publication of *Lependu*, McKay made a deliberate, self-conscious effort to retire the figure of the trickster from his poetry. In the years to come, he would treat both sequences like youthful indiscretions he would prefer not to revisit. Poems featuring overt manifestations of the trickster were omitted from his early/mid-career selected volume *Birding, or desire* (1983) as well as from *Camber: Selected Poems* (2004). I asked him why the first time we sat down together in a concrete bunker of a faculty lounge at Trent University. He said that both *Long Sault* and *Lependu* were shaped by the zeitgeist of the back-to-the-land literary movement of the 1960s and '70s, and shared in the privileged relationship many writers at the time assumed they had with nature. "When the magic happens," McKay said pointedly, "it's not because of you."[48] Yet the trickster didn't, in fact, disappear from his poems after 1978. What followed was not a divergence from his earlier poetics but a seamless continuation in another guise. The trickster would thin itself into the texture of the poem, and live on in its gestures of meaning.

McKay's fascination with birds began in the late 1970s, when he started participating in bird counts for a breeding guide organized by a local field naturalist club near London. He was given ten square kilometres to patrol and, for several years, got up most mornings before dawn to look for birds in conservation areas and on farmlands. Other more-experienced birders taught him how to identify the granular differences between birds with similar characteristics, and impressed upon him the need to get their names right. The birds themselves taught him how to insert himself into and move around a landscape without scaring them off. McKay started paying more attention to visitors to his feeder on his property near Coldstream, verifying his observations in *The Birds of Canada*, which became something of a bible to him. He was intrigued by the taxonomies ornithologists created to cage birds, how much those taxonomies left out, and how difficult it was to translate birdsong into human language without resorting to a kind of poetry.

These lessons changed the way McKay engaged with his surroundings, whether on camping trips with his family to the Bruce Peninsula, canoeing on the Thames River with Stan Dragland, or on longer excursions into places he'd always wanted to visit, including Algoma Provincial Park near Sault Ste Marie. While the canoe had been McKay's primary mode of connecting with the land dating back to his time at Kamp Kanawana, it was now supplanted by birding. The two activities didn't always harmonize easily. On one trip to Algoma with his colleague Alan Gedalof, very high water cut off the landings for a number of portages on the Goulais River. The two wound up shooting some rapids, more out of necessity than choice. "I couldn't resist grabbing the binoculars to spot some warbler as we sped past," McKay said. "I can still hear Alan shouting, 'Not now, you asshole!' as he tried, vainly, to keep the canoe on track."[49]

As his commitment to birdwatching intensified, McKay started making pilgrimages to some of the most important birding sites in southwestern Ontario. This included Hawk Cliff outside of Port

Stanley where a variety of hawks would pass through before setting out on the updrafts over Lake Erie on their seasonal migration. There he helped put up mist nests, working alongside biologists who were catching and banding various birds. On his first visit, he saw a man doubled over, hands on his knees, gazing intently at something on the ground, and wondered for a minute if he had lost something in the grass. It turned out that the veteran birder had been staring so long at the swirling cauldron of broad-winged hawks overhead he had strained his eyes. Not long after that came a primal moment when a bird looked back:

> The image, or icon, that is fixed in my memory is of one of the bird-banders standing in the back of a pickup truck with a small frozen-orange-juice can upside down in his hand. He whipped off the can, like this, and there was a kestrel. (I learned later that these small cans were just the right size to hold the kestrels, or sharp-shinned hawks, compressed and quiescent, as opposed to a cage, in which they would likely thrash about and damage their feathers.) Anyway, once the orange juice can was removed, the kestrel stared right through us – an atom of fierceness in the midst of all us binoculared birdwatchers. It was partly the suddenness of the montage: ordinary orange juice can then wild kestrel – Hopkins' windhover itself – incarnated on the back of a pickup truck.[50]

McKay realized that there was no way that language could presume to capture or do justice to the phenomenological frisson of such a moment. In the Romantic view, nature sung effortlessly through the poet, yet this simply did not accord with his experiences as a birder. He became increasingly disenchanted with the Romantic emphasis on emotionalism in which the poet's capacity to be moved by a non-human other threatened to supplant that other. For McKay, nature poetry had to avoid this kind of anthropocentrism and the one-way drain of energy it involved. His task was to actively acknowledge the reductive nature of the linguistic act – that "language is completely inadequate to the real" – while still trying to articulate *something* by way of response.[51] "I don't think there was any energy in my work until I got to that point," he told Ken Babstock. "Energy requires tension and paradox."[52]

When Dennis Lee, then poetry editor at McClelland & Stewart, came across McKay's next book, *Lightning Ball Bait* (1980), he

was struck by the poet's obvious intelligence but, moreover, how
"his rationality is comfortably linked and integrated with the rest
of his nervous system."[53] McKay, it seemed to Lee, was writing what
were recognizably nature poems, or short lyrics that took as their
central concern the non-human world, but with a twist. More often
than not, the lyric voice found itself on the verge of being overwhelmed by its subject matter, the nature poem exposed as little
more than a rickety contraption up against forces that threaten to
blow it to pieces. What resulted, Lee said of his colleague's work, was
"an intricate dance of consciousness-in-the-world, mimed in shifting
registers of voice."[54] He approached McKay about bringing together a
number of poems from across his oeuvre, including twenty-six poems
from *Lightning Ball Bait* alone, into an early volume of selected poems
published as *Birding, or desire* in 1983. This book earned McKay his
first of five nominations for a Governor General's Literary Award,
establishing him as a poet of coast-to-coast importance.

One of the signature poems from *Birding, or desire* is
"Identification." It enacts a moment of vertigo that results from an
encounter with a peregrine falcon the speaker spotted while digging
in his garden behind his house in Coldstream:

Yesterday a hawkish speck
above the cornfield moving
far too fast its where are those
binoculars sharp wings row row row the air above
the Campbell's bush it
                stooped and
vanished
          Peregrine
             I write it down because

I write it down because of too much sky
because I might have gone on digging the potatoes
never looking up because
I mean to bang this loneliness to speech you
jesus falcon
fix me to my feet and lock me in this
slow sad pocket of awe   because
my sinuses, those weary hoses,
have begun to stretch and grow, become

a catacomb my voice
would yodel into stratospheric octaves
                                            and because
such clarity is rare and inarticulate as you, o dangerous
endangered species.[55]

Here McKay aspires to give us both the falcon and the movements
of the speaker's inner world as he attends to her. We see what the
speaker himself sees, and eavesdrop on his interiority as it roils
in the excitement of the encounter. Note, for example, how he
uses the word "because" six times in a desperate attempt to translate
the bird's appearance into sense. In his profile of McKay in *The New
Canadian Poets 1970–1985*, Lee uses the term "phenomenological"
to describe this curious form of double-jointed knowing. "This is
an impulse to make the poem recreate a two-way process, in which
the world is known to consciousness and consciousness knows the
world," Lee writes. "We can meet both the birds and beings to which
the speaker devotes his attention, and also to the teasing play of his
consciousness *as* he attends to them."[56]

However, the poems of *Birding, or desire* make clear that cultivating
such permeability to the particulars of the world is not without risk.
The speakers of *Birding, or desire* are often staggered by the realization that the dimension of otherness they've only recently discovered
is imperilled. The peregrine falcon, for example, was extirpated from
large swaths of eastern North America because of widespread use of
DDT; it was identified as an endangered species in Canada in 1978,
shortly before this poem was written, and de-listed in 2017 after making an incredible comeback. Ecological grief has a peculiar isolating
quality to it, a mirroring of the breakdown in connectivity that inspires
it. Such "solastagia" adds to the gloom evident in McKay's poetry
from the beginning, shaping a poetics that is open to the earth, blis-
tered by what it finds there, and defaults to a sense of humility in the
face of the atrocities visited upon otherness by humankind. Moreover,
"Identification" suggests that we are incarcerated in language and surrounded by forms of life we will never understand. Isolated and alone,
the most we can hope for are moments of wonder in our encounters
with beings whose life spaces differ radically from our own. "In my
work," McKay told me, "the other remains other."[57]

Hints of domestic disharmony in *Birding, or desire* foreshadowed the
collapse of McKay's marriage around Christmas of 1984. He recovered

his rhythm through teaching, writing, and his ongoing responsibilities at Brick Books, which was still publishing a few volumes a year under "the thin bemused contempt" of the English department at Western.[58] He renewed his friendship with Jan Zwicky, whose manuscript *Where Have We Been* he edited in the summer of 1982. They had corresponded in a friendly way for a few years after the publication of her book, visited once or twice whenever they happened to be in the same place, and became romantically involved in the spring of 1985.

McKay gives crucial insight into his own poetics in the title poem from *Sanding Down This Rocking Chair on a Windy Night* (1987), one among several works set in or around the Williamstown farmhouse in eastern Ontario ("Plantation" from *Night Field* and "Forest Moon" from *Another Gravity* are other entries). He had long felt at home in Glengarry County and at ease with the folks who lived there – French-speaking people with English names and English-speaking people with French names. (The farmhouse remained in his family after his parents moved to Sarnia in 1961, and McKay continues to manage the tree plantation to this day.) A hybrid of poetry and prose that clocks in at thirteen pages – one of the longest single entries in his oeuvre – "Sanding" recounts a visit he made to an old woodsman while still working for Kamp Kanawana. The woodsman sold him some canoe paddles and a rocking chair that was covered in scenes he'd painted himself, including a river across the top of the chair back, fishermen in a red canoe, a bear, a moose "looking like / a cow with antlers," a forest fire, a formation of geese, and daubs and wavy lines between them all.[59] McKay was very fond of the chair's naïve art and the unself-conscious and unprepossessing nature of it, as if from some place "before talent was invented."[60] The chair went ahead of him to Montreal to a friend's house when he stayed on at Kamp Kanawana after the season ended. When he caught up with it, he made the disappointing discovery that his friend's parents had removed the art, perhaps thinking they were doing him a favour. McKay's affection for the chair's lost naïve art is central to his aesthetic. His own drawings, doodles, and deliberately imperfect maps appear in *Long Sault, Lependu,* and elsewhere in his work (his essay "The Impulse to Epic in Goderich, Ontario," published in *Brick* magazine in 1978, is packed with such sketches). "Being *amateur,*" he would later write, "is what it's all about."[61] A work of art should be alive to the circumstances of its creation, but should not aspire to supplant or upstage what inspired it.

A quiet and persistent Taoist influence augments this stance. It comes in part via the philosophy of Zhuangzi (or Chuang Tzu), the fourth-century BCE Taoist philosopher who McKay met through A.C. Graham's book of translations *The Seven Inner Chapters and Other Writings* (1981). If life moves like a galloping horse, as Zhuangzi wrote, our task is to somehow embrace its transformative energies regardless of where they might take us. In *Disputers of the Tao* (1989), another book of translations of Zhuangzi by A.C. Graham that McKay included on a booklist he sent me in 2003, the old master recounts a conversation between two monks on their deathbeds: "Wonderful, the process which fashions and transforms us! What is it going to turn you into, in what direction will you go? Will it make you a rat's liver? Or a fly's leg?"[62] For the poets of the rivers-and-mountains tradition of Ancient China who followed the example of Zhuangzi and other Taoist sages, their work could never constitute anything more than a bow to nature and to what Graham calls "the universal process of transformation" that governs it.[63] The "slightness and subtlety" of their gestures, McKay writes in a 2017 essay, contrasts with the "conventional humanism of Romanticism, which tends to focus on the human emotional response to nature rather than to bow toward nature itself."[64]

Meanwhile, the university was changing around McKay, and in ways that unsettled him. He had arrived at Western just ahead of a tidal wave of theory that turned the humanities upside down. By the late 1980s, his university had become a bastion of post-structural theory. Some of McKay's colleagues founded The Centre for Critical Theory, two others edited the *Princeton Encyclopedia of Literary Theory*, and graduate students began to value secondary texts over primary ones. The way people talked about books was changing, and this shift disillusioned a lot of people, McKay included.

Yet McKay did not let his misgivings prevent him from seeing what the hullabaloo was all about. He recognized genuine value in Jean-François Lyotard's suspicion of master narratives, Jean Baudrillard's descriptions of the erotic power of the "simulacra," Michel Foucault's investigations into the roots of power, and the problematics of reference articulated by Jacques Derrida. He shared in the sense of nimble-minded playfulness or jouissance with which Derrida and others made art out of their thinking. He agreed that perception is saturated with language and culture, leaving us essentially incarcerated in our humanity. Yet he still believed in the existence of a world *de hors-texte* and was against any theory skeptical of that basic fact. "The difficulty of postmodernism, at bottom, lies in skepticism having the function of a worldview and dominant modality of thought, rather than one implement in the tool kit of reason," he told me. "One might venture a (metaphorical) definition of cynicism as 'skepticism as CEO.'"[65]

As McKay became increasingly alienated from academia, his prose persona underwent a dramatic transformation. He replaced the staid discursive voice of his earlier scholarly writings with that of a loafer-wanderer type who strolls his way through a number of physical and intellectual ecosystems, moving seamlessly between anecdote, philosophical analysis, myth, pop culture, and whatever else is at hand. The opening line from "Some Remarks on Poetry and Poetic Attention," a brief but important essay published in 1989, essentially thumbs its nose at the academic convention of a thesis statement: "Things occur to me, in the midst of writing, following my nose into whatever, and I'll pass some of these along."[66] McKay, though, hadn't given up on *thinking*. In "Some Remarks," he introduces the notion of "poetic attention," a way of being in the world or "a species of longing that somehow evades the usual desire to possess."[67] He contrasts it with "the big-bullying theories of the schoolyard," or those intelligence systems that equate knowing with owning and deny the existence of a non-human order that radiates with its own meaning. "I'm not wild about the taste of paper or the narcissism of the 'signifier,' however free or ideologically correct the play may seem in those salons of the spirit where it is pursued," he writes.[68] In his view, post-structuralism ignores the fact that ecosystems are made out of relationships, relationships are held together by desire, and to negate desire is to cut deep into the connectedness of the world. "I don't believe that 'reference' is a consequence of imperialism, late capitalism, or the patriarchy," McKay writes. "Freeing words from the necessity to refer is equivalent to freeing Tundra swans from the necessity to migrate, or, getting down to it, freeing any creature from its longing for another."[69]

After nineteen years at Western, McKay moved to Fredericton in 1990 to take over the directorship of the Creative Writing program at the University of New Brunswick (UNB). His duties included editing *The Fiddlehead*, the country's oldest literary journal. He "weaseled" $300 from the Department of English to help get *QWERTY* started, an avant-garde journal run by students that took its name from the first six letters on a keyboard.[70] He also lobbied to reopen the fabled Ice House building as the centre of creative writing: "It really had been an ice house, and had been vacant for some time, though seminars had been held there in the past, and it was connected with Alden Nowlan, Fred Cogswell, and Bob Gibbs, who used it for writing sessions. I still recall the surge of energy I could sense when I was given the key, and warned about the erratic heating and the banging radiator. Perfect. It allowed us to step away from the institution slightly without leaving campus. A classroom edging its way toward hideout. Things went on there that I wot not of. Nor do I wish to wot."[71] McKay didn't simply want to build an institution but create a culture – one conversation at a time – that would protect and nourish young writers. Clare Goulet, a student in the program who joined the staff of *The Fiddlehead*, remembered one beginning-of-the-year party McKay and Zwicky hosted at the house they were renting outside of town at the end of a long dirt road. There they shared their music, their bookshelves, and the contents of their fridge with students. "Who's got the *bird* fetish?" one of them asked, staring at the paper mobile attached to the ceiling by scotch tape, unaware that his co-host had written a book called *Birding, or desire*. "McKay ambled over without introducing himself and quipped 'Some people call it ornithology,' and offered the person a beer and a species identification of the paper bird," Goulet recalled. "His respect for and toward people went deep, and it set a certain bar for how people treated one another."[72]

In spite of the social obligations that came with his job, McKay remained a deeply private person. He still needed an enormous amount of time on his own to read, think, listen to a lot of jazz (he admired Thelonious Monk and Bill Evans because they could surprise him), and, when he could, write. "Poetry is the introvert's art," he told me. "I need my solitude desperately."[73] He didn't talk much about his own work, even if pressed, so it came as something of a surprise when McKay – or Don as he was simply known to everyone – won a Governor General's Literary Award for his collection *Night Field* (1991), adding his name to the list of esteemed writers who'd been involved with creative writing at UNB.

Away from the university, McKay began learning about, and directly from, a set of landscapes that had been brutalized by colonization, industrialization, and militarization. "No one would be likely to mistake New Brunswick for pristine wilderness," he said.[74]

The province had a long history of settlement, predating that of both central and western Canada. The bush had been used and used again going back to the rule of "The King's Timber," in which the monarch owned by right all trees of a certain girth for use in servicing his navy. "This meant that Buddy would generally cut down any of his trees before they got that large, which put a crimp in the ecosystem."[75]

Another huge crimp in local ecology, and the one that affected McKay the most, was the establishment of the Canadian Forces Base at Gagetown, "a tract of land larger than a small European country, dedicated to its own destruction."[76] He was introduced to the concept of *matériel*, a military term for tools and personnel that it possesses absolutely (an ex-soldier friend of his used to joke that he could be prosecuted for getting a sunburn, having thus damaged military property). As a "military forest," the Gagetown forest was renovated extensively with a number of large shapes visible from the air sculpted into it, including a giant maple leaf and a Scottie dog, and then subjected to repeated and ongoing heavy artillery bombardment. McKay got in touch with authorities about going on a guided tour of the bombed-out, chemically saturated forest, where it was said moose and deer took refuge during hunting season. He was told that such a tour was possible so long as he didn't slag the military. "I declined, as you can imagine," he said, and decided to enter the forest illegally.[77]

McKay began to realize that absolute ownership not only involved the permanent deformation of entire landscapes but also their conversion into symbols. He'd seen such happen years earlier with the drowning of the Long Sault Rapids in the name of power and progress, and then with the massacre of sixteen women and one man at the École Polytechnique in Montreal in December 1989 when the deranged gunman Marc Lepine "took it upon himself to own the deaths of people, imprisoning them as symbols in his own system."[78] McKay made a pair of road trips to deepen his understanding of *matériel*, first to an open pit mine in the northern United States and then to the Alamogordo Desert in New Mexico, where the first atom bomb, named "Trinity" after the seventeenth-century English poet John Donne, was detonated in July 1945. Alamogordo left a powerful impression. The drive along the desert was mostly nondescript, though here and there were ranches with signs warning that trespassers would be shot on sight. "The country seemed hyper-rational, sun-swept, clean, and constantly at the edge of violence," McKay said.[79] In one of the small towns he passed through, he found the husk of a Fat Boy prototype set proudly in a public park for all to see, like a piece of modern sculpture. This wasn't a memorial to the human and non-human beings affected or destroyed by the blast, but a monument that signalled the beginning of a new era – one in which humankind possessed a technology powerful enough to crater the planet.

In "Baler Twine: Thoughts on Ravens, Home and Nature Poetry," first published in 1993 and revised for Tim Lilburn's anthology *Poetry and Knowing* (1995), McKay elaborates on the ideas he introduced in his micro-essay "Some Remarks on Poetry and Poetic Attention." In place of the Romantic notion of the poet who can preserve a vestige of the other in words, he finds the basis for an alternative nature poetics in the give-and-take nature of home making. To make a home requires what Emmanuel Levinas called "the primordial grasp" as we reach out and pull non-human others out of the material world and into our dwelling places. Yet home is also where we celebrate the world as we have come to love it, lining our walls and filling our rooms with mementos and artifacts. "To make a home is to establish identity with a primordial grasp, yes; but it is also, in some measure, to give it away with an extended palm," he writes.[80] McKay proposes that the nature poet can emulate this two-way relationship – drawing on the world for creative inspiration and offering a gift in return – so long as he does not presume too effortless a connection with it. He returns to the stance he calls "poetic attention," which acknowledges the difference between things as we know them and things as they actually are. When we look without seeking to own and master, we encounter a remarkable strangeness in even the most familiar of objects. This is wilderness, he writes, recasting the term to mean "not just a set of endangered spaces, but the capacity of all things to elude the mind's appropriations."[81] The poet aspires to translate wilderness, haltingly and imperfectly, into his own idiosyncratic terms of reference, aware of his own anthropocentrism while "enacting it, thoughtfully."[82] The key is to carry out this task lightly, in the spirit of "anthropomorphic play"; language surrenders its authority and risks breaking up altogether. He writes: "Poets are supremely interested in what language can't do; in order to gesture outside, they use language in a way that flirts with its own destruction."[83]

McKay brought this spirit of anthropomorphic play to his poems of the early to mid-nineties, a number of which celebrate the residual wilderness in the most familiar everyday tools and objects. When the field naturalist's flow of attention is redirected to the built environment or "the nest of the mundane," as Alanna Bondar called it, personhood can be glimpsed all around us.[84] A great number of the poems of *Apparatus* (1997) extend warmth and affection for these overlooked and taken-for-granted others who mediate our relationship with our surroundings, for, as Pablo Neruda wrote in "Ode to My Socks," "beauty is twice / beauty / and what is good is doubly / good / when it is a matter of two socks / made of wool / in winter."[85] Sitting before a table setting, McKay doesn't see the plate, the glass, the knife, fork, and spoon, but some under-resonance in things that makes audible the historical, cultural, and material processes that shaped them. He doesn't presume to communicate in verse the interior life of what he is contemplating, as did French poet Francis Ponge in books like *Le Parti Pris des Choses* (1942), which McKay included on his syllabus for a contemporary literature class at Western. Rather, he offers a song of his own inspired by that material being. Here is "Spoon" from "Setting The Table," a poem whose spatial arrangement hints (ever so slightly) at the shape of the object it celebrates:

> whose eloquence
> is tongueless, witless, fingerless,
> an absent egg.
> Hi Ho, sing knife and fork, as off they go,
> chummy as good cop and bad cop,
> to interrogate the supper. Spoon waits
> and reflects your expression,
> inverted, in its tarnished moonlight. It knows
> what it knows. It knows hunger
> from the inside
> out.[86]

McKay gives the name "apparatus" to the processes that pull other beings and things out of their orbits and into ours, where they are melted down into forms that suit our needs and wants. Even after they have been transformed into throughput for the material economy, something of their original selves remains. There is still a chance they might revert back to something of their former selves. Sometimes, though, the act of appropriation is so complete and total that human and non-human others can never go back to their original selves. In the *"Matériel"* sequence from *Apparatus*, McKay traces this impulse to total appropriation back to Cain from the Book of Genesis, the first farmer who kills his brother and is cursed by God to perpetual homelessness. Achilles, from *The Iliad* by Homer, adds to the violence by not only killing Hektor but also desecrating his body, denying him "access to decomposition" and turning him into a symbol.[87] The illicit visit to the Gagetown military forest is recounted in "The Base," complete with the sprained wrist he got jumping over a creek and a cutting he took of pussy willow branches. The final poem in the sequence, "Stretto," shifts into manic overdrive, each section borrowing from the last and rising in intensity as the voice of Cain mangles the English language and the poetic traditions it has sponsored. *Matériel* is the expression of a masculinity so terrified of its own mortality and the anonymity of death that it would rather declare war against natural processes than be subject to them. In modernity, this male rage thins itself into a methodical, organized violence that hides behind the mask of value-free rationality, spreads out over the land like a metallic rhizome, and threatens all our efforts at home making.

It was through the unlikely event of a yard sale he organized that McKay began to assemble something of a poetic response to *matériel*. He was delighted to find an old forgotten Latin word to refer to the stuff he wanted to sell – *incunabula*, or rare, precious objects – and gave that word pride of place on the posters he put up around campus. On the day of the sale, though, inclement weather set in – "first chill then lashing rain and sleet" – and McKay had to hustle rare, precious objects like a 1950s floor lamp, a royal wedding souvenir plate, and an archaic meat grinder back to the garage.[88] As he recalls in his essay "Remembering Apparatus: Poetry and the Visibility of Tools," a strange transformation took place once inside. Temporarily released from ownership, "each thing emerged from the general mess into its own identity," asserting itself with an autonomy and individuality to which he'd become oblivious.[89]

We have to take our tools and technologies outside, McKay realized, if we are to come to terms with their hidden operations and the power they contain. Some act of de-familiarization – some pause in everyday experience – is needed to remove them from the comfortable contexts in which they are so seamlessly embedded so that we might see them in a more critical light (*Pause* was the original name for the book that became *Apparatus*).

Language, the technology McKay is most interested in, also needs to be taken outside and reassessed. As George Grant pointed out, though, how are we to gain perspective on something that saturates every corner of our thinking? Here McKay zeroes in on the contraption of metaphor, which oscillates between is and is not "re-opening the question of reference" and reinvigorating words with a small dose of wilderness.[90] Metaphor is that pause in language reminding it of its nature as apparatus. Metaphor prevents language from becoming a closed system. It is, essentially, the trickster after his metamorphosis into a trick-turning figure of speech. He writes: "We might think of metaphor as the raven of language, a member of the mythological community who ensures that its tendency toward totality never succeeds."[91]

Back at UNB, McKay's relationship with the university was beginning to unravel. He and Zwicky wanted to share his academic position, offering themselves as a two-for-one package, but were stymied by an inflexible administration unable or unwilling to process the logistics. At a deeper level, the professionalism and respect with which McKay treated his colleagues and students – and the affection he received in return – was resented by other members of the English department. In the spring of 1996, when Zwicky landed a coveted position in the Department of Philosophy at the University of Victoria, McKay decided that after twenty-five years in the academy he'd had enough of what his colleague Stan Dragland called "the smallness of smart people."[92] His last act as an academic was to fling open his office door and let students help themselves to whatever they wanted – shelves of books, files, notes, back copies of *The Fiddlehead*, beer coasters, hockey game ticket stubs, paper mobiles. While McKay initially thought of his departure as a "quasi-disaster," it was in retrospect "just the shift my work needed."[93]

McKay was still figuring out how to insert himself into the West Coast landscapes around him when he received a phone call from a tiny commercial press out of Kentville, Nova Scotia, that wanted to venture into literary publishing. Andrew Steeves, co-founder of Gaspereau Press, knew of McKay through his work at UNB and asked if he might have anything to contribute to the new press. Especially something that strayed from the beaten path. As it happened, McKay had just finished a poetry-prose hybrid that included new and previously published work, including "Baler Twine," "Remembering Apparatus," and the *"Matériel"* sequence. A year later, Gaspereau published *Vis à Vis: Field Notes on Poetry and Wilderness* (2001), a little blue book that earned McKay his fifth nomination for a Governor General's Literary Award and became something of a minor classic, giving the new academic sub-field of "ecocriticism" one of its first Made-in-Canada texts. McKay's poetics appealed to a younger generation of thinkers who had passed through the postmodern critical moment, absorbed many of its lessons, and yet still believed in the existence of a world beyond language and culture. The book's iconic cover features two binocular-like eyeholes through which we can see a skewed excerpt from one of McKay's poems and a row of black feathers belonging to a dead raven wrapped in baler twine, its beak slightly open. The suggestion here is of two things face to face: a destabilized nature poem and a ravaged real world, or, as Steeves told me, "our expectations of the outside and what we find when we're actually there."[94] This anticipates the central dilemma of *Vis à Vis*: is nature poetry even possible in a time of environmental crisis?

The heart of the book is McKay's sustained engagement with the Lithuanian phenomenologist Emmanuel Levinas (1906–1995). He first encountered Levinas's work in the early 1980s and remembered urging Dennis Lee to read it, for here was "the antidote to Heidegger," or a philosophy that privileged our ethical responsibility to one another instead of trying to capture the entire world in a single ontological superstructure.[95] Levinas studied under Edmund Husserl at the University of Freiburg and became a French citizen in 1931. When France fell to the Nazis in June 1940, he was captured along with more than a million other servicemen and sent to a labour camp near Hanover, Germany. There he lived for five years under the constant threat of deportation and execution, circumstances that prompted him to think about the obligations human beings have to one another. After the war, and inspired by his apprenticeship to Monsieur Chouchani, a vagabond spiritual teacher who may well be one of the most enigmatic and apocryphal figures of post-war Europe, Levinas developed an ethical philosophy based on radical empathy and responsibility to the other. To move beyond a preoccupation with ourselves and discover that other lives have meaning is the central transformation of human consciousness. Crucial to that transformation is "The Face," as Levinas put it – not necessarily someone's actual face, but anything about them that allows us to glimpse their essential humanity. The Face of the other calls out to us; it asserts itself with tremendous power; it compels us to respond to its summons. "I am he who finds the resources to respond to the call," Levinas writes.[96] Such responsiveness brings us into contact with the true miracle of existence: not that there is something instead of nothing, as Heidegger argued, but that kindness still moves through the world. Thus Levinas's philosophy circles back to the paradox known to wisdom teachers throughout the centuries: those who empty themselves out for the other receive "all the wonder of giving."[97]

One day over tea in his backyard, McKay talked about the protracted arguments of environmental ethicists and how they can take away from our ability to engage directly with our surroundings. "What we need," he told me, "is a way of inserting ourselves in the world in a flash."[98] In "The Bushtits' Nest," the final essay from *Vis à Vis*, he suggests that we look for faces among the non-human others around us, in effect extending Levinas's ethical philosophy to the natural world. McKay acknowledges that projecting faces onto trees and rocks might strike us as an inherently anthropocentric act, yet argues that the human perspective is impossible to escape. Human categories are all we have to work with. The challenge is to use those categories knowingly and playfully, and in the spirit of the gift: "We can perform artistic acts in such a way that, in 'giving things a face' the emphasis falls on the gift, the way, for example, a linguistic community might honour a stranger by conferring upon her a name in their language. Homage is, perhaps, simply appropriation with the current reversed; 'here' we say to the thing, 'is a tribute from our culture, in which having a face is the premier sign of status.'"[99] Such tributes completely transform our perception of our surroundings. We enter into a world of persons, and one in which everything looks back at us. "When a lake or a pine marten looks back, when we are – however momentarily – *vis à vis*, the pause is always electric. Are we not right to sense, in such meetings, that envisaging flows both ways?"[100] McKay is suggesting that when we give other beings a face, our essential humanity is gifted back to us through their gaze. "Only in the mirror of other life can we understand our own lives. Only in the eyes of the other can we become ourselves," writes Andreas Weber.[101] Hence the delicate, even faint notes of symbiosis McKay offers in the coda to his essay – the bushtits' nest he found in a forsythia bush hanging over his driveway, woven together from whatever materials the pair could find; an enigmatic passage from Zhuangzi about the need to fast the heart in order to listen for the energies of the Tao; the botanist Trevor Goward's colourful descriptions of the complex relationship between fungi and algae that make up lichen.

Levinas's influence on McKay's poetry is most audible in the "Song for the Song of" poems, a long-running series that can be traced back through several collections and grew out of one of McKay's earliest impulses as a poet: the need to address the non-human other with a human gesture of meaning. One of the first times this impulse expressed itself was in "The Great Blue Heron" from *Long Sault*, which speaks of a memorable encounter between a father, his young son, and a heron "that rose / like its name over the marsh."[102] Another important forerunner is "Twinflower" from *Apparatus*, in which the speaker comes across a community of tiny pink-white flowers, crouches down beside them with his field guide, and promptly begins reading the field guide entry out loud to them. "Listen now, / *Linnaea borealis*, while I read of how / you have been loved – with keys and adjectives and numbers, all the teeth / the mind can muster."[103]

McKay acknowledges that such gestures are part of his practice. He told Ken Babstock: "I've actually done this, you don't want anyone to come up the trail while you're doing it, but I have, and it puts you in an interesting place, especially if you're thinking of yourself as the creature with language approaching the non-linguistic entity."[104] For the "Song for the Song of" poems, the task was to go beyond the field guide and fashion his own idiosyncratic responses to the beings that inspired him, without resorting to description or imitation. What he wanted, in other words, was to offer tribute, to sing back to the land in his own voice. A glance at the index of poem titles from *Angular Unconformity* gives us a sense of the diversity of his gestures: domesticated animals, fallen leaves, coyote, the wind, and a dozen entries for different species of birds. The "Song for the Song of" has become something of a fixture in McKay's work, which says a lot about someone who is otherwise predisposed to avoid such things.

Back home in Victoria, McKay was looking over a map of southern Vancouver Island when the name "Loss Creek" caught his eye. Alert to the peculiarities of nomenclature and eager to make a dent in his own ignorance, he started to sniff around. He learned that the creek followed an enormous fault line that ran from the Juan de Fuca nature preserve on the west coast of the island to Metchosin just outside Victoria, marking the place where the most recent geological arrival to North America, the Crescent Terrane, had rear-ended the rest of the continent. When he drove out to see the fault, he found himself in a canyon that was both beautiful and forlorn, for the Loss Creek area, like much of southern Vancouver Island, had been designated a "working forest" and thoroughly logged. McKay decided to walk the entire fault, one segment at a time, without any agenda other than to see what it had to teach him. His curiosity about the gold rush, early twentieth-century logging practices, and a rumour he'd heard about a locomotive abandoned in the woods because of an inventory glitch pushed him into the provincial archives in Victoria. The sight of black bears eating flowers and cougar tracks frozen in ice led him to studies of mammal behaviour. Encounters with the columbines and alders dominating the secondary growth sent him to *Plants of Coastal British Columbia* (1994). The dramatic sight of a bed of schist tilted on its side – a phenomenon geologists call an angular unconformity – sent him to the university bookstore where he found *Earth System History* by Steven M. Stanley (1998), an introductory textbook that contained "a wonder on every page."[105] He writes: "You could say that Loss Creek assigned meditational exercises; you could say it gave me homework: both would be true, and I did not bother distinguishing between them."[106]

Loss Creek first came up in my conversations with McKay in July 2005. We were sitting at a rickety picnic table in his backyard in Victoria and looking over a large geological map of Vancouver Island. As he talked about the map, he got more and more excited, and so on a whim I asked him if he would take me to Loss Creek so that I could see it for myself. Three weeks later, we met outside my bed and breakfast in Sooke and made our way up the southwestern side of Vancouver Island. We pulled over on the height of land so that I could get my bearings – though fog rolling in off the Pacific obscured everything – and from there we drove some distance along the West 100, a decommissioned logging road that ran alongside Loss Creek. When washouts slowed us to a crawl, we got out of the car and proceeded on foot. My initial impression was of a place as grim as its name. We found a clearing filled with garbage left by backcountry campers and beneath that the rusting detritus of long-ago logging operations. When we stepped out onto the exposed riverbed, a massive clear-cut – at an impossibly steep and very likely illegal incline – came into view. The place was eerily quiet. It felt used up and lifeless. After letting me take in the devastation without saying anything, McKay gently redirected my attention to the landforms around us. He had stories, it seemed, for everything. A tiny handful of pebbles spoke of the massive collision between two terranes that shaped southern Vancouver Island. Speckled rocks poking up through the blue-grey basalt at our feet migrated there on the backs of glaciers several thousand years earlier. Ancient powers were still very much alive and active beneath the wreckage. My perception of the place was totally reversed. The place came to life and reared on its hindquarters right in front of my eyes. "It's like we live on the back of an animal," he said when we got back to the car.

Deactivated West 100 (2005), the richly elegiac follow-up to *Vis à Vis*, appeared two months after our visit. The damaged landscapes of southwestern Vancouver Island, which few Canadians would ever see, were now on the country's literary map. At the core of that book is McKay's notion of "geopoetry." He found the term in the writings of Harry Hess, one of the scientists whose work led to the acceptance of plate tectonics. Hess had offered the word "poetry" as a concession to those skeptical of the idea that the land existed in a state of perpetual motion. McKay writes: "Earth is dynamic, constantly forming and reforming its features, building and leveling mountains, rifting continents to open oceans between the two sides and closing them up again."[107] Such processes, gargantuan as they are, should disavow us of anything except a sense of our own insignificance. Our appropriate relationship to place, he goes on to suggest in the book's opening essay, should be one of catch-and-release, holding a place close to our hearts as surely as we let it go. McKay enacts this stance in his practice of choosing a small, coin-sized rock from an unnamed beach on Vancouver Island, carrying it with him everywhere for a few years, then returning to the place where he found it and throwing it "as casually as I can manage" back among its fellows.[108] Implicit in this stance is an inescapable existential loneliness. In "Limestone," one of twenty-four prose poems that make up the abecedarian sequence "Between Rock and Stone: A Geopoetic Alphabet," he recounts waking up beside the Goulais River to the sound of a chorus of voices outside his tent. While he couldn't understand the language they were chattering away in, "every so often, out of the hubbub, my name would appear, inflected by the accents of the mystery language."[109] By the time he stumbled through the dark to the water's edge, the voices had transformed back into the river's "protomusical purl and rush,"

which, he notes, was "very beautiful in itself, but not even remotely
addressed to me, or anyone."[110] He concludes that the experience was
nothing more than an auditory hallucination. "Since we are doggedly
linguistic as a species, our brains naturally process any continuous
sound as a language," he writes. "And since we are also, as a species,
lonely, we are primed to hear ourselves called by name."[111] Is McKay
suggesting that the world can't, in fact, reach out and assuage us of
our loneliness?

As Andrew Steeves told me, "wilderness wins" in the final pages
of *Deactivated West 100*.[112] Elegy gives way to renewal. A stump
suddenly turns into a bear; the songs of Swainson's thrushes, juncos,
and "the subliminal drumming of a grouse" fill the valley.[113] Now
that the industrial project has moved on, life returns unimpeded to
Loss Creek. The green fuse cannot be stopped, even as the losses
pile up around us. In McKay's case, these include the passing of his
father in 2002, his mother in 2004, and the end of his relationship
with Jan Zwicky in 2006.

For the publication of the poetry collection *Strike/Slip* (2006),
McKay was asked by a staffer at McClelland & Stewart to update
his author's photograph for the book's jacket. It was a seemingly
innocuous request, but having his picture taken for mass consump-
tion counts among McKay's least favourite things. (While at Loss
Creek, I made the mistake of taking his picture without asking him,
and the hawk-like glare I got in return was fierce enough to burn
the film in my camera.) McKay dislikes being singled out. He isn't
beguiled by literary celebrity. He doesn't want to be transformed into
an iconic, that is to say fixed, version of himself. He refused the
request for a new photograph, but after his publisher pushed back,
he went to Victoria and got some done in a photo booth: "I sent one
... which they complained about, saying it looked like it had been
taken in a photo booth. I responded, feigning injury over the fact
that I had in fact spent a good deal of money hiring a photographer
whose shtick was to make high-end 'photo booth' pictures. Anyhow,
they published it (probably to call my bluff rather than because they
bought my story)."[114] When *Strike/Slip* was nominated for the Griffin
Poetry Prize in 2007, McKay's low-resolution headshot, already
grainy to begin with, was enlarged to gigantic proportions and
mounted alongside the professional photographs of other nominees
at the MacMillan Theatre in downtown Toronto. "After the reading
a friend remarked that, as the audience surveyed the poets onstage, I

was the only one who looked better than his or her photograph," he told me.[115] Being at the centre of the largest poetry circus in the world – especially for someone who preferred to spend his time honing his senses to non-human beings and energies – made McKay feel "like a specimen on a pin," said his colleague Maureen Scott Harris.[116] His conundrum, she added, was that he doesn't like publicity, but has something to say. All the same, the applause was rapturous when he was announced winner of the 2007 Griffin Poetry Prize three days later, such was the respect and affection he'd earned through his writing, teaching, and editing ("Rare is the poet in Canada who has not felt Don McKay's kindness," writes Eric Miller).[117] When he took to the podium to accept his award, as awkward and rumpled as ever in jeans and black blazer, McKay commented on the perceived fragility and durability of the craft of poetry. "I don't think poetry is in any danger, that it runs deep and will always be here," he said. "It will survive, with cockroaches, beyond us."[118]

It was something of a straightforward decision to move to St John's in the fall of 2006. McKay had visited the city before and had friends who had settled there, including Stan Dragland, who lived just down the street from the newly renovated century home he'd bought. Books he was reading on his arrival include J.P. Howley's *Reminiscences*, which opened a window onto Newfoundland culture and geology in the late nineteenth century, and *Reading The Rocks: The Autobiography of the Earth* (2006), Marcia Bjornerud's lively account of the earth through deep time (he actually read Bjornerud's book three times, cover to cover, on acquiring it).

When McKay started to read the land under St John's, he found evidence all around him of Avalonia, the Paleozoic micro-continent that had been broken up and scattered in a geological diaspora as far-flung as Ireland, Wales, New Brunswick, and Massachusetts. There were traces of Avalonia in the *Aspidella terranovica* fossil in the out-crop kitty-corner from Tim Hortons, in the syncline whose northern edge formed the narrows that ships passed through on their way to the Atlantic, and in the remarkable fossil beds at Mistaken Point, two hours south of St John's on the other side of a desolate expanse known as the Barrens. Mistaken Point was home to the Ediacarans, "an entirely unread chapter in the history of life" that predated the Cambrian explosion by some 50 million years, added a whole new time period to the geological scale, and has been likened to the dis-covery of a new planet in the solar system.[119]

McKay's apprenticeship to Avalonia gave him a helpful perspective on our own troubled moment. In the opening essay from *The Shell of the Tortoise* (2011), his third book of prose, he continues to press the point that an awareness of deep time can dislodge whatever pretensions of mastery we might have. This allows us to graduate beyond anthropocentrism to a stance he calls "membership," whereby we see ourselves as "one expression of the ever-evolving planet."[120] In "Great Flint Singing," the next essay in that book, McKay surveys the impulse to membership as it arose among a number of non-Indigenous Canadian poets over the last two centuries, many of whom were aware of a "primal power" that could not be easily accommodated within the aesthetic categories of colonial culture.[121] He tracks how a poetics based on observation and attention to detail emerged alongside the "peak moments and grand unifying themes" associated with English Romanticism and American Transcendentalism.[122] "Epiphanic vision" gave way to "ecosystem" as many poets began to bow toward their subject matter instead of using it to validate their own emotions.[123] This poetics of place will remain out of reach, though, so long as ownership of the land remains the dominant mode through which we think about and relate to it. In "The Muskwa Assemblage," inspired by a week spent among fellow artists in a remote corner of British Columbia, McKay pushes against the impulse to ownership by reversing the colonial practice of naming places after people. "Is it possible," he asks, "to imagine being named by a place?"[124] Anyone attempting to move from colonialism to membership would do well to keep in mind the trickster, McKay writes in the book's title essay, "the only figure at home" in times of difficult transition.[125] He does not borrow from First Nations oral traditions for his trickster, but looks to Hermes from Ancient Greek mythology to let loose that "primal otherness" inside Western culture.[126] He focuses on Hermes's theft of the sacred cattle herd belonging to Apollo, an act that the trickster makes up for by gifting the sun god with the lyre (Apollo was so pleased with the beautiful music the lyre produced that he let Hermes keep the cattle). The sacred cattle that the trickster might steal from colonial society is our sense of entitlement to the land and the ideas of human exceptionalism and dominion that buttress it. In return for this land theft – the reverse of the colonial theft of Indigenous land – we are given back the ability to co-create with our surroundings, for as McKay points out, "it was the very dynamism of the natural world that animated the lyre in the first place."[127]

As for the shapeshifter, he makes one final, daring, and, as it happened, short-lived literal appearance in "Paradoxides," one of the first of McKay's Newfoundland poems published in *The Fiddlehead* in 2010 and revised substantially for inclusion in his 2012 collection of the same name. *Paradoxides* is a species of trilobite that identifies the middle Cambrian period and thus serves as an "index fossil" or "guide fossil" to that period. McKay first came across this strange being in J.P. Hawley's *Reminiscences*, where the author tells of a visit to Cape St Mary's in 1870 and includes a description of several specimens and a sketch. When McKay and his new partner, land artist Marlene Creates, visited the area for a picnic, he turned to her at one point and said something like, "You know, Hawley said there were *Paradoxides* fossils alongside this shore – big extravagant trilobites." Without missing a beat, Creates pointed to a nearby rock and said: "You mean like that?"[128] McKay recounts this picnic in his poem as well as the discovery of the fossil, described as "bold, declarative, big as my hand and just as complicated."[129] Even as a photograph on his desk, *Paradoxides* asserts its influence over the speaker, who marvels over its eyes of calcite crystals "unique / in all of animalia" and is compelled to offer a gesture in response: "Friend, stranger, paradoxidid, / I wave one jointed arm. / I wink one endothermic lid."[130] The 2012 version of the poem ends here, and in a manner consistent with McKay's ethics of respectful address. The version of "Paradoxides" published in *The Fiddlehead* two years earlier, though, veers off in a totally different direction. There the speaker dreams that he metamorphoses into the trilobite, complete with compound vision, "reminiscent of the stacked T.V. sets in Zellers or Future Shop," and celaphon, "the extra-long spines sprouting from my cheeks like misapplied armour."[131] Kafka, Don Cherry, and Zhuangzi's tale of the man who dreamed himself a butterfly all slide together as the psychopomp from the middle Cambrian conducts a late-night raid on the hapless inhabitant of the Anthropocene. It was as if the shapeshifter that manifests so readily in McKay's earlier sequences had somehow smuggled itself back into his poetry. When I asked about what is for him the unusual move of making major alterations to a work already in print, he replied: "In recent years, I've been content to have projects live for lengthy periods in notebooks, fermenting and recombining. But in this instance, it seems I rushed not only into 'coherent' poetic form but print. Let it be a lesson to me."[132]

McKay's twelfth collection of poems is crowded with other beings whose presence circumvents our categories of knowing. "Gjall" was inspired by a trip to Iceland that McKay took in the fall of 2009 (a place, he said, that was "constantly revelatory in the sense of a dynamic, mobile earth").[133] Gjall is described in an endnote as "a very light rock formed when lava solidifies while flying through the air during an eruption."[134] In the poem inspired by this astonishing fact, McKay likens its organic form to "the material pelt of a burst bubble or the chrysalis left behind when some rock-moth hatched and flew off."[135] Some rocks are liquid at birth and capable of flight; others are lit from within by their own iridescence created by the internal reflection of minerals, a property known as "schiller." In "Labradorite," spirit, supposedly lighter than air, reveals itself in that which is most solid. "Spirit beings of aurora borealis, / say the Inuit, remain / trapped in the rock, still / dancing the dancerless dance."[136]

In some of the most emotionally resonant moments in *Paradoxides*, McKay leaps from quotidian life to deep time and back again – like the Taoist sage whose meditations lead out into the cosmos and home to his garden gate – with a renewed sense of gratitude and awe. "Eddy Out" dismisses, with great wit, the neuroticisms accompanying the onset of winter (summarized here as "snow tire– / firewood–long john frenzy") and comes to rest in the memory of a gathering of young families, a sing-a-long to "Good Night Irene," and a night sky alive with the colours of the Northern Lights.[137] The poem "Snowball Earth" tells the story of a time "when winter won," a reference to a planetary deep-freeze that lasted for 100 million years, and then celebrates the fact that the green fuse pushed through and prevailed:

> Let all who dwell
> on the blue-green planet celebrate
> the mother magma churning at its heart,
> the home fires that kept burning and at length undid
> that cold Precambrian spell.[138]

Like Dennis Lee, Don McKay remained eagle-minded and productive into his seventies. He published *Angular Unconformity: Collected Poems 1970–2014* in October 2014, which includes new poems and a Borges-esque afterword, "Brief Encounter," in which McKay and his younger self quarrel over their respective preoccupations with shape-changing and wilderness (each leaves the encounter disgusted with the other). The ten poems of *Larix*, a chapbook published in 2015, continue his exploration of those facets of the world mostly invisible to modern culture. His gift for seeing beneath daily aware-ness to the broad contours of the land and the processes that churn through it is on hand in the title poem. There, his speaker takes note of the lurch in the lane near the Williamstown farmhouse – a "dis-tinct jog" in the road that confirms the existence of an old elm tree long lost to Dutch elm disease.[139] The warmth of "Larix" is reversed in "How It Got Dark," which traces in rapid-fire progression the evolution from tools to *matériel*, and then corkscrews into an apoc-alyptically funny encounter with a red squirrel who jumped into the speaker's stew pot on a camping trip, and then had the gall to sass him from a nearby pine tree. "I said that's it, / let's get the little bugger and picked / up the first stone."[140]

One of the most intriguing poems in *Larix* speaks to McKay's third-act fascination with biosemiosis, the study of the vast web through which the earth communicates with itself. In "Biosemiosis: some issues," he asks "Sign, sing, signify, what / are they up to?"[141] Everything communicates; everything means; "it seems forests / bristle with encrypted messages / we seldom intercept."[142] Jesper Hoffmeyer (1997) calls this web the "semiosphere," which incor-porates "all forms of communication: sounds, smells, movements, colors, shapes, electrical fields, thermal radiation, waves of all kinds, chemical signals, touching, and so on."[143] What biosemiotics offers us, McKay said, is the opportunity to shift away from human lan-guage as the paradigm through which we measure and credit other beings according to how well they can perform in that arena (in a letter he cited the disastrous Nim Chimpsky experiment in which a chimpanzee was raised as a human child). Instead of insisting that other species have linguistic capability – orangutans learning American Sign Language or the well-publicized skills of Kanzi the bonobo at the Great Ape Trust – we might talk about the communi-cative strategies found among different species. The linguistic model might be dropped in order to focus on our different capacities as message bearers and receivers. "If we shift from a linguistic to a semi-otic model," he said, "then we have effectively stopped the dubious practice of inviting them in our *Umwelt* for assessment and begun to appreciate the incredibly vast set of interconnecting messages which make up an ecosystem."[144] McKay explored some of these issues as one of the co-hosts of "Enlichenment, Enlivement, and the Poetics of Place," an intimate, five-day workshop held at Trevor Goward's house in the Clearwater Valley in April 2017.

In terms of his other activities, McKay contributed poems used as source texts and libretto material for *Song of Extinction*, an experimental film directed by Marc de Guerre that premiered at the Luminato Festival in June 2016. He was an enthusiastic participant at the Gros Morne Summer Music Festival, where he read his work alongside performances by the musical group Dark by Five, whose members were wearing bird masks inspired by his poetry; in a letter he compared the experience to "being (willingly) kidnapped by the circus."[145] McKay retired from his editorial responsibilities at Brick Books in January 2018 after more than forty years. He resurfaced in public in March, when he gave a lecture at the University of Prince Edward Island called "Dragon, or Tectonic Lithofacies Map of the Appalachian Orogen" ("I used Power Point and survived!" he told me afterwards).[146] In October 2018, he was the Page Lecturer at Queen's University; his talk, "Play and Work in the Work of Joanne Page," honoured the contributions of the late poet, journalist, and literary organizer. McKay has also been working with Rosalind Gill on a polyglottal manuscript about the Eskimo Curlew, a bird that migrates between North and South America and passes through a host of living languages on its migration, including Portuguese, Spanish, and English, as well as the homelands of the now-extinguished Aztec and Beothuk civilizations. He has written a memoir, or "sketches from memory," which engaged "departed parents in a mode of writing where unfinished tensions could be aired and a form of redress attempted."[147] He shelved the memoir after he became aware of his own motives, acknowledging it as a "strange endeavour" he is "loathe to publish."[148] Is there perhaps another collection of poems or essays on the horizon? When I asked him as much in an exchange of letters in late 2018, McKay filled some five pages with comments addressed to an imaginary James Reaney ("Jamie Reaney, thou shouldst be living at this hour"), along with reflections on the botched nature of university politics and an assortment of other jokes and gags involving the moose horn ("nature's revenge on music").[149] It was a perfect answer, so full of dodging and weaving and mirth that I almost forgot the question.

3

Robert Bringhurst

Renaissance Man

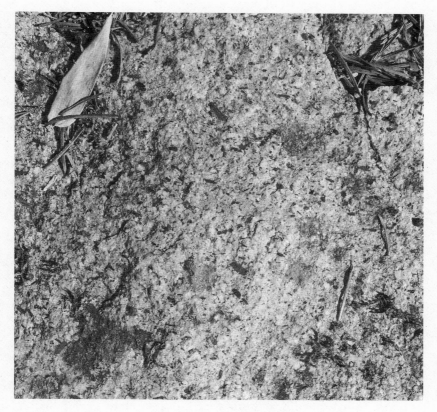

Rock, moss, Douglas-fir needles, and willow leaf, Quadra Island, British Columbia. Courtesy of Robert Bringhurst.

Among the poets of this book, Robert Bringhurst's biography is
without compare. There are epic travels, encounters with sages and
teachers from across human history, walk-on parts for some of the
most important figures of twentieth-century cultural and intellectual life, and a roiling controversy that rocked the CanLit world. He
has made important contributions to a number of fields – poetry,
philosophy, translation, cultural history, typography, and book
design – all the while guided by an arresting vision, alluded to in an
essay written at mid-career. "Home," Bringhurst writes, "is where
the stones have not stopped breathing and the light is still alive."[1]
This perception of a world defined by its aliveness is all but dead in
our time. The enormous task he has taken on is to help us recover
the ability to perceive and participate in "the beauty of being."[2]

To do this, Bringhurst has consistently sought the help of "the old
in their knowing," or elders from a number of pre-modern civilizations who knew very well they were surrounded by a world that was
so much more than a collection of natural resources.[3] His search,
which he acknowledges is nowhere near comprehensive or complete,
has led him to the poet-philosophers of pre-Socratic Greece, the
prophets of the Levant of the Old Testament, the teachers and sages
of Taoist and Buddhist Asia, the artist-thinkers of the Florentine
Renaissance, and the mythtellers of Indigenous North America.
Whether in the form of literal translations or creative imaginings
of their works, Bringhurst urges us to remember that other people
also moved to the patterns and movements of a living world. His
re-imagined Lianhua Fengxian says: "Stop writing the guidebook.
/ Our ancestors reached here as well. / They tasted this wind, and
they left us / this cache of old footsteps."[4] Following their footprints
allowed Bringhurst to experience for himself what he'd only dimly
sensed in his formative years: the earth as a multi-levelled, many-
voiced, poly-temporal being whose intricacy of structure could
somehow be explored through human consciousness. "I came to
realize clearly," writes Dōgen, the founder of Soto Zen Buddhism,
"that mind is not other than mountains, rivers, and the great wide
earth, the sun and moon and stars."[5]

These encounters with some of humankind's most perceptive
teachers transformed Bringhurst's sense of himself as a poet. Had he
not immersed himself in the works of Herakleitos, Dōgen, Skaay, and
others, it seems unlikely that he would have gone on to reconceive
poetry as a polyphonic medium, or a place where overlapping words

aspire to emulate the interwoven music and boxes-in-boxes structure of the non-human world. Poems like *The Blue Roofs of Japan, New World Suite No. 3,* and *Ursa Major* not only reconfigure the medium of print but also invite our surroundings into the act of reading. Such activities – and so many others – are among Bringhurst's ways of reseeding an awareness of the earth into a culture predisposed to ignore it. Hence his friend Gary Snyder's description of him as a "Renaissance man ... a solitary artist and thinker who's in touch with almost everything."[6]

Dislocations, upheavals, and long migrations characterize Robert Bringhurst's family background. His maternal grandfather was abandoned as an infant in a field in Oklahoma, making him "the perfect ancestor," Bringhurst said, because he wasn't from anywhere, had no inherited traditions to keep alive, and could start from scratch.[7] His mother, Marion Large, was sixteen when she left Idaho for Los Angeles with her sister. She lied about her age and found work as a typist. Bringhurst's father's side of the family took their name from a small village in the English Midlands. The Bringhursts, who were Quakers, left England toward the end of the seventeenth century, going first to the Netherlands and then to Philadelphia in 1699. Bringhurst's father, George, grew up in Garland, Wyoming, a town that was abandoned in his own lifetime. George had a certain aptitude with machines and worked as an electrician, carpenter, and inventor while in his twenties. When the United States entered the Second World War in 1941, he tried to enlist as a paratrooper but was denied entry to jump school when it was discovered he did not have thirty-two teeth.

Robert Bringhurst was born on 16 October 1946 in Los Angeles, "a city of migrants where everyone was from somewhere else, and trying to get someplace else."[8] His arrival, he said, "ruined" George's life because his father was forced to find full-time work to support his family.[9] After a year in South Central living in the black ghetto, George moved the family to Salt Lake City, Utah, for work. He applied at Lennox Furnace Co. for a job in the warehouse and was so persistent in his application for a job with no future that they took him on as a salesman instead. Between 1947 and 1952, he moved his family another five times, around the state of Montana. Their sixth move in that same time span saw them cross the border into Canada, where George was given the job of regional general manager for the company's western Canadian division, based out of Calgary.

What Bringhurst remembered about the quick succession of towns and cities he passed through as a child was how phony they seemed. Western North America looked like an enormous construction site, perpetually building itself up and tearing itself down in a hyper-accelerated parody of growth and decay. Nothing looked as though it had been there for very long and couldn't be brushed aside in short order. People did not seem aware of, or responsive to, the enormous, elemental presences around them. "There was no sense of being surrounded by something outside of your control, nothing to wonder at," he said. "I felt like I was drowning."[10]

Growing up in a house without books, Bringhurst learned to write before he could read, identifying individual letters of the alphabet and then writing pages and pages of them, his mother circling the words that formed accidently in the stream. George, who wanted his wife to himself, sent his son to live with relatives in Wyoming every summer. When Bringhurst was seven, his father packed him off to 'Ooléé'jtó, a Navajo community in southern Utah, to spend two months with a family that had converted to Mormonism (one side effect of this early exposure to Indigenous life in the Southwest, Bringhurst said, is that he doesn't feel like "an alien in a native household").[11] In Calgary, he skipped grade 4, changed schools, was introduced to two sports he had never seen before (soccer and hockey), and learned French from a one-armed Irish teacher who had an imaginary dog named Hypothesis. His schoolyard was unusually diverse: his first friend was Polish; he fell in love with a girl who was Estonian and whose best friend was Latvian; and in time his circle widened to include Blackfoot and Cree children.

In 1959, when Bringhurst was thirteen, his father was transferred back to the Salt Lake Valley. He entered grade 9 at Olympus High School in the suburb of Cottonwood, already having been put ahead yet another year, making him the youngest person in the class. Michael Peglau, who lived a couple of doors down the street, remembers Bringhurst showing up as if his personality was already fully formed, a teenager who preferred classical guitar and drums to '60s popular music, and rarely spoke in class.

Bringhurst fell in with a group of friends who were both academically and athletically gifted. He was fearless, but not talented, at sports. His inner compass was already pointing somewhere else, away from the playing fields to the sheer vertical rise of the mountains beyond. While in Calgary, his parents had sent him to a camp in the Rockies where climbing was taught. Since then, he had been reading books on the subject and going on solo expeditions to put into practice what he learned. One weekend, he decided to climb Mount Olympus, a bone-dry peak that towered some 5,000 feet over the Salt Lake Valley. There was no trail, Peglau told me; Bringhurst just found his way up there, and made little noise of it on his return. Another set of landscapes that beckoned him were the slick rock canyons of southern Utah, home to mysterious pictographs that were like tiny windows onto some other reality he felt drawn to but could not understand. Once he had his driver's licence, he would often disappear with his car – a used Triumph TR3 – and explore those canyons at length.

Around this time, Bringhurst discovered *The Cantos* by Ezra Pound. He was tipped off by a reference in Jack Kerouac's *The Dharma Bums* and tracked down a beautiful hardcover copy of Pound's eclectic masterwork in a used bookstore in the suburbs of Salt Lake City. He likened *The Cantos* to "a great sprawling landscape of quotations and sentences as if a bomb had gone off in a polylingual library."[12] He understood very little of what he encountered, and told Michael Peglau that he had to go and "chew nails" after every few pages.[13] "I had a sense that there was something going on, and I wanted to know what it was."[14]

In September 1962, aged fifteen, Bringhurst began taking philosophy courses at the University of Utah in the afternoon while still attending Olympus High in the morning. The following spring, he published his first poems (under the name "Bob Bringhurst") in *Pegasus*, the school magazine, and graduated from high school that June. He spent much of the summer climbing in Wyoming's Teton Range, making a solo ascent of Grand Teton, the second-highest mountain in the state at just over 13,000 feet. He also began reading Daisetsu Suzuki, who beginning in the 1920s had almost single-handedly introduced Zen Buddhism to North American audiences hungry for a different way of thinking of being.

In the fall of 1963, Bringhurst moved to Boston by himself to begin his undergraduate career at the Massachusetts Institute of Technology (MIT) on a scholarship to study architecture. He wasn't yet seventeen years old and was "about as socially awkward as they come."[15] He quickly left the program when he realized that there was no room

for electives and that he wasn't interested in designing large spaces
for 500 people that he himself wouldn't want to be in (he gravitated
immediately to Bernard Rudofsky's *Architecture without Architects*
when it was published the following year). He used an exemption
from freshman math to take a course in Milton, a decision that did
not go over well at home. "I remember a phone conversation with
my father in which he asked what courses I was taking. I said physics, psychology, etc., etc., and Milton. 'What's Milton?' he asked.
'An English poet,' I said. And the line went silent."[16] By his second
semester, Bringhurst was filling his schedule with almost nothing but
humanities courses. He encountered Chaucer and Dante for the first
time. He listened to tapes of a "quite drunk" Dylan Thomas reading
poetry. "These impressed me greatly," he said.[17]

Bringhurst's instinct was to approach the study of literature from
an unusual angle – linguistics, a discipline that traditionally did not
concern itself with anything beyond the individual sentence. He
wanted to know what language was, how it knew what it did, where
it came from. His interest in linguistics brought him into conversation with Noam Chomsky, whose classes he would sit in on from
time to time. Already a major figure in the field, Chomsky gave him
the all-important advice that one cannot know anything about language if all the languages you know are from the same family. For
the necessary perspective, Chomsky suggested, Bringhurst had to get
outside Indo-European languages altogether.

Bringhurst left MIT after a year, returned to Utah, and in the summer of 1964 attended an intensive course in Arabic at the University
of Utah. "Arabic was hard," he said, "The first thing I had ever done
that was hard."[18] He became enthralled with T.E. Lawrence, the
self-styled, larger-than-life British soldier and archaeologist whose
activities in the Arab Revolt in the Sinai were described in his book
The Seven Pillars of Wisdom (1922). That fall, Bringhurst officially
transferred to Utah and spent the year studying philosophy and
Arabic. After a stint working on a rail dock in Salt Lake City, he
caught a freighter for Casablanca in the spring of 1965; upon land-
ing, his use of Arabic startled a tout who approached him in French.
He passed through Italy, detouring to Rapallo to stop at Ezra
Pound's house. When he realized that he had nothing to ask Pound,
who at the time wasn't talking to many people anyway, he walked
on past Pound's gate and made his way to Greece and Egypt. He
spent May to September in Beirut before moving to a small village

near Bcharré in the mountains of Lebanon, where he set about his errand in the Middle East with characteristic single-minded purpose. He imbibed the culture and the language, yet was more concerned with finding his way to the roots of such things. Letters to friends at the time, tersely worded and beautifully crafted, testified to his ability to internalize a landscape and find a few right phrases with which to evoke it.

In December of that year, as the war in Vietnam began taking its disturbing form, the US draft board came looking for Bringhurst. George relayed the message to his son, who pondered his options: he could declare himself a stateless person, re-enroll at MIT, or move to Canada or France as a draft dodger. "What bothered me most about it," Bringhurst said, "was the wholesale submission to authority."[19] While he wasn't a pacifist, Bringhurst thought it was pointless for the United States to be fighting a peasant culture, and ludicrous to be doing so with heavy industrial weapons, burning up forests, harassing villages, and counting bodies to keep score. He decided on an unlikely course of action. He learned that if he joined up instead of being drafted, he would have some say in where he went and what he did, though he would have to serve for a longer term. He returned to the United States and, on 15 January 1966, enlisted with the army as a military linguist to escape the draft. Much to the worry of his friends, he entered the army enthusiastically, seeing it as another domain of experience to plumb. After basic training, he went directly to the Defense Language Institute at the Presidio of Monterey, where he worked as an assistant to instructors of Arabic ("the teachers included some wise old émigrés," he said).[20] His schedule was generous, with weekends off, and he devoted much of his free time to hiking and rock climbing.

On one such leave, Bringhurst and Peglau wanted to go south to Big Sur. They caught a ride with beatnik icon Neal Cassady, who at that point was only two years removed from his stint as the main driver of "Further," Ken Kesey's psychedelic bus immortalized in *The Electric Kool-Aid Acid Test*. On their way down the coast, Cassady made a detour to an isolated farmhouse in search of a legendary cocaine stash and, once back on the highway, drove over a hundred miles an hour, often on the wrong side of the road, taking corners on two wheels. When one of the other passengers – a young woman from Stanford University – begged him to slow down, Cassady opened the driver's side door, touched the asphalt with the back of his hand, and, now bloodied, warned her: "Don't bother me when I'm driving." The party of five headed to yet another isolated farmhouse near Big Sur, where Cassady believed the Merry Pranksters would be arriving later that night. Bringhurst and Peglau disembarked and headed into the mountains. Five miles in, and well up the mountainside with a stunning view of the Pacific, they stopped and talked for some time before noticing heavy fog rolling in off the ocean. When they returned to the farm just before nightfall, the Pranksters had indeed arrived en masse from Oregon. In the LSD-fuelled chaos that ensued, which at one point involved an axe and a suspected witch, the two hikers slipped back to the car to wait out the night. Bringhurst had nothing against psychedelics – at fourteen he had tried peyote, "the drug in vogue at the time" – but he had no interest in '60s counterculture beyond his interest in Cassady, whom he described as "a fascinating study in human functionality."

Early in the summer of 1967, Bringhurst was on leave visiting his parents, now living in Portland, when the Six-Day War broke out in the Middle East. He was immediately transferred from Monterey to the Army Security Agency detachment at National Security Agency (NSA) headquarters at Fort Meade, Maryland, where he did "ELINT," or electronic intelligence, work – intercepting, decrypting, and translating radio traffic worldwide. Not long after his arrival, he was asked if he wanted to go and work for the Israelis. Bringhurst soon found himself based in Netanya, Israel, making short forays into the Sinai Peninsula. A broad expanse of land nominally claimed and colonized by Egypt, the Sinai had been seized by Israel in the war, even though it was home to just a few towns of settlers and otherwise inhabited by Bedouin nomads. When the Israel Defense Forces (IDF) ran the Egyptian garrisons out of the Sinai in June, they found themselves with a vast collection of captured equipment, some pedestrian, some quite sophisticated. They also came into possession of Russian manuals on chemical warfare with process or operating instructions in Arabic taped next to a dial or control knob. The convoy's orders were to bring in as much of the hardware, and as many of the documents, to Netanya. Like the other Americans in the convoy, Bringhurst had to dress as an Israeli soldier and speak only Arabic or French to disguise his country's presence in the region. Unlike the munitions experts or the specialists in weapons design and electronics, though, no one quite knew what to do with the linguists on these forays, meaning that Bringhurst had no orders to follow other than watch and observe.

This suited him fine, for he considered himself temperamentally an anthropologist, not a participant, in the conflict.

Bringhurst returned to Fort Meade via London, England, in December, expecting to be reassigned to the IDF, even though he had strong misgivings about it. He was by now clashing on a regular basis with NSA administrators and other military authorities. During one confrontation, his eyes were repeatedly drawn to the large map of the world that his boss kept on his wall. It was in black and white: the world as it existed in the minds of many during the Cold War. "I did not want to be working to reinforce that notion of the human species," he said.[21] He told the man with the map that he wanted to resign his security clearance, a request that raised a number of eyebrows because no one had ever said such a thing before. He sat in limbo for a few months – the NSA building off limits to him – and mostly read books.

As the Vietnam War continued to intensify, Bringhurst asked to be transferred there as a combat photographer. He wanted a way of seeing what was going on "without having to shoot anyone to do it."[22] To his considerable disappointment, he was sent to Panama for a year and a half instead to serve as a military police photographer, even though he knew nothing about photography. He was quickly reassigned to the legal office at base headquarters as a law clerk, a job for which he had no qualifications. He was given a pleasant office lined with books on military law and regulations, and encouraged to start reading. A few months later, the command legal officer left, and when no qualified lawyer appeared to take his place, Bringhurst was put in charge of the legal office at HQ Fort Clayton. He organized courts martial, wrote wills and powers of attorney, and freed American soldiers imprisoned for minor marijuana possession. Because he had to become an expert on all manner of military regulations, he discovered that he could actually be discharged from the army six months early to accept an offer of seasonal employment in civilian life. When he learned that his parents, once again on the move, had begun operating a fishing camp in the village of Quinault on the Olympic Peninsula in Washington, he saw his chance. In October 1969, three months before his four-year hitch was up, Bringhurst was discharged from active military service. He put his car on a ship, put himself on a plane, and moved into a cabin not far from his parents' new home.

Ten months later, Bringhurst moved to Boston, re-enrolled at MIT to study linguistics with the GI Bill covering his tuition and providing a living allowance, and started to look for work as a part-time journalist. He joined *Time* magazine as a low-level stringer, contributing "files" converted into stories by staff writers in New York. He moved to Bloomington, Indiana, the following year, accompanied by his wife-to-be, Miki Sheffield, whom he had known since high school. They settled outside of the city in an old farmhouse, where she worked with horses and he set out to finish, once and for all, his undergraduate degree. Indiana University had an experimental program called Independent Learning that allowed a student to design their own plan of study so long as they could find professors willing to tutor them. Their education was to be conducted in the library, not the classroom, an approach that suited Bringhurst perfectly. He invented a degree in comparative literature and tracked down three capable tutors to help him find his way. These were Robert Gross, a scholar of Ezra Pound; Mohammad Alwan, whose specialty was Arabic poetry; and Willis Barnstone, a poet and translator who produced a steady stream of award-winning books and who demonstrated by example how the two vocations could coexist and inform one another.

Bringhurst completed his first translations of French and Arabic poets, including works by Villon and Badr Shakir al-Sayyab, in 1972. He, Sheffield, and a few other friends set up Kanchenjunga Press (named after the third-highest mountain in the world) to publish their own work. Because he had studied a bit of architecture, his friends assumed he knew something about typography and book-making as well, and appointed him the press's designer. He accepted the role without complaint, went to the library, and gave himself a crash course in the field, beginning with Daniel Berkeley Updike's *Printing Types: Their History, Forms and Use*. His climb to the summit of typography had begun.

In *The Shipwright's Log* (1972), the first of his books to appear under the Kanchenjunga imprint, Bringhurst tries out a number of different genres, triggering a number of gaffes and misfires (including groaners like "I need your love to make my hate come true").[23] Most of the poems are written from his personal perspective, in the voice of the lyric ego; this is noteworthy because "I the writer" all but disappears from his later work. He experiments with social satire in "Haruspications in a Whorehouse" (that's "Private Bungburst" at the bar); elsewhere he measures himself against modernist masters Ezra Pound, Basil Bunting, and, in the following excerpt from "Sinai," the T.S. Eliot of *Four Quartets*: "And there is time if not tomorrow / in the stillness, and tomorrow if not time / above the flutter in the hull."[24] There are also signs of an emerging poetic sensibility that is recognizably his, including his eye for the elements underlying the human social sphere, a voice with the emotional texture of gunmetal, and, in "The Sun and the Moon," the mythic landscapes that would figure prominently in his later work:

> In the night's darkness there was once no moon,
> and no sun rose into the dawn's light, no sun
> sucked the color from the grass.
> No moon opened the empty womb,
> no moon frosted water, leaf and stone.
> No sun burned into the upturned eye at noon
> or polished the sparrowhawk's skull
> or the coyote's bone.[25]

A second apprentice book, *Cadastre*, followed in 1973. There Bringhurst moves away from the confessions and impressions of the lyric ego to begin a sustained engagement with the voices of the past. This lifelong practice, he explains in a little-seen foreword from the 2001 edition of *Book of Silences*, involves "rooting through the library, digging up the dead, holding their bones to my ears like shells, and pulling their skulls down over my head."[26] Translating their work allowed him to see through their eyes, commingle with their consciousness, and explore the world as they knew it. Bringhurst's first group of adopted elders, introduced in *Cadastre*, hail from the fishing villages of Ancient Greece before Socrates and Plato. These "nature-thinkers," or *physikói* as they were known to later Greek thinkers, saw the world as a constantly moving and changing entity the likes of which, according to Aristotle, they felt "nothing at all could be truthfully said."[27] Bringhurst met the pre-Socratics, as they are now remembered, through Bertrand Russell's *History of Western Philosophy*, and told me that he has been "rooting for them" all his life (following Heidegger, Bringhurst includes the dramatist Sophocles among their ranks).[28] While their thought had been ground to fragments, the tradition they belonged to could grow again through translation and creative interpretation – a service Bringhurst begins to provide in *Cadastre* through dramatic monologues inspired by their work. His poem "Herakleitos," for example, reworks and expands a single fragment, translated here by classicist

Charles Kahn: "Immortals are mortal, mortals immortal, living the
other's death, dead in the other's life."[29] This mysterious little fragment seems to suggest that the dead possess some of the attributes of
the living and vice versa, and that while they may be separated, there
can also be exchange between them. After a number of drafts and
rewrites, here is what Bringhurst makes of this fragment:

Dead men are gods; men are dead gods, said
Herakleitos. Immortals are mortal, mortals immortal.
The birth of the one is the death of the other;
the dying of one gives life to the other.

The living are dying. The dead live forever,
except when the living disturb them, and this
they must do. The gods die
when men live forever. Air, earth and fire
die too. Dying, we mother and sire

the other: our only and own
incarnation.[30]

It is worth noting that Bringhurst's communion with the dead
began at exactly the same moment he discovered the need for roots.
In 1973, he returned to Canada to begin an MFA in writing at the
University of British Columbia. "When I rolled into Vancouver to go
to grad school, I had not only never lived on the Northwest Coast; I
had never lived in any particular place for very long. The idea of staying put seemed stranger to me than going to the moon."[31] Canadian
writers, he noticed, seemed especially preoccupied with place. This
fascination was shared by two of his new friends, fellow-American
expats J. Michael Yates and Charles Lillard, renegades associated
with the creative writing program. And with that, Bringhurst began
to wonder where he was. He found a clue of sorts in the library
basement, which was where the collection of Northwest Coast and
Oceanic art was being stored prior to the construction of the new
Museum of Anthropology. As impressed as he was by those artifacts,
he didn't respond to them in any noticeable way. "I hadn't taken up
the challenge they posed."[32]

For his three areas of concentration, Bringhurst chose poetry,
translation, and screenwriting. He wrote one of his finest early poems

during this time, "Deuteronomy," which re-enacts Moses' ascent up
Mount Sinai, his encounter with a presence that utterly defies mental categories, and his return from the summit with two flat stones
that said "what it seemed to me two stones / should say."[33] Another
early project was a screenplay adaptation of Ovid's *Metamorphoses*,
a hopelessly sprawling affair that was "twenty times the size of a
documentary."[34] Bringhurst's thesis, "Carmina propria et opuscula
translata," defended in 1975, was a combination of his own poems
and some translations from Arabic and other languages.

While Bringhurst did not aspire to become an academic, mis-
fortune intervened to keep him at the university after finishing his
degree. Pat Lowther, a gifted poet who had just started teaching in
the department, was murdered by her husband in September 1975;
with twenty-four hours' notice, Bringhurst was asked to step in and
take over her course load. He inherited a group of students – not all
of whom stuck it out over that difficult semester – that included Erin
Mouré, Daniel David Moses, and lifelong friends Roo Borson and
Kim Maltman.

Bringhurst's next book-length collection was *Bergschrund*, published in 1975. The title refers to a crevasse that forms at the head of
a glacier when moving ice breaks away from the snowpack above.
"This is a book largely about mountains," he explained, "and the
condition of the mind in the mountains, which is one of predominant clarity, I hope."[35]

The difference is nothing you can see – only
the dressed edge of the air
over those stones, and the air goes

deeper into the lung, like a long fang,
clean as magnesium.[36]

In poem after poem, Bringhurst continues to engage with and
occasionally dispute the modernist poets he carried with him
on his forays into the Coast Mountains around Vancouver. His
"Gods immersed in the masked / North American air" from "The
Greenland Stone," for example, re-imagines Pound's "Gods float in
the azure air."[37] In its first six sections, one of the most elliptical
sequences in the collection, "Hachadura," is an image-by-image,
stanza-by-stanza response to "Le Monocle de Mon Oncle" by

Wallace Stevens. Elsewhere in *Bergschrund*, Bringhurst continues his practice of disappearing behind the mask of one historical or mythological figure after another, using them as personae and composing dramatic monologues in their voices to explore cultures and landscapes far removed from his own. This was the equivalent, he told me, of "passing one brain through the inside of another," a form of mutual thinking or compound intelligence that transcended the limits of individual consciousness.[38] "It's just my way of hanging out with some of my dead friends – buying the ghosts a drink and letting them talk if they want to."[39]

His engagement with the dead is similar in spirit to that of Ezra Pound, the American expatriate and iconoclast whose work Bringhurst found in his teens. He shared Pound's conviction that literature might serve as "the guide and lamp of civilization," a regenerative force in a culture hollowed out by the rapid transformations and upheavals of the twentieth century.[40] The modern experience had moved forward so rapidly, Pound argued, that teachings from earlier generations had been forgotten or ignored, leaving great gaps or lacunae in the consciousness of our time. The central task of the writer is to fill these gaps by auditing the works of the past, sifting for insights that extended the reach of human understanding. Those "luminous details" might eventually be incorporated as accepted truths that govern knowledge "as the switchboard the electric circuit," Pound wrote.[41] Yet recovering forgotten wisdom was only the first part of Pound's salvage project. The writer, wherever necessary, had to "make it new," restoring to past works their potency so that they might sing in the minds of another generation. Translation, as the central task of the cultural historian, involved less a literal rendering from one language to another and more the revitalization of the spirit of the original in a new form. The aim, Pound wrote, was to drive "the reader's perception further into the original than it would without them have penetrated."[42]

In the years after *Bergschrund*, Bringhurst continued to experiment with different personae, using the poem as a kind of manned submersible to explore lost or submerged worlds. He gravitated consistently to thinkers, prophets, and artists who understood themselves to be surrounded by a world populated with gods, ghosts, and numinous landforms that could intrude upon the lives of human beings with impunity. He attempted a translation of the *Persae* of Aeschylus at the invitation of editor and classicist William Arrowsmith, but neither he nor his sponsor were happy with the results and the manuscript was destroyed. He meditated on angelology and mountains in "Jacob Singing," looked out at the Florentine Renaissance from Francesco Petrarch's deathbed in "The Stonecutter's Horses," and visited Fifth Dynasty Egypt through the eyes of a government minister in "The Song of Ptahhotep." "Bone Flute Breathing" revisits the gruesome consequences of the musical duel between Apollo and Marsyas, and in "Leda and the Swan," Bringhurst asks what a mortal human female might be able to teach a male god. He made his first attempt to engage with Indigenous realities in "Tzuhalem's Mountain," a sequence based on a historical account of a Qu'wutsun' warrior and iconoclast who took refuge with more than two dozen kidnapped wives on the east side of Vancouver Island.

Bringhurst's term as a visiting lecturer at the University of British Columbia came to an end in 1977. "It was not unpleasant work, but it was not my kind of life," he said. "If I'd stayed, it would have destroyed me."[43] He spent the next year running a Vancouver typesetting firm owned by George Payerle where he continued his apprenticeship to letterforms, "as organic in their secondary way as seashells, hoofprints, fossils."[44] After that, he began making his living as a freelance typographer and editor. One of his chief clients was Douglas & McIntyre, and many of the books he worked on at this time took as their subject matter "the culture of place," as Scott McIntyre writes, of British Columbia.[45] Three of the most important of these were books about the art and cultural traditions of West Coast Indigenous cultures: *Looking at Indian Art of the Northwest Coast* (1979), *Salish Weaving* (1980), and *Gathering What the Great Nature Provided: Food Traditions of the Gitskan* (1980). Preparing each of these texts gave Bringhurst something of a crash course in the history of his adopted province, sensitizing him to both the existence of marginalized Indigenous peoples and the relationships they had cultivated with the land down through the millennia. If North American civilization were to ever go sustainable, he realized, it would have to learn how to listen to these land-based traditions and the cultural authorities who maintained them. In an interview with Jane Munro published in 1980, Bringhurst described himself as "very eager" to learn about these traditions, and talked about the need as well as the impossibility of settler culture "Indianizing" itself. "That doesn't really work very well either because it's false," he said. "So we're vagrants, we're migrants, we're intruders, although the land is ours now as much as it is anybody's and we have to do the best we can by it."[46]

In the spring of 1980, and still unsure how to be where he was, Bringhurst began dividing his time between a garret in Vancouver and a cabin in Garibaldi, a township in the Coast Mountains that had been abandoned because of the threat of rock slides. He used the cabin as a writing retreat and base camp for parts of the next two years, setting out into the Garibaldi and Mamquam mountains on solo hikes that lasted for weeks at a time. He was acutely aware of the fact that he didn't know the names let alone the defining qualities of most of the species and landforms around him. He studied the natural architecture of the highlands, grieved the view of clear-cuts they revealed, experimented with freeze-dried foods, and read ancient sages and philosophers in his sleeping bag when fog rolling in off the Georgia Strait made hiking impossible. "There's no place on the planet that I've ever been happier," he said. "Being there, for me, is like being in one of those Renaissance paintings where humans and gods are permitted to mingle on equal terms."[47] His time among the gods was not without dangerous incident. He once saw an uprooted tree come down a mountain stream in a flood and tear out a roadbed, ripping a six-foot-diameter steel culvert out of the ground and tossing it aside like a toilet paper tube. He put a crampon through an air mattress on one of his climbs, a mistake with potentially disastrous consequences when sleeping on snow and ice with no insulation. When he forgot to bring gloves, he climbed an ice cliff with socks on his hands. He fell down a long steep snow slope – "I had only travelled that fast in an automobile" – and was spared at the last moment when he dug in his heels just above some jagged rocks at the bottom.[48]

Bringhurst also took refuge in the mountains for personal reasons. He and Miki Sheffield had gotten married in 1974, but their relationship was all but over when their daughter was conceived a few years later ("Human relationships all too rarely have clean, sharp beginnings and endings," he said).[49] While his marriage staggered on for a little while longer – he and Sheffield were not legally divorced until 1981 – he couldn't save it nor form a bond with his daughter, from whom he became permanently estranged. The emotional catastrophe of a family unravelling is the subject of "These Poems, She Said," one of the only poems in his entire oeuvre in which he comes out from behind a mask:

These poems, these poems,
these poems, she said, are poems
with no love in them. These are the poems of a man
who would leave his wife and child because
they made noise in his study. These are the poems
of a man who would murder his mother to claim
the inheritance. These are the poems of a man
like Plato, she said, meaning something I did not
comprehend but which nevertheless
offended me. These are the poems of a man
who would rather sleep with himself than with women,
she said. These are the poems of a man
with eyes like a drawknife, with hands like a pickpocket's
hands, woven of water and logic
and hunger, with no strand of love in them.[50]

"These Poems, She Said" is the frontispiece of *The Beauty of the Weapons: Selected Poems 1972–82*, which began its life when Dennis Lee, newly installed as editor of the Modern Canadian Poets series at McClelland & Stewart, got in touch with Bringhurst and suggested that they pull together an early/mid-career volume of selected poems out of work that had been published in a number of hard-to-find magazines, periodicals, and chapbooks. In November of that year, Lee flew out to Vancouver and the two of them sat together, sixteen hours a day for four days, going over the text of *The Beauty of the Weapons* one word at a time (Bringhurst's account of the time the two poets spent under one roof, recounted in *Tasks of Passion: Dennis Lee at Mid-Career* (1982), is an understated comic gem). At Lee's insistence, he compiled a glossary with definitions of key words, phrases, and historical personalities that appear in the book. Knowing that Lee would edit him ruthlessly, he made an eight-hour trip from Vancouver to Clearwater Valley to track down Trevor Goward, who was holed up with friends in a remote cabin even further back in the bush. All this was done to inquire after a species of lichen, *Alectoria sarmentosa*, that makes the briefest of appearances in "Tzuhalem's Mountain." When I asked him why he made the trip, Bringhurst shrugged and said: "I had to know what I was talking about."[51]

Bringhurst was sworn in as a Canadian citizen on 24 July 1982, yet still felt far removed from the country's Indigenous realities. He was well aware of the *fact* of Indigenous North America, having cultivated what his colleague Crispin Elsted called a "self-conscious anti-colonial passionate interest" in the subject.[52] He also knew of the existence of Indigenous oral literature, having come across a dusty, olive-green relic of a book called *Haida Texts and Myths: Skidegate Dialect* (1905) in the stacks of the UBC Library in the late 1970s. *Haida Texts and Myths* is a collection of oral narratives dictated to John Swanton, a linguist and career employee of the Bureau of American Ethnology, in the winter of 1900–01 on Haida Gwaii. Swanton had taken the essential step of Boasian anthropology and linguistics by transcribing word-for-word the stories he heard from Haida mythtellers. He didn't collapse them into tidy summaries scrubbed free of anything that might scandalize a Victorian sensibility, which was common practice among anthropologists at the time. What Swanton did that was truly unusual was that he did not stop. He went on to take thousands of pages of dictation when he realized that the mythtellers had something to say (Boas himself would have lost interest after a few hundred pages at most). "Reading Swanton's translations is what stopped me in my tracks and forced me to start thinking," Bringhurst said.[53] Yet he couldn't help but notice that Swanton's stories were dimmed somewhat by the linguist's faithful but flat prose and stilted sentence structure. His reliance on the convention of the paragraph seemed to blot out their structural intricacies. Swanton, Bringhurst realized, had laid an excellent foundation for a much bigger project he had been unable to complete.

In Bill Reid (1920–1998), Bringhurst found a guide and mentor to help him make sense of Haida mythology, and how individual myths lived in the minds of those who told and retold them. Reid first appeared on his horizon in 1976, when Bringhurst was still teaching as a sessional instructor at UBC. He used to bring his students over to the newly constructed Museum of Anthropology for his practical workshop on how to give a poetry reading – using an old machine-gun mount left over from the Second World War for a podium ("Nowadays, no ragtag bunch of poets would be allowed to do any such thing in the gallery space," he said).[54] From time to time, Bringhurst would see Reid, Jim Hart, and others working on the iconic *Raven and the First Men* sculpture, which was destined to occupy the very gun mount he and his students were using for their rehearsals. "I hadn't yet been introduced to Reid, and had never spoken to him. I just watched. He had his own key to the museum, and he came and went as he pleased," he said.[55] Scott McIntyre introduced the two in 1983 when he asked Bringhurst to assist Reid on *The Raven Steals the Light* (1984), a collection of ten traditional stories accompanied by ten of Reid's spectral graphite drawings. It was a stroke of good fortune for both men. Bringhurst had the opportunity to speak with a cultural authority who seemed to have internalized everything he was fascinated with; Reid met someone who could preserve the tradition's greatest literary accomplishments.

Although in his sixties and slowed by the onset of Parkinson's disease, Reid was nevertheless at his most artistically mature at the time of their meeting. He grew up at a distance from the landscape of his mother's people, learning the artistic traditions of the Haida by studying exemplary works of the past. As a young man, he'd been introduced to some of the elders who had listened in on John Swanton's work a half-century earlier. Then, while in Toronto apprenticing as a jeweller, he had spent long hours at the Royal Ontario Museum, where a mortuary pole from his grandmother's village jutted up through the stairwell, reawakening him to his ancestry. Often credited with helping to revive Haida monumental art, Reid himself frequently scoffed at such a prospect because, as Bringhurst writes, "he knew well how hard it is to make a work of art that measures up to the classical Haida standard."[56]

Working on *The Raven Steals the Light* gave the two men a chance to get to know one another, and before long, Reid became something of "a stand-in for the father" Bringhurst had earlier disowned.[57] Reid himself had been abandoned by his own father, an American of Scottish and German descent who moved to northern British Columbia to run a couple of hotels. "Reid was well acquainted with the hard and brittle silences that form from time to time between child and father, or father and child, and he too took a quizzical delight in the immediate and mutable relationships that now and then replace them," Bringhurst writes.[58] Reid introduced him to a circle of friends and associates that for Bringhurst became something of a surrogate family among the living: a grandfather in the structural anthropologist Claude Lévi-Strauss, an uncle in the visual anthropologist Edmund Carpenter, and a sister in Reid's wife Martine, herself an anthropologist and protégé of Lévi-Strauss.

Bringhurst became a regular fixture at Reid's studio on Granville Island, where he embarked on an artistic and spiritual apprenticeship

with the man known to some as Yaahl Sghwaansing or "Solitary
Raven." He learned how to use a crooked knife ("don't bleed on
the finished part," Reid offered helpfully), did some carving, and
received something of a crash course in Indigenous cultural politics.[59] Because of his own mixed heritage, Reid had no time for
anyone who hid behind their ethnicity or cited it as evidence of their
virtue. "Haida only means human being," he said, "and as far as I'm
concerned, a human being is anyone who respects the needs of his
fellow man, and the earth which nurtures and shelters us all."[60]

In the spring of 1984, Bringhurst accompanied Reid on one of
his annual pilgrimages to Haida Gwaii on board the *Norsal*, an old
wooden boat he frequently chartered. Bringhurst had his collapsible
kayak with him, "a French boat that makes up as either a double
or a big, cavernous single," which the poet and the sculptor put
to good use exploring the coastline.[61] They also spent time talking
about the stories that John Swanton had collected. Bringhurst was to
some degree stuck – he didn't have the capacity to read them in their
original language and couldn't make translations of his own. Reid
suggested to Bringhurst that he get inside the stories by approaching them from an unexpected direction: European classical music.
Bach and Mozart were important influences in his studio, and not
simply background music; both composers, working in a medium
seemingly far-flung from Haida sculpture, taught him so much about
how to carve overlapping forms. One night in the *Norsal*'s lounge,
Reid played Bach's *Unaccompanied Cello Suites* for the poet, saying:
"Those solo cello pieces are like those myths you were talking about.
It's hard to follow the pattern, but they make a kind of sense."[62]

When Bringhurst went back to Swanton's book with Reid's
advice in mind, one mythteller in particular seemed to be using his
voice the way Bach composed for solo cello. This person danced
rapidly back and forth between different voices, creating and jumping between multiple through-lines in a story at the same time. The
man's Christian name was John Sky, and he was clearly a remarkable talent. Other voices began to emerge out of *Haida Texts and
Myths*, each with their own distinct narrative signature and sense
of the world. Walter McGregor, for example, told stories that were
not as long or multi-layered as those by Sky, but were "lyrical, clear,
and deep," and charged with a sense of the pathos of the human predicament.[63] Abraham Jones was the historian of the group and, like
Herodotus, spoke "a language of beautiful simplicity" buttressed by

a sense of "the tragedy, the humor and the curious persistence of all-too-human history."[64] Yet the Indigenous identities of these and other authors remained masked by the Christian names assigned to them by missionaries. What scant biographical details Swanton offered about his informants hinted at the civilizational collapse they had lived through, but no more. "Told by Moses McKay," reads one heart-stopping entry, "sole survivor of the Seaward-Sqoa'ladas."[65] And out of seventy stories in total, only thirteen appeared in English with accompanying texts in the Haida language. Without those original texts, Bringhurst could not really preserve this tract of old-growth knowledge he'd stumbled into, nor add to it in any meaningful way.

Later that summer, Bringhurst visited the American Philosophical Society Library in Philadelphia, where a large collection of Swanton's papers was housed. Without much difficulty, he was able to find the Haida versions of the other stories from *Haida Texts and Myths*. It was a primal moment for him, confirming his classicist impulse. "I felt then an excitement such as I think Gian Francesco Poggio Bracciolini felt in 1417, when, poking through manuscripts at a monastery in Italy, he recovered the lost text of Lucretius' *De rerum natura*," he recalls.[66] Yet the Haida papers were incomplete. The opening page from John Sky's epic "Raven Traveling," which just so happened to describe the creation of the world, was missing. When Bringhurst found that page eight years later at the Smithsonian Institution in Washington, DC – in the form of a ninety-year-old carbon copy stuffed in a binder misfiled as a letterpress book – it wasn't so much euphoria he felt but a sense of hush. Decades had passed since anyone had seen that page, and it had been hauled in from the very brink of oblivion.

Bringhurst now turned to the task of learning the language as it had been spoken in southern Haida Gwaii a century earlier in order to rebuild the stories in English. Circa the mid-1980s, though, there were no existing dictionaries, grammars, or commentaries to read, nor were there any professors of Haida language or literature to consult. Bringhurst arranged to meet with some of the remaining fluent speakers of Haida, of which there were only a dozen or so. He described them as "wonderful people, fountains of knowledge," but noted that colonization and proselytization had cut them off from their own cultural heritage.[67] "Their language was different from the language Swanton heard because they used it in different ways and lived in a different world," Bringhurst said.[68] Reid was of limited help since he wasn't a fluent speaker, but he did pass on tapes of one of his teachers that had been recorded in the late 1950s. Henry Young had been present at some of the sessions between Swanton and the mythtellers at the turn of the century and spoke the same kind of language Bringhurst was reading in the Swanton book. Young, he said, became his "instructor in Haida elocution."[69]

By learning the Haida language from bits of paper and old recordings, Bringhurst started to push his mind deep into the stories Swanton had transcribed. What he found was a fascinating world, or a number of intersecting worlds, where everything was alive, was capable of speech, and could engage directly with human beings "eye to eye and face to face."[70] Spirit-beings, or *sghaana*, were everywhere, and their relationships and intrigues were responsible for the ongoing creation of the earth. The most powerful *sghaana* lived beneath the water, which may be why Sky referred to human beings, who counted for very little in the scheme of things, as *xhaaydla xhitiit ghidaay*, "good-for-nothing surface birds."[71] Shamans were of especial concern to Sky. They were those human beings who sought to accumulate their own store of spiritual power, and who dared engage with the *sghaana*, often travelling underwater to do so. Whole sequences in Sky's stories are set under the sea; or by lakes, creeks, and streams; or in a blurring of the realms of water and earth where movement through time and space becomes increasingly dream-like and hard to follow.

Reid's advice that Western polyphonic music offered a way into Haida myth continued to resonate. Bringhurst found no shortage of examples in Sky's stories where more than one being could occupy the same space at the same time. The interpenetration of bodies was a constant theme. "You become something else by putting on someone else's skin, or by stepping out of a skin that you normally wear," he explained. This, he added, was a "very hunterly vision."[72] And whenever two bodies shared the same space, it seemed that there was a corresponding overlap in terms of consciousness as well. Two or more minds could pass through one another like voices in a motet. This was emblematic of the kind of mutual thinking that Bringhurst was familiar with from decades of work as a translator. Was it possible to enact that interpenetration of bodies and minds in his own idiom?

The breakthrough came in 1985, a year in which Bringhurst travelled so much that all the places he visited began blurring together inside him. He spent most of February and March in Australia and New Zealand, a trip that gave him his first substantial contact with Indigenous Australians, their rock art and music, and Maori culture. "I saw very powerful resemblances between Maori and Haida cultures."[73] He returned to Vancouver by way of Fiji, then flew across the country to northern Ontario for a workshop for aspiring Cree and Anishinaabe writers. There he met Tomson Highway and Richard Wagamese, spent time with elders Louis Bird and Henry Frogg ("a first-rate storyteller"), and had his first exposure to Indigenous people who spoke no colonial languages.[74] These included Jemima Morris, who gave Bringhurst his Anishinaabe name, *Kijianabit*, or "Big Robert," a name that had originally belonged to one of Morris's relations, a young man who had been able to move effortlessly across cultural boundaries and who had died shortly before Bringhurst's visit. A week later, it was Chile and Peru by way of Vancouver, a memorable illegal night visit to Machu Picchu by way of a precarious back route, and then on to Japan for a reading tour with Audrey Thomas sponsored by the Writers' Union of Canada. Later that fall, he met Gary Snyder after a poetry reading the latter gave in Vancouver. Snyder was sixteen years older than Bringhurst and had written his undergraduate thesis on one of Walter McGregor's stories (published in 1979 as *He Who Hunted Birds In His Father's Village*). The two connected immediately through their love of climbing, poetry, and nineteenth-century Haida myth. All of these "pieces of map, pieces of music" collapsed together in Bringhurst's mind, creating a many-stranded texture that he came to recognize as a paradigm for his mental life. "'Topic = TOPOS = place," he wrote in his journal while in Bangor that November, "so a man with more than one idea, more than one imagination, must somehow be in more than one location."[75] Thus he found himself in Quetico, Ontario, reading about Peru and thinking about rock art in northern Australia; studying Fujiwara architecture in Cuzco and Inca stonework in Tokyo; and soaking everything in memories from Navajo country and the BC coast and thoughts from ancient Greece and China.

In May of that year, Bringhurst was travelling by train through Honshu – the most populated of the Japanese islands – with Audrey Thomas and Eleanor Wachtel, who went on to host the popular CBC Radio program *Writers and Company*. At one point, Thomas made a comment about the blue-tiled roofs dotting the countryside, one that, heard above the chatter of the crowded passenger car, lodged itself in Bringhurst's mind as the opening line of a new poem: "In a house with such a blue roof, you'd wake up cheerful every morning."[76] When he set out to write the poem, the voice seemed to split into two. This second voice seemed to tease the first, echoing and sometimes reversing its words, acting as both trickster and conscience. "I wanted to take full advantage of this problem," he writes, "so I made no attempt to shut out either of these voices. They would alternate, I thought. But they refused. They kept trying to talk at the same time – and kept succeeding."[77]

Composing a poem for more than one voice meant that Bringhurst had to rethink the logic of the medium of print, which had evolved to showcase voices sequentially, one at a time, like cars taking turns at a four-way stop. Was it possible to imagine a different way of reading a book? Bringhurst's early efforts were rudimentary. He began by copying each of the speakers' parts onto separate acetate transparencies and then layering the sheets on top of one another with translucent blue paper behind them. This allowed him to experiment with how two voices might fit together visually. For clues he turned to other artists who worked with overlapping voices or melodies, just as Reid relied on Bach and Mozart in his studio. He listened with new-found interest to Bill Evans's *Conversations with Myself*, to African and Afro-Cuban polyphonic percussion, and to Bach's works for solo lute.

The Blue Roofs of Japan, described by Bringhurst as a "duet for interpenetrating voices," features a male and a female speaker whose words occupy the same space at the same time.[78] In the version printed in *Pieces of Map, Pieces of Music* (1987), he makes use of both sides of each page spread. The male voice dominates the left-hand page, his lines printed in black and superimposed over the female voice's lines, which are printed in a ghostly blue showing out from underneath. On the right-hand page, the female voice dominates, printed in black, with the male voice in blue this time. By overprinting the two texts, Bringhurst's intention was to provide both speakers with a visual point of reference whereby they could continually place themselves in relation to one another as the poem progresses. It is the female voice that ghosts around that of the male, troubling his assumptions about social and natural order. The earth is "rich" and "disordered" to the male speaker, while, for her, it is simply ordered.[79] When the male says, "The garden prefigures the table and page," she shoots back, "Is a woman's body / the garden?"[80] Such are the "patterns of interference" that form when two voices intersect in a polyphonic poem, their interactions creating all kinds of interesting textures on the surface of the poem, not unlike two pebbles tossed into a pond at the same time.[81] Across the five sections of the poem, the male and female speakers explore some of Bringhurst's pressing concerns: the parallels between writing and agriculture; the role of the artist and for whom he or she performs; a meditation on being and the elements. In its most serene moments, the voices of *Blue Roofs* settle together like the quiet gestures of a Zen tea ceremony around which the entire poem is structured. *Blue Roofs*, first performed in public at the University of Montana in 1985, went on to win the CBC Poetry Prize a year later. Other performances soon followed. Bringhurst presented Reid with a copy of *Blue Roofs* on the occasion of his sixty-sixth birthday, and was somewhat surprised when the master carver simply grunted and tossed it aside. "It was the perfect Zen master's gesture," he recalled, "as if to say our relationship has nothing to do with such pious formalities. Now get your head back where it belongs."[82]

In 1987, Bringhurst was awarded a Guggenheim Fellowship. His initial thought was to make poems out of the stories he'd come across in *Haida Texts and Myths*. Reading those stories in the original Haida, though, convinced him that "they already were poems" and "they didn't need me or any other smartass to turn them into literature."[83] Yet John Sky, Walter McGregor, and others didn't use metrical lines, stanzas, or other structural units traditionally associated with poetry. What was the basis for his claim? Bringhurst called the works of Sky and company "poems" because their chief distinguishing characteristic was a form of music that registered not in the ear but in the mind. "Poetry isn't a way of speaking; it's a way of thinking," he said.[84] This "noetic prosody," or thought-music, defined the literary works of non-agricultural peoples nearly everywhere. "Verse in the sense of a measured, repetitive pattern of syllables is scarcely to be found among paleolithic cultures, though poetry there is usually abundant," he writes. "Peoples who choose not to domesticate plants and animals typically choose not to domesticate language either."[85] Instead, they pay attention to the measured motion of earth itself and respond with patterns of their own making. Those patterns are often fractal-like in nature, recurring at different levels across a work of art, forming an "organic geometry" akin to "a snowflake or a tree."[86] For example, he noted that Haida oral literature is broadly organized around units of meaning or significant details that occur in suites of five (in Navajo and Chipewyan oral literature, by way of comparison, significant events often happen in fours). "Those patterns are very much like time signatures: 3:4, 4:4, 5:4, and so on," he told me. "Very much like, but also very different, because *time* is not what they regulate. They are the shapes of conceptual space, narrative space. They are the branching and leafing and flowering of ideas in the mind."[87]

After the publication of *The Blue Roofs of Japan*, Bringhurst wanted to expand his understanding of polyphonic texture, so he gave himself a crash course in musical history. He traced polyphony back to its European origins in organum and Gregorian chant, following it through to the Renaissance in the motets of Josquin des Prez, Nicolas Gombert, and Thomas Tallis. He listened to recordings of their works for hours every day, covering hundreds of polyphonic Masses. He had no interest in the Christian theology invoked in those Masses; rather, he wanted to understand the structural principles behind that theology. He found it astonishing how composers could build entire musical architectures from just a handful of phrases, slowing down and stretching out individual words and the pauses between them, creating spaces that expanded and contracted not unlike the formline of Northwest Coast visual art or the subterranean passages of the cave complex at Altamira he'd recently visited. From des Prez, Gombert, and Tallis, he graduated on to the fugues and string quartets of Bach, Haydn, and Mozart. He listened closely to John Lewis's work with the Modern Jazz Quartet, John Cage's experimental soundscapes, and, on Dennis Lee's recommendation, Glenn Gould's largely forgotten contrapuntal radio documentaries known collectively as *The Solitude Trilogy*. He found his way to different polyphonic traditions around the world, including Inuit *katajjait* throat singing, and puzzled over the words of an anonymous thinker from Pond Inlet who told the anthropologist Bernard Saladin d'Anglure that "human beings learned the *sounds* of these songs from wild geese but learned the *meanings* of the sounds from the aurora."[88]

Bringhurst's hunch that polyphonic music modelled a fundamental characteristic of reality was confirmed for him during an extended stay in the highlands of Bali in 1988. He was forty-two years old at the time and travelling with his second wife, an Englishwoman named Charlotte Bagshawe, who was conducting informal research on traditional *ikat* weaving. "It was the music, more than the weaving, that impressed me in Bali," he said.[89] Having installed themselves in a little cottage near Ubud, the artistic capital of Bali, he spent "prodigious amounts of time" listening to *gamelan* rehearsals in the local temple.[90] One night as he watched a dance-drama version of the story of Rajapala, he realized with a start that this was the Balinese counterpart of the Swan Maiden tale that Walter McGregor told in *Haida Texts and Myths.* The *gamelan* was itself a polyphonic marvel. Involving anywhere from a dozen to forty or more performers, a *gamelan* orchestra consists of drums and gongs sometimes accompanied by flutes, fiddles, and singers. The orchestra itself is thought of as a living entity, its instruments said to be given names dreamed by their players, and what mattered most was pleasing not the human audience but the spirit-beings who might be listening in. The *gamelan* also had a peculiar relationship with the Balinese landscape itself. "Night after night in Indonesia I have walked between the village, where the humans boomed and chirped with their bogglingly complex polyphonic tuned percussion, and the rice fields, where the frogs, just as earnestly and skillfully, were polyphonically croaking," he writes. "Nothing but human arrogance allows us to insist that these activities be given different names."[91]

   Back in Vancouver, Bill Reid was preoccupied with what would become one of his most enduring and recognizable masterworks, *The Spirit of Haida Gwaii.* A massive bronze sculpture commissioned by the Canadian Embassy in Washington, the "Black Canoe," as it was known to its makers, took Reid and a team of assistants four years to complete. It depicts a boatload of refugees from the Haida mythworld – including Mouse Woman, Wolf, and Raven – who are all tangled up with each other, jostling for position in a traditional canoe set adrift into an uncertain future. Reid, with typical "Raven-like understatement," said that the piece was inspired by Sunday drives with the family, with "dogs and children lunging at one another across the station-wagon seats while mother stares out placidly and father resolutely at the road."[92] The title of the work points beyond Reid's deflection to his belief that carving was a "technology of enchantment." A well-made sculpture of a mythic being wasn't simply a representation of that being; if it had been "deeply carved," it participated in that being's energies.[93] Thus the best of Reid's works communicate an intensity of presence that only comes when an artist has gone beyond tradition and touched its animating source (the first time I sat with "Raven and the First Men" in the UBC Museum of Anthropology in December 2000, I felt the trickster's eyes on me wherever I went and that night had strange and portentous dreams). If there is a sliver of hope in Reid's canoe of refugees, it is that they might be carried to some corner of the imagination untouched by the ravages of colonialism and there find a home among human beings still alert to their existence.

Throughout the construction of the Black Canoe, Bringhurst watched, asked questions, did a bit of carving, and later accompanied his mentor to New York to visit the foundry that was casting the sculpture. There he met a long-time associate of Marshall McLuhan, Edmund Carpenter (1922–2011), who helped him understand Reid's work in the context of a philosophy of making tens of thousands of years old. Carpenter had just finished editing *Social Symbolism in Ancient and Tribal Art* (1986–88), a massive set of tomes that offered evidence of a complex symbolic system of great antiquity shared among indigenous artisans from around the Pacific Rim. Within that system, he and his late colleague Carl Schuster distinguished between "patterned animation" and "animated pattern," two approaches to making that, in Bringhurst's words, make visible "what we know to be there but cannot see, and to capture for long inspection and contemplation what we would otherwise only know through fleeting glimpses."[94]

As Bringhurst understands it, patterned animation is centred around a predetermined structure – the iambic pentameter grid, the five-or-seven-syllable grid, the pointillist or cubist painting grid, a Native American stepwise narrative grid – that serves to trap, or attract, or reveal certain aspects of reality. "Seems to me that anytime you set up a grid it's likely to tell you things," he told me. "Set up a window screen, the bugs will land on it. Drop a fishnet into the sea, the fish will swim into it."[95] With animated pattern, though, otherness does not pass through a pre-existing grid as much as it is allowed to converse with and reorder it. The artist begins with an intuition of the work, and then experiments with flourishes and details that might coax it into shape. "Now your system of representation and the things it might represent are starting to talk back and forth, and maybe your chances of getting somewhere are improving."[96] Over supper one night in New York, Carpenter put on a memorable demonstration of animated pattern by standing up in the middle of the restaurant and slapping his shins and upper arms all the while talking about patterns of chiefly descent. "In a flash, he explained weavings and carvings I'd seen in Indonesia and had not, until then, understood," Bringhurst said.[97] Animated pattern quickly moved close to the centre of his own lexicon. "I had the idea that I had used the phrase so often I was in danger of wearing it out."[98] The term appears exactly once in his published writings.

Created alongside the construction of the Black Canoe and influenced by it on multiple levels, *New World Suite No. 3*, Bringhurst's next major polyphonic composition, tells the story of the retreat of the civilizations of the Americas and the dispersal of their resident myth-creatures before the deluge of European explorers and settlers. Newcomers saw the land as the staging ground for the victory of the Western spirit and turned it into a continent-wide construction site of pit mines, logging slash, urban sprawl, and the "acres of radioactive glass" at the Alamogordo nuclear test site; in this new reality, one speaker asks, "what is there to listen for, or to sing of?"[99] The deluge of modernity is slowed to some degree in the later movements of the *Suite*, when spirit-beings like Coyote and Kokopelli are overheard lingering around the edges of the poem and fragments of Eastern thought are carried like driftwood on the tide. In the poem's last movement, mythic time begins to reassert itself as history gives way to the measured movements of seasons and celestial bodies. "The sun burns to the ground. / It is kindled again. There is one lesson / deeper than hunger," says one of the speakers.[100] In the poem's final unsettling line, the image of Reid's boatload of refugees is inverted, for it is now the descendants of colonists who are the ones adrift, orphaned by a culture that stripped the land of meaning and then collapsed upon its own achievements. "We who have traded our voices for words / circle back to the pool / of alkaline silence / to listen."[101] Bringhurst has modern human beings attempting to restore a dialogue with the earth by looking in the wrong place: "Alkaline pools are silent because the water is not what it seems," he explained. "Nothing much comes there, and nothing much grows there. Which I guess means the folks who have traded their voices for words are misdirected; they habitually go (if we can believe what they say) to the wrong water hole."[102]

After *Suite*'s debut at the Vancouver Writers Festival in 1990, Bringhurst worked on and off for the next five years to translate it for the page. How to compose a poem for three voices that speak together at the same time? For the version published in *The Calling* in 1995, he makes recourse to musical notation: the voices are organized into staves, stacked in successive bars, and printed in bold, italic, and roman fonts. Braiding them together creates a rich, sumptuous texture made up of echoes, divergences, and innumerable shared rhymes or half-rhymes that can be heard both in the ear and the mind. One of the most sonorous moments in the *Suite*, in the middle of the first movement, occurs when the first speaker says: "History here is a clock ticking, a blade / sliding between the earth and our shoes." The second speaker says: "Therefore the deer remain dead, / and the pronghorn are spooked by the fences."[103] When these two lines are spoken together, they walk side by side during the first clause, and then jump clean through each other on that shared half-rhyme in the second clause, the words "shoes" and "spooked" echoing through one another on the whistle-like sound of the "s" and the long "oo."

If we move from the level of the line to that of the movement, we may see that whole ontologies, and not just individual speakers, are also gliding around and through one another. Technological civilization's one-dimensional program of world mastery, explored in the long first movement, is contrasted with the rhythms of the Pueblo mythworld and the more abstract Buddhist ontology of being and non-being in the second and third movements. In the fourth movement, Orion from the Greek mythworld and Prajapati from the Indian *Rig Veda* are seen to occupy the same constellation in the night sky. Different meanings overlap and cohere if we allow them to. There is room in the night sky and, more importantly, room in our minds for more than one story. For Bringhurst, cultivating polyphonic consciousness in ourselves is an ecological imperative. Bodies within bodies, processes within processes, ecosystems within ecosystems: the nature of reality is nested, like matryoshka dolls, one being inside another. Enacting that essential fact in our own gestures of meaning invites the multi-dimensional character of the earth to reassert itself in our presence. In a letter to Robyn Sarah, he asked: "When you are standing in the middle of a clear-cut or a parking lot, how polyphonic does a poem have to be in order to be helpful in calling the forest back?"[104]

Bringhurst begins his essay "That Is Also You: Some Classics of Native Canadian Literature," published in *Canadian Literature* in 1990, with a scene from John Sky's epic *Raven Travelling* that demonstrates both the mythteller's familiarity with the polyphonic nature of reality and his ability to encode that reality in his work. Early on in his misadventures, which include moving between different levels of the Haida mythworld, baby-snatching, and eye-stealing, the Raven is summoned to a house at the bottom of the sea where an old man waits by a fire. His first words to the Raven leave him puzzled. "'I am you,' the Old Man said, 'and that is also you.'"[105] He gestures to something "blue as air and green as beachgrass" that can be seen moving behind a screen at the back of the house.[106] Some sort of underlying elemental subjectivity is being invoked, one that links the Raven to the old man to the creature behind the screen. The old man then asks after a box hanging in the corner. "On the sides of the box which the Raven brought were faces, with faces in the eyes, and in the eyes of the faces in the eyes, another set of faces. Inside the box was another box, and inside that box was another. Five in all, and inside the fifth box, side by side, were two round objects, one black and one speckled" (it is a short distance from this moment to the 2005 version of *New World Suite No. 3*, which comes in a large black box that contains within itself – and serves as a lectern for – the three speakers' scripts).[107] The boxes-in-boxes motif is suggestive of both the multi-scalar nature of the Haida mythworld and the concentric nature of meaning itself. As Bringhurst writes elsewhere, the image of the blue-green creature behind the screen and the image of the mysterious objects retrieved from the innermost box are meant to overlap in our minds like acetate transparencies. In so doing, the identities of both the Raven and the blue-green creature behind the screen are revealed to be one and the same. "A raven that is slim and blue is a yearling," he writes.[108] It is a testament to Sky and his artistry that such information isn't given away thoughtlessly, but results from his unique style of thought-music.

"That Is Also You" is the first in a series of academic journal articles and lectures in which Bringhurst argues that Sky and Walter McGregor are deserving of inclusion in the colonial literary canon on the basis of such artistry. This attempt to indigenize the university curriculum, some twenty-five years before it became an academic imperative, is part of an effort to create a critical context within which his translations might be received. Bringhurst introduces readers to the complexities of early-contact-era Haida civilization. He describes the smallpox epidemics of the nineteenth century that decimated the population of the islands by over ninety per cent.

He writes of the advent of the residential school system and the
Canadian government's long-standing ban on ceremonial gatherings
and activities, and how waves of missionaries, Indian agents, and
traders swept over the remnants of one of the most sophisticated,
materially affluent, and artistic cultures of the Northwest Coast.
John Swanton is introduced, standing out against this chaotic back-
drop all the more because of the way he gave the mythtellers the
space to be themselves, transcribed everything they said, and paid
them an hourly wage equal to what he himself was earning. The
stories that Sky, McGregor, and others shared with him deserve
to be studied alongside other classic literary works in universities,
Bringhurst writes, "not because that is the purpose for which they
were made, but because that is the best response and acknowledgement we can now offer them."[109]

Bringhurst's Ashley Lectures, given at Trent University in the
winter of 1994, constituted something of a coming-out party for
Sky and McGregor, who for the first time were referred to by their
Haida names – Skaay of the Qquuna Qiigghawaay and Ghandl of
the Qayahl Llaanas – releasing them from their Anglo-Christian
personae. In the last of these lectures, "The Polyhistorical Mind,"
published in the *Journal of Canadian Studies*, Bringhurst reiter-
ates his claim that their works deserve to be recognized as part of
Canadian literature, even if such cultural overlap might compli-
cate non-Indigenous Canadians' sense of identity. "One story is not
enough. One history is not enough. One literature, in a country such
as this, is not enough. Nor two."[110]

Bringhurst was now aware of the existence of other pockets of
mythtellers, poets, singers, and historians from across Indigenous
North America who had been carefully transcribed word-for-word
by a small cadre of anthropologists, almost all of whom worked
under the aegis of Franz Boas at the Bureau of American Ethnology
(Boas himself did not believe in the individual talents of these
artists). Brilliant works of oral literature from across the continent
were mouldering away in archives, libraries, and rare book collections around the world. Bringhurst began insisting to anyone who
would listen that the long-term viability of North American civilization depended on a respectful engagement with these works and the
traditions that birthed them. They alone could help non-Indigenous
people see that they did not have the world surrounded but were
surrounded by it, and belonged to it, in every conceivable way. "If

I could send a generation of young Canadian writers off now on a grand tour, it would not be a tour of European capitals. It would be a journey through time, mind and landscape involving the serious study of these ancestral North American languages and literatures This may sound like a romantic project, but I mean it as a very classical one indeed. I would expect results as valuable as those produced in Europe five centuries ago by Erasmus and his colleagues, through the secular study of Latin and Greek."[111]

Bringhurst found another "elective grandparent" among the present-day inheritors of those literary traditions in Sèdayà of the Yanyèdí (1915–1999), whose Christian name was Elizabeth Nyman. She was at first "a voice from the oral world that came to me on paper" courtesy of an invitation Bringhurst received to write the introduction to *Gágiwdul.àt: Brought Forth to Reconfirm The Legacy of a Taku River Tlingit Clan* (1993), a collection of personal, historical, and mythological narratives shared with and recorded by linguist Jeff Leer, her non-Indigenous adopted nephew.[112] Sèdayà was herself an orphan, her mother having died while she was an infant, and so she was not taught "as eagerly and generously" by her elders as she might have been ("Some orphans make it through, / and some don't," her prospective mother-in-law told her bluntly).[113] As a result, Sèdayà had to "stand herself up," and she did so by looking to the Taku River valley, which was the source and depository of all teachings. "For her," Bringhurst said, "the Taku country wasn't just a succession of landforms; it was an enormous library shelf, a living body of oral literature."[114] She gave Leer the remarkable advice that whatever he could not learn from his own mother or from the stories of the elders in their community could be learned from the river itself. The river, she said, knew "what happened to you in your past" and could tell him who he was.[115] Because most of us are orphans of one sort or another, Bringhurst told me, we would do well to follow Sèdayà's example and "stand ourselves up." There exist a number of books from Indigenous North America by elders who "will teach you what they can"; these voices, he said, "fit together – polyphonically – with the landforms" they spoke about, each illuminating the other and teaching us "a lot of things that cultural orphans don't otherwise get taught."[116]

Circa the mid-1990s, Bringhurst was now heading into the most intensive phase of his work on Skaay, Ghandl, and the other oral artists he had encountered in the Swanton book. In 1995, he published

The Calling: Selected Poems 1970–1995, which features all three of his polyphonic compositions and a number of fascinating poems and poem-fragments that speak to the ongoing necessity of reciprocal relations between different realities. Hence, in one of the book's epigraphs, from hereditary headman Job Moody to John Swanton, the myth-creature Loon is asked why he keeps calling out over the water in a time of the great deluge. "I am not speaking only from my own mind," Loon replies. "The gods tell me they need places to live. That is the reason I am speaking."[117] An answer of sorts to Moody's fragment is offered thirteen pages later by a contemporary of Confucius, Zuŏqiū Míng, who says: "When spiritual beings have a place to return to, they need not become malicious. I have allowed them a place to return to."[118] Bringhurst's attempt to provide such spirit-beings a literary safe house hit a snag shortly after publication, though, when McClelland & Stewart lost several hundred copies of *The Calling* in a shipping mishap and refused to reprint it. His most substantial collection since *The Beauty of the Weapons* was suddenly a rare commodity. "I wasn't counting on the royalties," he told me. "No living poet makes enough from any one poetry book for it to matter financially. I was counting on the book to keep my name alive in the poetry world while I went off for five or six years on the Haida translations."[119] Another volume of selected poems would not appear until 2009.

Bringhurst was one of the key players at the symposium on literary polyphony held at Trent University in September 1996, a major event that brought together all the poets of this book (due to a scheduling conflict, their visits did not overlap). He published a lengthy article inspired by that gathering called "Singing with the Frogs: The Theory and Practice of Literary Polyphony," which appeared in the journal *Canadian Literature* a year later. There he moves decisively against Dennis Lee's sense of literary polyphony, which in his view resembles modulation in music, and makes the case for a "literal" literary polyphony that claims Western polyphonic music as its direct ancestor. "Polyphony is a precisely identifiable characteristic of certain musical compositions, or parts of compositions, and by extension also certain poems and plays, paintings, and sculptures, and so on," he told me.[120] He summons Russian critic Mikhail Bakhtin, who understood polyphony as the autonomous coexistence of characters and viewpoints in a literary work, yet just as quickly dismisses him for insisting that the novel was the only authentic form of literary polyphony. Beyond Western polyphonic music, what validates literal literary polyphony, he argues, is the world itself. "The world is a polyphonic place," he writes. "The polyphonic music and the polyphonic poetry and fiction humans make is an answer to that world."[121]

Bringhurst marshals support for "natural polyphony" by making recourse to the writings of Estonian biologist Jakob von Uexküll (1864–1944), who argued that all creatures are immersed in a constant perceptual reciprocity with their environments. Beings are forever reading and responding to a range of shifts and changes around them, from a slight drop in temperature or the momentary absence of the sun to the arrival of a predator or a tree-toppling storm. They do so from the lifeworld or *Umwelt* they each inhabit, a kind of bubble through which they experience the world from their own unique angle of perception. A single tree, for example, is different things to the different beings that inhabit it – the fox who builds a lair in its roots, the ant who lays its eggs beneath its bark, the owl who hunts from its branches, and so on. Reality, from this perspective, is really a multiplicity of realities, a "heterogeneous mosaic of places," as environmental philosopher Neil Evernden put it.[122] This, according to Bringhurst, is the deep structure of reality that literary polyphony emulates and enacts, a structure shared by the human mind as well. "Works of polyphonic art – Josquin's motets, Bach's fugues and the Lion Panel [at Chauvet Cave] for example – don't just express emotions or mental states," he writes in the final lines of his essay. "They are models and exemplars of the ground of mind itself.[123]

Bill Reid died on 13 March 1998 after suffering from Parkinson's disease for decades. He had been in "passable shape" during the early years of his friendship with Bringhurst, but by the mid-1990s his health had declined precipitously.[124] When not on the road, Bringhurst helped out whenever he could, and was often first in line as substitute caregiver and nurse. The two saw a lot of each other during this immensely sad and difficult time, mostly in the hospital or at home where Reid lay immobilized and suffered under the slightest touch. "I learned more from Reid than from anyone else I've ever known about how to tolerate pain."[125] Reid was as stoic as he could be in the face of these trials and, despite the degradations of palliative care, never lost his dignity. There was also anger toward the end, as he realized the tradition he'd given so much to was leaving him behind. Other conversations between sculptor and poet, which left the latter speechless, confirmed that theirs was an apprenticeship of spirit. After Reid passed, Bringhurst found himself without a friend, a teacher, a father figure, and, of crucial importance when it came to the publication of his Haida translations, a protector.

In 1999, more than twenty years after he had stumbled across John Swanton's book of Haida translations in the stacks of the UBC Library, Bringhurst completed *A Story as Sharp as a Knife: The Classical Haida Mythtellers and Their World.* He had originally intended to write a short introduction to accompany his translations of Skaay and Ghandl, but when that introduction hit 500 pages, he realized that it had evolved into a book in its own right. "I wish I did not understand how much of your soul resides within this manuscript," Bringhurst's publisher, Scott McIntyre, told him upon receiving it, for here was a book laboured over for so long it was lit from within.[126]

A Story as Sharp as a Knife is built around excerpts and, in some cases, entire stories as told by Skaay, Ghandl, and others. These are interwoven with biographical portraits of the major mythtellers and historians Swanton encountered, along with an unsparing account of the civilizational collapse they lived through. Bringhurst also explores in detail the painstaking approach John Swanton took with those elders, how that approach differed from the collecting methods of most anthropologists and linguists of his era, and the byzantine institutional politics he had to navigate to ensure that the stories he recorded were preserved in the way, and in the order, their tellers intended.

Reaction to *A Story as Sharp as a Knife* shifted within weeks of publication from lavish praise to accusations of cultural appropriation made by a couple of members of the Haida Grand Council. Not all Haida, it seemed, were pleased to see some of their ancestors scooped up into Bringhurst's adoptive family tree. These accusations were amplified by a large number of non-Indigenous critics and academics who proceeded to castigate Bringhurst for various offences, including a failure to consult with Haida cultural authorities, Romanticism, and deficient scholarship. The situation quickly turned toxic. A leading linguistics journal was forced to issue a retraction for reprinting without scrutiny false statements posted online by one of Bringhurst's most vociferous non-Indigenous critics, a linguist named John Enrico. Four years earlier, and with the blessing of the Haida community, Enrico had published his own translations of Skaay's and Ghandl's stories. Bringhurst and Enrico had actually corresponded in a friendly way until it became clear the former wasn't simply asking questions but actually intended to publish something. The controversy entered the public eye in the fall of 1999, when Adele Weder, herself a friend of Bill Reid, published a long piece in *The Globe and Mail* calling Bringhurst's credentials into question. It was resurrected in November 2001 when journalist Dorothy Bartoszewski produced the two-part radio documentary, "Land to Stand On," for the CBC program *Ideas*, repeating without question a number of the false statements that had already been made and refuted by that point. Almost overnight, Bringhurst had gone from obscure poet to one of the most controversial figures in Canadian letters since Grey Owl – minus, of course, the charade.

A year after the book's publication, a number of Indigenous authors and cultural authorities began coming forward to recognize the value of the translations, complicating a simplistic reading of the controversy. In a letter to *Books in Canada*, the late Cree elder Christine Wilna Hodgson, herself a noted bridge-builder between nations, called Bringhurst's work a "gift to First Nation peoples across this land" and "a masterpiece in the growing genre of spoken texts."[127] Ishmael Hope, who is of Inupiaq and Tlingit heritage, described Bringhurst's Haida books as "so finely made" the spirit-beings featured in the stories chose to live in them.[128] Woodrow Morrison, one of the last speakers of the Northern Haida dialect who teaches Haida in Vancouver, wanted to know what all the fuss was about, so he attended a reading Bringhurst gave at the University of British Columbia; he stood up afterwards and praised him openly. In a written commentary published in *Listening for the Heartbeat of Being* (2015), Morrison chastised Bringhurst's detractors for running to the media and suggested they ought to consider looking at his work from another angle. The Haida artist and writer Michael Nicholl Yahgulanaas, originally a steadfast opponent of Bringhurst's Haida project, later reversed his opinion and tried to secure from the Haida community an official foreword endorsing the second version of *A Story as Sharp as a Knife*, published in 2011. Yahgulanaas's own endorsement was nuanced: "Robert might have selected to do a more socially sensitive outreach," he wrote in an e-mail. "This was, after all, a time when our tiny but robust Nation was much engaged in defining our own public cultural persona in a world that likes to garnish its predatorial behaviour with dollops of myth. But his choice not to ask the living does not in and of itself damn his work with the dead."[129]

One irony of the Haida controversy is that it completely overshadowed any discussion of the translations themselves. Ghandl and Skaay were silenced a second time. It remains for us to ask, though, why they chose to work with John Swanton in the first place. Did they have a salvage agenda of their own? It seems unlikely they would have sat through transcription sessions that proceeded in such painstaking fashion, one sentence at a time, hour after hour, day after day, and week after week had they not sensed an opportunity in Swanton's method. They were, after all, artists. They knew that a well-made story can travel widely, outrun cultural upheaval, and might even circle back to its point of origin to someday find new generations of listeners. "Literature is a kind of intellectual and emotional Red Cross," Bringhurst said. "It sends care packages to the people in the future, who are going to be refugees in their own world, and who will need the kind of intellectual food that literature provides."[130] Gary Snyder was electrified by the idea of this reversal of the Eurocentric notion of the salvage agenda, and said as much to Bringhurst in a letter from 2002: "It gave me a chill when you suggested that the Haida elders knew what they were doing once they saw Swanton's transcribing system worked and they used this for their own purpose ... establishing a body of cultural lore for the future," he wrote. "That's a brilliant insight, and I feel deeply that it is true."[131]

Two volumes of translations followed the publication of *A Story as Sharp as a Knife*. *Nine Visits to the Mythworld* by Ghandl of the Qayahl Llaanas appeared in 2000 and was nominated for the inaugural Griffin Poetry Prize (Dennis Lee was one of the judges; the prize went to Anne Carson for *Men in the Off Hours*). *Being in Being* by Skaay of the Qquuna Qiighawaay was published a year later. The book's title grew out of its cover, which features a photograph of a shaman's rattle described by George Emmons, the ethnographer who sold it to be the American Museum of Natural History, as "one spirit within another, both singing." When Bringhurst saw that photograph, he told me he thought "it had an awful lot in common with Skaay's vision of the world."[132] The centerpiece of all three books is the *Qquuna Cycle*, which takes up more than half of *Being in Being* and deserves to be recognized as a literary achievement of global importance. The *Cycle* is 5,000 lines long, or roughly half the length of the *Odyssey*, and takes ten hours to read out loud.

Its narrative architecture is as rich and complex as the cosmos it explores, consisting of five parts made up, with one exception, of smaller trilogies of poems. Bringhurst likens this structure to that of a human hand, with each of the four fingers containing three segments and the thumb only two.[133]

At first blush, the *Cycle* reads like a series of unrelated and ambiguous vignettes or "a novel that is constantly losing its way."[134] The three poems in the first trilogy, "The One They Hand Along," "A Wolverine For a Mother," and "Ghaawaxh," tell of the establishment of covenants linking the Haida to the *sghaana* of the sea, forest, and sky upon whom their survival depends. Poems in the second trilogy describe the establishment of a totemic relationship with bears as well as the tragic consequences of transgressing the boundaries of that relationship. The third poem, "The Sapsucker," is a tiny but memorable meditation on the relationship between a creator-being who lives in the hollow of a spruce tree and the being he shapes, colours, and adorns with feathers. The third trilogy takes as its subject the figure of the shaman who aspires to mediate the relationship between the human community and the more-than-human world. "Standing Traveler" describes what a successful shamanic apprenticeship looks like, while "Quartz Ribs" and "Floating Overhead" examine what happens to those who substitute hubris for humility and attempt to acquire spiritual power for their own self-aggrandizement.

Skaay asks us to acquaint ourselves with the signature images and events from these first three trilogies because they provide the grammar of thought we'll need to make sense of "Spirit Being Going Naked," the mind-bending fourth finger of the *Cycle*. The protagonist of "Spirit Being Going Naked" is a would-be shaman who, over the course of his adventures, ends up tangling with some very powerful *sghaana* and has his mind turned inside out as a result. In this respect, Spirit Being is a figure not unlike Harold Ladoo, teaching us by negative example about the risks of engaging with realms of active powers beyond human understanding. To compose this poem – the only part of the *Cycle* with a single continuous character and plot – Skaay borrows freely from his own oeuvre, making use of scenes from elsewhere in the *Cycle*. Spirit Being's training regime, for example, mirrors that of Standing Traveler, so much so that at certain moments we might think we are reading the same poem. The two scenes unfold in near-identical manner, almost verbatim, before veering off in different directions and with very different outcomes. Later in the poem, a powerful creator figure named Voicehandler paints Spirit Being a pair of new faces. It is a scene that recalls the Sapsucker, and how that diminutive bird accepted his new feathers with a reverent exclamation of "Wah!" or "Oooooooooooh my!" (Bringhurst's use of ten os in his translation of the Sapsucker's exclamative is in keeping with Haida numerology, in which the next unit of major significance after five is ten).[135] Spirit Being, however, is incapable of so expansive an emotion as gratitude. He rejects Voicehandler's gifts, calling one of them "awful," and this *after* he has defecated in his host's water supply.[136] Spirit Being drowns during an ill-fated walk across the water and, in a final nod to the Sapsucker, is given a new form in the final lines of the poem. Instead of becoming a powerful shaman, as he aspired to do, Voicehandler turns him into the Varied Thrush, one more "good-for-nothing surface bird."[137]

In his fourth polyphonic poem, *Ursa Major* (2003/2009), Bringhurst restages the primal encounter between Indigenous and non-Indigenous civilizations in North America, but with a twist. Composed in four languages (English, Cree, Greek, and Latin), *Ursa Major* brings together two mythological texts from different parts of the world featuring the motif of the great bear. The first of these texts is Ovid's version of the story of Callisto and Arcturus, which survives only in fragments. Callisto the huntress, part of the company of Artemis, is raped by Zeus and punished by Hera, who transforms her into a bear. She gives birth to a son, Arcturus, who grows up among human beings, unaware of the events of his conception. One day he unknowingly hunts his mother, but Zeus intervenes at the last moment to turn them both into constellations, leaving them to endlessly re-enact their chase through the skies. Counterpart to Ovid's story is "Bear Woman," dictated by Sweet Grass Cree mythteller Kâ-kîsikâw-pîhtokêw (or "Coming Day") to the linguist Leonard Bloomfield on the Sweet Grass Reserve in 1925. Reprinted here in its entirety, "Bear Woman" is about a careless but lonely buffalo hunter who, upon returning home one evening, finds a beautiful woman tending the fire in his teepee. They fall in love, and she teaches him to be less wasteful in his hunting. Soon after, they travel to her father's village, loaded with provisions – her village, she tells him, is starving. They receive a joyous welcome from her family, but the hunter soon realizes that his wife and her kin are bears. The story, which is a marvel of understatement, ends simply: "And he was sorry he could stay with them no longer."

Ursa Major builds on one of the structural principles of *New World Suite No. 3* – that whole ontologies can pass through one another in the listener's mind and commingle without losing their distinctiveness or autonomy. Characters from the Greek and Cree mythworlds pick up fragments of each other's speech. The names of species native to the prairies, where the poem is set, begin showing up in the mouths of Greek characters. Each mythworld remains secure on its ontological foundations. Ovid, for example, was fascinated by the concept of a world in constant change and transformation, even if in his stories the metamorphosis from human to non-human is perceived as an irreversible punishment. For Kâ-kîsikâw-pîhtokêw, change is simply part of the order of things. Identity is permeable and fluid. In a gathering and hunting culture, where human life intersects with the larger life of the land on a daily basis, a certain etiquette is required because one is never truly sure what – or whom – one is gathering or hunting. As Bringhurst pointed out at a discussion of *Ursa Major* at Acadia University, when you skin a bear, it looks remarkably like a human being. Yet the notion that more than one being can occupy the same place at the same time is, for Kâ-kîsikâw-pîhtokêw, not just an ontological tenet but also a basic emotional truth. His hunter will never be the same after finding and then losing a wife who happens to be a bear. He has learned not to be wasteful, and that other beings struggle to hold onto their place in the larger order of things. Even though they have gone their separate ways, the hunter and the bear woman will remain in each other's hearts.

When Arcturus comes into contact with Kâ-kîsikâw-pîhtokêw's poignant vision, something extraordinary happens. He becomes aware of the relative nature of his parent culture and is no longer willing to accept the primacy of its worldview. The son doomed to chase his mother through the sky comes back to earth and continues to learn. The most poignant lines in *Ursa Major* belong to him, and they amount to a universal truth: "You can have what you want but can't have it for long. / That's the rule."[138] Arcturus's ability to change, even after thousands of years of incarceration in the Greek mythworld, suggests that ancestors are not static beings. Regardless of whether we classify them as historical or mythological figures, they can grow if given the opportunity. Their development does not unfold through time, but in relationship. To modify what Zuǒqiū Míng once wrote, they need not become malicious so long as we provide them with the opportunity to live through us and go on learning from our world. They, in turn, can help us make sense of our own journeys through time, and help us figure out how to be home.

Bringhurst's largest, most sprawling, and ambitious polyphonic project to date isn't a poem per se, but the application of his poetics to a specific place. In 2003, looking to break with the Rinzai master's admonition that "the true man has no name and no address," he and his partner at the time, Louise Mercer, bought a shabby old house on Quadra Island, a short ferry ride from Vancouver Island. In keeping with most of his major projects, he set out to renovate someone else's work. He tore down the massive perimeter fence that cut the house and yard off from the forest. Deer moved in by nightfall and laid waste to the vegetable garden. Several truckloads worth of garbage that had been dumped around the property were ferried off to the dump. He hired someone with a backhoe to dig out a decent-sized pond for the island's native frog population. He erected a car shelter on the other side of the forest out of Douglas-fir logs that looks like a cross between a pagoda and a longhouse. He bushwhacked a network of trails connecting carport to house. When Tim Lilburn and Don McKay came calling not long after Bringhurst moved in – before he had a chance to line the trail with gravel – the two poets got lost in the forest between the two. Later, when Bringhurst took them on a hike along Heriot Ridge, he ignored the trail signs and all three of them got lost ("I was too proud to look at the signs," he admitted. "The experience didn't do much to enhance my reputation as a great woodsman").[139] Closer to the house, he added a two-storey building designed in the manner of a *zendo* or Buddhist meditation hall that contains a writing studio, woodshop, and floor-to-ceiling library. He moved his literary ancestors into the latter, making good on his long-standing promise to provide a home for them to go back to. Bringhurst also gave the shabby house a complete facelift and installed a number of bridges, stairways, ladders, and elevated decks that allow for views of the "hermitage" from various angles. Finds from his travels can be spotted here and there (the upper stairway in the house is guarded by a pair of Indonesian Cyclops). Despite all this architectural ingenuity, the hermitage feels completely surrounded by a landscape returning to natural possibilities. A solitary raven *toks* from the top of a Douglas fir; the wind roars over the ridge; families of deer clop their way through the forest; the singing of the frogs is sometimes so loud that the humans in the house have called up friends and relatives and simply held out the telephone for them to hear.

Alongside his work on the hermitage, Bringhurst continued to produce books at a dizzying pace. He rethought and revised a number of his public lectures and essays, publishing them as *The Tree of Meaning* (2006) and *Everywhere Being is Dancing* (2007), and produced two more editions of his industry classic *The Elements of Typographic Style* (2008, 2012). He directed some of his resources to salvaging half-finished manuscripts on subjects dear to him, including Athapaskan oral narrative in *This Is What They Say* (2009) and Renaissance French typography in *The Scythe and the Rabbit* (2012), after their original authors, Ron Scollon and Kay Amert, passed away. "I would never have gotten involved in the Scollon book or the Amert book except for my sense that we owe the dead a serious debt," he told me.[140] His *Selected Poems* appeared in Canada in 2009, while British and American editions followed in 2010 and 2011. A second edition of *A Story as Sharp as a Knife* was published in Canada in 2011 and a long-awaited British version, with an introduction by Margaret Atwood and illustrations by Dan Yeomans, an artist of Haida and Métis descent, followed in 2015. That same year, he prepared a slim volume of translations of ten of the late poems of Michelangelo, called *Hard High-Country Poems* (after the "hard high-country stone" that was the Renaissance artist's preferred carving medium), and a year later came the book-length *Palatino: The Natural History of a Typeface*, which honours the work of Hermann Zapf, the renowned typographer who passed away in 2015. Another collector's item, the nine-part poem *Going Down Singing*, a collaboration with California artist Joseph Goldyne, appeared in 2017. He has also been compiling a new manuscript of poems that by early 2020 had reached nearly 300 pages in length. The centerpiece of that manuscript is "The Ridge," which when completed will be the longest poem in his oeuvre. He is also at work on a retelling of Dante's *Inferno* with present-day political players, and told me that he had found the "texture" for a new polyphonic poem but not the words.

Meanwhile, a new voice joined the hermitage. Bringhurst first met Jan Zwicky in 1985 after a reading he gave at Wilfred Laurier University, and a second time around Thanksgiving of that year when she and Don McKay passed through Vancouver on the way to Saltspring Island, where McKay was using Phyllis Webb's cabin as a writing retreat. While Bringhurst and Zwicky disagree in retrospect on whether he had a kayak or kayak paddles hanging from the ceiling of his apartment, the two of them soon became close friends and intellectual allies (he maintains the kayak was upside down and strapped to the railing of his balcony at the top of three flights of stairs). They would get together for sprawling and intellectually nourishing conversations over food whenever they happened to be in the same city. Some months after each of their previous relationships ended in 2006, Zwicky began dividing her time between Quadra Island and Victoria. She moved there full-time two years later after retiring from her position at the University of Victoria. They often give readings together and have collaborated on a number of projects, the first of which was a series of meditations on timelessness that, appropriately enough, have been slow to come to light. They were invited by Early Music Vancouver to contribute poems to accompany Haydn's "Seven Last Words," a string quartet that took as its theme the Crucifixion. Bringhurst and Zwicky modified that theme to the Crucifixion of the earth (the performance I saw in Vancouver in January 2015 was all the more haunting because of the "Pineapple Express" tropical storm that rolled in and turned the city into a swamp). Their most recent collaboration is *Learning to Die: Wisdom in the Age of Climate Crisis* (2018).

Another project that Bringhurst has been working on for decades, *Voices in the Land*, awaits completion. Originally intended as something of a field guide to the oral literatures and major authors of early-contact Indigenous North America, *Voices* is a mammoth effort that he started compiling, in bits and pieces, when he began sleuthing around in archives and rare book collections in the 1980s. He was able to find about 400 books in all, plus photocopies and microfilms of another 100 unpublished texts and roughly 200 volumes of dictionaries, grammars, and ethnographies. Many of them surfaced around the turn of the millennium, when the antique book market collided with the emergence of abebooks.com and other online services. These days, there is nothing left to buy. "All the books are gone," he said.[141] What he had assumed would be a permanent state was really just a blip, a convergence of market forces and technology that has since passed. In its present form, *Voices in the Land* contains entries on most of the Indigenous languages of the continent, complete with lists of notable speakers and transcriptions of their works. Nearly a thousand pages long, the manuscript is, in his estimation, still only skeletal; to finish it, Bringhurst had hoped to write small essays on some 200 or more major authors and significant minor ones (a handful of these essays can be found in W.H. New's *Encyclopedia of Literature in Canada* (2003)). Doing this would require going to all the places these people lived, seeing for himself what they saw when they looked up in the morning, and "drinking from the same rivers they did."[142] *Voices in the Land*, he said, remains "a lifetime's work."[143] He admitted that no one would likely publish such an enormous undertaking, and was considering putting the whole thing online as a free electronic resource.

Bringhurst still holds out hope, however faint, for a North American cultural and ecological renaissance based on a respectful engagement with these literatures. While the idealism he once had for this prospect is gone – a consequence of the controversy around his Haida translations – he still sees it as a *conceptual* possibility, however slim the chances of its realization. "What could be done now is to put that big body of transcribed literature to use. It could be edited and re-edited, published and republished, read and reread. If it were internalized by a generation of readers, North American society would be fundamentally changed. A basically deracinated and mercantile culture, disrespectful and inconsiderate toward the land in which it lives, might be changed into a culture that feels a real and articulate kinship with the ground beneath its feet. The USA and Canada and Mexico could outgrow the colonial mindset at last."[144]

Even without such an engagement, the source of those literatures remains. It is possible to learn directly from the land without the assistance of human intermediaries. At the end of "The Mind of the Wild" from *Learning to Die*, Bringhurst raises the prospect of "thinking like an ecosystem," which involves calibrating the mind "by spending a day in the wild – alone with reality, keeping quiet and letting things unfold."[145] Of particular importance to him is a grove of Douglas firs, some 600 to 800 years old, a twenty-minute hike from the house. He calls these trees "the ancestors" because they are among the very few to have survived the 1925 conflagration that swept over the island. For him, any being is an ancestor if it outlived the epoch it was born into, and thus has one foot in the world that was and another in the world that is. If we apply this notion to his elective grandparents among his own kind, we may see that almost all of them lived through moments of profound cultural rupture and transformation, including the dramatic collision of the oral and the written and everything that came with it. The notion of non-human beings as elders – or that in certain places we can be surrounded by grandmothers and grandfathers of all shapes and sizes – is a source of deep meaning for Bringhurst. "Standing among those trees is quite a lot like sitting with the elders at Wāwākapewin or Kwanlin Dün or 'Ooléé'jtó," he told me. "If you spend any time alone with those trees, and you know how to listen, something will happen."[146] It is the job of the elder to pass on what they know, broadcasting their insights beyond the boundaries of their own culture or species, inspiring in human beings those ways of thinking that are similarly open-minded.

4

Jan Zwicky

Lyric Philosopher

Summer, family farm near Mayerthorpe, Alberta. Courtesy of Jan Zwicky.

Jan Zwicky is equally accomplished as a philosopher, poet, and musician. She earned a PhD in philosophy from the University of Toronto, taught for several years at the University of Victoria, and lectured at a number of institutions across North America, including Princeton, Harvard, and Stanford. She is a professionally trained violinist and has played with orchestras and symphonies from coast to coast. She has published eleven collections of poetry; one of these, *Songs for Relinquishing the Earth*, began its life as a plain hand-sewn book printed on recycled stock and went on to win a Governor General's Literary Award in 1999.

As disparate as these vocations may seem, Zwicky sees no separations between them. The same thinking and experience go into all three. They are different approaches to the same core concerns. Among those concerns is the land itself. "My love for land – for landscapes, for plants, for stones, for farming, for weather, for walking and hiking, for non-human animals – is one of the major headwaters of my own project," she told me.[1] By the time she was nine or ten years old, she had already discovered for herself certain primal truths. She knew the land was an endless source of generosity, delight, and patience. She knew it was her parent, and that it loved her as much as she loved it. She found no affirmation for these impressions in school, which threatened to bury them before they could fully flower. Like the speaker of Rainer Maria Rilke's poem "There Stands Death" who sees a shooting star and feels it fall through his eyes and body, she sensed that her task was "not to forget you. To endure."[2]

At first glance, the discipline of philosophy seemed like a good place to honour that commitment. As originally conceived by Plato and company, philosophy meant "love of wisdom." It involved a quest whereby a person might follow a desire initially experienced as loss or confusion right out of the cave of their ignorance and into an encounter with the source of a meaningful life. As an undergraduate, Zwicky was immediately attracted to the discipline's emphasis on clarity. Yet she couldn't help but notice that something was not quite right in the halls of institutional philosophy. Her professors were preoccupied with a particularly narrow notion of clarity, which led to the practice of philosophy as a set of word games, or what Plato called sophistry. It is a testament to the strength of her commitment that Zwicky didn't give up but set out to develop her own alternative approach, one that would remind the discipline of its original task.

Later, as an independent scholar, she began experimenting with a polyphonic mode of philosophy that brought together fragments of her own writing with those from other thinkers, along with reproductions of paintings, poems, photographs, and musical scores. Books like *Lyric Philosophy* and *Wisdom & Metaphor* invite readers to puzzle over the connections between these voices, allowing them to enter into an intellectual and emotional ecology that not only emulated but also pointed to "the being of the world" and all its interwoven wonders.[3]

Yet Zwicky's thesis found few supporters among academic philosophers who were by and large already committed to their own anti-ecological and disintegrative points of view. After a while, she got tired of pushing against the limitations of the discipline and, like other reformers who got fed up, including her exemplar Ludwig Wittgenstein, quit the discipline altogether, retiring to Quadra Island to garden, play music, and write. Thus in Zwicky's artistic and intellectual biography we find a profound reversal of the model of the philosopher sketched out by Plato in Book Seven of *The Republic*. Zwicky didn't begin her journey shackled in the dark but *started* outside the cave and, armed with a clear and unshakeable sense of the source of wisdom, ventured inside. Plato warned that those who do this – those who enter the cave after having glimpsed something more – risk being perceived of as bumbling idiots because their eyes haven't adjusted to the dark and may receive a hostile reception.

Jan Zwicky's father, Robert, came from an itinerant background. He'd lost his mother at an early age, did not take to his new stepmother, and left home as soon as he could, making his way through the southern United States before graduating from college at nineteen and finding work as a hard rock mining engineer for Shell Oil in Calgary. Her mother, Jean Keeley, grew up on a farm west of Mayerthorpe, Alberta, that her parents, Charlie and Marie Keeley, bought in 1927. She was teaching music at a satellite campus of the University of Alberta in Calgary when she and Robert met on a blind date set up by mutual friends. They were married in May 1954.

Their first of two daughters, Janine Louise Zwicky, was born almost a year later, on 10 May 1955 in Calgary. Three months later, Robert was transferred to Houston, then on to Oklahoma City within a year (when Charlie Keeley came to visit the family in Oklahoma, he made the trip by train and brought with him in his

suitcase a freshly killed and plucked chicken). From Oklahoma it
was back to Calgary in 1959, then on to Edmonton in 1962. By the
time Zwicky was halfway through grade 1, she had already moved
five times. Luminous details from those early landscapes stand out
in her mind decades later: the mountains beyond Calgary; a climbing rose on the east side of their first house in Edmonton; the North
Saskatchewan River as it ran through the city, subject of the very
first picture she tried to paint.

As often as possible, Robert and Jean Zwicky brought their daughters to the Keeley's farm outside of Mayerthorpe, a homesteaded
quarter just beyond the northernmost edge of wheat cultivation.
"Northern Alberta gumbo" is how the speaker of Zwicky's poem
"Leaving Home" from *The New Room* (1989) describes the muskeg, "that joke of a topsoil, slick cold soup / slopped over thousands
of square miles of hardpan."[4] Zwicky was conscripted into the
farm's daily operations as soon as she was physically capable. She
learned how to take care of the animals, from simple tasks like feeding, mucking out stalls, and milking the cows to minor veterinary
skills like pulling stitches and puncturing the stomach of a bloated
calf. She learned everything she could about how to ride and care
for horses, how to tell when a crop was ready to come in, how to
preserve vegetables. She operated all the farm machinery except the
swather and the auger ("too many people lost too many fingers"),
and learned simple electrical wiring and basic carpentry (when she
left home in her late teens, her father gave her a toolbox of basic
tools, a gift she still treasures).[5]

Farm life was by no means bucolic. Later poems bear witness to
complicated and oppressive relationships with certain members of
her extended family – of "unwelcome dressed as welcome."[6] These
experiences accentuated the larger, elemental world around her and,
in a very real way, pushed her deeper into it. When the emotional
weather inside the farmhouse became too stormy, she retreated to
the untilled places around the farm and to the Little Paddle River
itself, only minutes away through the windbreaks. There she got
to know many of the non-human beings for whom those places
were home, including individual birds, foxes, deer, and coyotes. The
one-time discovery of a freshwater clamshell in the creek was like
finding a pearl in an oyster. She kept a weather journal and tried to
understand what was happening in that vast prairie sky. Berry picking was another fascination. "One of the things I was enraptured by

as a child, was continually delighted and awestruck by, was the fact
that the land, unaided, produced fruit you could eat. This was one
of my most memorable experiences of a kind of ontological beauty,"
she said.[7] These impressions were heightened by her mild synesthesia
– tones she heard in the presence of certain saturated colours and
intense light. "Places where there is a lot of living, non-human
nature, a substantial amount of it wild, seem to me literally to hum.
They have distinctive musics, distinctive keys and tonalities; but they
all sing," she said.[8]

Music was central to Zwicky's upbringing from the very beginning. Jean was a choral conductor and pianist, and taught her
daughter how to play the piano as soon as she started reaching for
the keys. "I actually don't remember learning to play the piano and
there are pictures of me as a tiny baby sitting on my dad's knee,
banging away," she said.[9] Zwicky also sang in choirs as a kid and, at
the age of ten, started violin lessons.

Her musical training, as well as her effectiveness on the farm, were
curtailed when Zwicky fell off her horse and broke her wrist badly
at the age of twelve. While ending any dreams she may have had
about becoming a soloist, her accident opened up more space for
books. She and her younger sister were huge readers, had library
cards, and looked forward to trips to the library with great anticipa-
tion. At one point, her great-grandfather, who lived with his wife in
a small cottage near the main farmhouse, gave her a copy of one of
Teilhard de Chardin's books and said, "I bet you can't read this." He
was right – she couldn't make sense of it but tried all the same and,
for the first time, felt the pull of a philosophical text.[10]

When Zwicky was thirteen, the family moved from Edmonton
back to Calgary, settling into a house on the outskirts of the city on
the east slope below Nose Hill (her father, who devoted himself to
community service work wherever they happened to be living, was
instrumental in the fight to save Nose Hill from development). It
was wild prairie beyond the back fence, and Zwicky spent countless
hours roaming around there. Wind and sky! Melting slabs and crusts
of packed snow in winter! Wild grass in subtle shades of brown,
grey, and tan in summer!

There was never a time when Zwicky did not excel in school.
She was always a straight-A student. "My mother was terrified I
wouldn't have any friends, so she taught me to be terrified of anyone
finding out what was on my report card," she said. "I lied about its

contents."[11] She had the sense of not being like other kids – most other children back in the city were not sewing their own clothes, driving tractors on the weekends, stooking bales of hay, or helping their grandparents butcher chickens (an experience that drove her into vegetarianism as soon as she moved out). She was drawn to conceptual geometry from an early age. "I found abstract concepts beautiful, and I wondered about them, and I sensed connections among them, and was interested in what those connections were," she said.[12] Later, she thought she might go into archaeology – her father was fascinated by the pre-modern civilizations of North America, including the Viking presence on the east coast – and then developed an interest in astrophysics. In high school, she also got into theatre. The drama club was made up of about eight honour-roll math and physics students and half a dozen others who were into smoking, drinking, having sex, and cutting class. "It was a fantastic mix," she said.[13]

Zwicky's interest in poetry began around this time. Her mother had a fondness for Alden Nowlan's work and had copies of most of his books. She was struck by the emotional intensity of Nowlan's poems; wrote some of them out in an enormous scrapbook she kept, alongside works by other poets such as John Donne and Andrew Marvell; and tried to imitate that intensity in her own early free verse. After grade 11, Zwicky felt that studying literature in school was a waste of time and decided to take English 12 on her own. "Those were the days when you could still get out of high school by passing a set of provincial examinations, no coursework strings attached."[14] One of her teachers, sympathetic to her frustrations, helped her prepare for the provincial exam by coaching her to read for the pattern in the questions and not the selections themselves. This strategic shortcut allowed her to finish with the highest score in the province, earning her a Lieutenant Governor's Award.

Zwicky began undergraduate studies in September 1972 at the University of Calgary. She started in physics but switched to philosophy in her second year after discovering there were better teachers in the latter field, along with a level of abstraction in which she felt more comfortable. Her training consisted almost entirely of analytic philosophy, which had been on the ascent since the turn of the century and, following the Second World War, had consolidated itself as the predominant branch of philosophy in English-speaking departments around the world. Analytic philosophy emphasized clarity and argument through formal logic and language analysis, and looked longingly to the certainty of meaning available in science and mathematics over what it regarded as the murky metaphysics of continental philosophy. It found an early expression in logical positivism, many of whose chief practitioners restricted statements of genuine meaning to those anchored in mathematics or empirical observation and expressed in logico-linguistic syntax (for example, "Lemons are yellow" or "2 + 2 = 4"). Such empirical statements or analytic propositions encouraged one to approach complex philosophical problems by breaking them down into their simple constituent parts. Logical positivists aspired to create an ideal language for philosophical analysis, one that had been scrubbed clean of the ambiguities and uncertainties of ordinary language, including metaphor and paradox (A.J. Ayer's *Language, Truth and Logic* (1936/1946), one of the lodestones of British logical positivism, went further and denied meaning to statements of ethics and religion as well). While the reductivism intrinsic to analytic philosophy would grate on Zwicky before long, its emphasis on clarity would remain a source of lifelong inspiration.

Zwicky's interest in the performing arts flourished during this time. She chose drama as her minor, studied with a movement teacher who convinced her that she could do the basics of modern dance, and won leading roles in a number of student productions. She joined the Calgary Philharmonic Orchestra in 1973, playing second violin on a per service contract ("the lowest of the low," she said) for the next three years.[15] Because of the injury she'd sustained early in her training, her teachers had concluded she could never be a soloist, yet the orchestral and standard chamber repertoire was still within reach. Even so, she remained something of an outsider within the culture of classical music. She did not graduate from a conservatory or a university performance program, and it was only after she joined the Philharmonic that she found her way to a moderately famous teacher, Moshe Hammer, with whom she studied briefly in the mid-1970s. Her real musical education took place outside the institution, in the form of a three-way friendship between Zwicky and two other young members of the Philharmonic, violinist Sheldon Nadler and solo trumpet player Eric Schultz. After rehearsals, the three would return to Nadler's basement apartment and his collection of thousands of rare classical vinyl LPs: "When I think back, I realize what absolutely amazing, formative nights those were: we listened, hard, until 1:00 or 2:00 a.m. at least once, sometimes twice, a week for three years. It was my 'conservatory.' Sheldon knew the recordings inside out and taught both Schultz and me so much. We drank together, high-spiritedly, after concerts when we could afford it. All three of us were pointlessly or stupidly or misguidedly in love with people outside the friendship; but that stuff never came up. In Sheldon's basement, we were just ourselves, just musicians crazy about classical music."[16]

In her third year at the University of Calgary, Zwicky enrolled in a seminar in creative writing taught by Christopher Wiseman, who'd brought to Calgary the innovative workshop approach he'd learned first-hand in the writing program at the University of Iowa. In his class, she experimented with voice, line lengths, and the confessional mode. For the class anthology, which she edited, she wrote a funny satire of the class in Longfellow's trochaic tetrameter under the pseudonym Alonzo Freud. Wiseman's class, Zwicky told me, "shaved five years off my development as a poet."[17]

When Zwicky arrived in Toronto in the fall of 1976 to begin graduate work in philosophy, one of her first purchases was a small wooden collapsible drafting table that served as both desk and eating surface. "I was terrifically intellectually hungry; I ate books for breakfast, and I had no doubt that philosophy was the discipline I wanted to pursue," she said.[18] The Department of Philosophy at the University of Toronto was primarily analytic in orientation, but it was also one of the few English-speaking departments on the continent that offered courses in continental philosophy. For the first time, she came across a number of authors whose very existence in the course calendar spoke to other intellectual encampments within the discipline. "Who are all these *H*s?" she remembered thinking, upon finding names like Hegel, Heidegger, and Husserl on the reading list for the placement exams she had to sit.[19]

One of the courses Zwicky signed up for was a graduate seminar on Ludwig Wittgenstein (1889–1951), a peculiar and contested figure within analytic philosophy whom she'd been introduced to in dribs and drabs during her undergrad, but who had not made any impression on her up to that point. "I wasn't exactly chafing to dig in, but I knew I had to study more Wittgenstein if I wanted to be a serious philosopher," she recalls.[20] It was early September – the leaves were still on the trees and the seminar hadn't even begun – when she went out and got all of the books on the syllabus in order to read ahead. She sat down with the first of these, the *Tractatus Logico-Philosophicus* (1922), and read it from cover to cover in one incandescent afternoon.

> I open it now and am still amazed by its beauty. The ferocious intensity; the chiselled, but grounded, purity of its language. It maybe looked abstract; but this guy was talking about the real world! The project to describe the outline of das Mystiche by showing how to say everything that could be said. Brilliant. The way in which passion was fused with insight. And I hadn't read two pages before I'd fallen in love with the structure, the numbered aphorisms: yes! This was the way to think! Absolutely transparent! And the emotion, the emotion everywhere – not rhetorically explicit but apparent in the pressure under which the sentences had been sculpted. I'd never encountered anything that was as complex, as philosophically deep, that was also as effortless to understand. It was as though Wittgenstein had read my mind before I'd known I had one.[21]

Wittgenstein, who grew up in one of Vienna's wealthiest families, showed up like an apparition at the door of Bertrand Russell's quarters at Cambridge University in 1911, speaking almost no English but curious about a future in philosophy having spurned one in aeronautical engineering. Totally raw and untrained yet relentless in his questioning, Wittgenstein was quickly claimed by Russell as his intellectual understudy and moulded in the tradition of logical positivism ("He is *the* young man one hopes for," Russell confided).[22] Early in his career, Wittgenstein sided with Russell and others in arguing that the role of philosophy was not to offer up knowledge about reality – that task belonged to science – but rather to clear away the misunderstandings that arose when the legitimate limits of language had been transgressed. To that end, Wittgenstein asserted that the only meaningful language was one rooted in the clarity of analytic propositions and empirical statements, and thus shared in analytic philosophy's dream of creating a logically ideal language. Yet he did not wish to celebrate analysis. Rather, he wanted to safeguard everything he felt was truly important outside of science and language – goodness, beauty, ineffable truth. If everything that could be said were said in his analytically clarified way, then everyone would be able to see what couldn't be said. "If only you do not try to utter what is unutterable," he wrote, "then *nothing* gets lost."[23] "What was important about his work was that it drew limits to analysis; it put everything meaningful and valuable (correctly, in my view) outside the domain of direct articulation," Zwicky writes. "Crucially, this didn't mean we couldn't *know* things about beauty or the good life. It just meant that if we tried to talk about them, we'd distort the truth."[24] The memorable last line of the *Tractatus* was actually a *validation* of the knowledge, though not the metaphysics, that analytic philosophy rejected from the outset: "Whereof one cannot speak, thereof must one be silent."[25] Wittgenstein remained in agreement with his colleagues that metaphysical discussions had no place in philosophy.

When her graduate seminar on Wittgenstein started shortly after her encounter with the *Tractatus*, Zwicky encountered her first major institutional disappointment. Her professor neither understood nor was moved by Wittgenstein's work, and she dropped the course after two weeks. Her love for Wittgenstein, however, meant that she simply had to keep studying him, so she began to read him on the side with another graduate student. "Wittgenstein was neither a cynic nor a skeptic; he'd lived a life of tremendous moral intensity," she writes. "And this is what I thought philosophy *ought* to do to a person: its study *ought* to help you see what mattered and what didn't; it should hone your appetite for a life saturated with the good."[26]

Coinciding with her discovery of Wittgenstein, Zwicky became aware of the urgency of the environmental crisis. There had always been a degree of ecological awareness in her family. Life on the farm depended on an intimate familiarity with the land, and her great-grandmother had been passionately outspoken in her opposition to DDT long before Rachel Carson sounded the alarm in *Silent Spring* (1962). Three events consolidated Zwicky's lifelong commitment to environmental activism. The OPEC oil embargo of the early 1970s had completely rocked North American society, leading to all kinds of emergency conservation efforts and long lineups at gas stations. Media coverage of the ecological crisis had grown exponentially since the first Earth Day celebrations in 1970, spurred on by activist groups like Greenpeace, which formed in Vancouver a year later. In the fall of 1976, she became aware of a startling prediction made by David Suzuki, then the host of *Quirks and Quarks* on CBC, about the need to drastically reduce carbon dioxide emissions by the early 1990s in order to stave off radical climate change. "If there's a triggering thinker here, it's Suzuki," she said, stressing that he was not so much an influence as a "crucial informant."[27] She'd always loved the land, knew it was her parent, and didn't need to be told it was important. Once she grasped that it was at risk, she knew she had to do something. Were there avenues for positive change available to the philosopher?

Two years into her graduate studies at the University of Toronto, Zwicky was beginning to chafe against a philosophical environment that was closed to anything outside its purview – including its own historical development. Late in her undergrad, she had written a paper proposing a non-analytic understory to the views of a famous analytic philosopher, which earned her an A+, but she had not realized just how closed the borders of her discipline were. Many of her professors in both Calgary and Toronto, products of Oxford University, enforced the myopic view that philosophy was not in fact a body of thought that had evolved over time, but a cluster of problems that one learned to attack head-on through a set of technical moves. "I was beginning to see analytic philosophy not as revealed truth but as a kind of academic culture," she said. "Were there other cultures?"[28]

As she had discovered her first year there, U of T was home to a small number of continental philosophers and their students. As much as Zwicky was critiquing the analytic camp, though, she could not bring herself to sign up with the opposition. When among analytic philosophers, she felt keenly their rejection of a world beyond the grasp of positivist language. Among the continentalists, even with their flair for the literary, she missed the precision of thought and commitment to clarity of the analytics. The continentalists seemed insufficiently disciplined – they used the literary licence inherent in their conception of philosophy as an excuse to indulge in inconsistency, vagueness, sloppiness, in language for its own sake. The postmodernists and poststructuralists among them were, in their own way, as fascinated with language in as narrow a sense as the analytic philosophers were. While she had an increasingly clear sense of the kind of philosophy she wanted to practice, she began to wonder if there existed an intellectual culture – anywhere – in which she might feel at home. She wanted her work grounded in the real world, and capable of speaking to real life; at the same time, she was certain that the most meaningful experiences in her life were beyond words. "This, more than anything else, pushed me outside both camps and forced me to think outside contemporary intellectual fashions," she said.[29]

Zwicky found a sympathetic ear in Dennis Lee, who for the
1977–78 academic year was the writer-in-residence at the University
of Toronto. *Civil Elegies* made a profound impression on her when
she read it that Christmas. She loved the poem for its intense engagement with philosophical issues, its critique of technological society,
and its sense that there were experiences of reality to be had outside the purview of technological consciousness. "That poetry was
fundamentally engaged with philosophy, *and* that both these things,
together, forced moral responsibility on the person who experienced
them – all this echoed my own deepest convictions."[30] Lee, for his
part, looked over a manuscript of poems she had been working on
and offered vital early encouragement: "I think you've got a manuscript here."[31] As they got to know each other, she shared with him
her growing frustration with analytic philosophy and the apparent
absence of any viable alternatives to it. They met from time to time
in his office and, on a memorable walk around the St George campus
later that winter, connected on the subject of ineffability. Lee knew
first-hand the difficulties of writing about experiences that seemed
to resist translation into language altogether. "Dennis's idea of body
music makes great sense to me, though I would say that his judders
and splurts don't show up in my experience," Zwicky told me. "For
me, it's more like feeling music than like driving a corduroy road
in a truck with worn out shocks."[32] Her primal experience of that
music remained the farm in northwestern Alberta. "I can remember first hearing passages in Shostakovich's Symphony No. 10 in
E Minor and being startled that they sounded like the farm," she
said. "It wasn't that I'd known all along that the landscape was in
E minor; it's that hearing the Shostakovich showed me it was."[33]
She couldn't hear that music in Toronto – "the tempo is too fast and
there's too much noise" – but picked up on it in Vancouver when
she spent a summer there in the late 1970s, so much so that she can
still hear it when she visits, "even though it is now buried under
overpopulation, the standard capitalist distortions of urban life, and
traffic."[34] It was increasingly clear to Zwicky that such experiences
were not beneath analysis, but constituted equally legitimate forms
of thinking.

In 1979, Zwicky realized she needed to get out of Toronto and
decided to relocate to Waterloo, Ontario, where she had a number of friends. One of these, Jan Narveson, was a senior member
of the Department of Philosophy at Waterloo. He was also a gifted

impresario who ran a chamber music series out of his living room
and a board member of the Kitchener-Waterloo Symphony. Zwicky
had met Narveson through philosophical circles before moving to
Toronto, and then once out east would visit him and his partner in
Waterloo. Before long, she was making the trip on a regular basis,
staying at his place and playing with the orchestra. When Narveson
told her he could get her office space in the department as well as
a library card, she decided to make the jump, ending up in a great
apartment – the second floor of a big old farmhouse in a little town
called Bridgeport – where she had her first garden (her tomatoes
ended up on the cover of one of the local agricultural newsletters).

Zwicky made a home for herself in the graduate student culture
at Waterloo in a way she never had at the University of Toronto. She
began hosting small but convivial lunches at the farmhouse, creating
a space in which philosophy students could get together outside of
the seminar room to hash things out. James O. Young, who at the
time was doing his master's in philosophy there (he later became a
colleague of Zwicky's at the University of Victoria), attended some
of these lunches. There was a certain energy and intensity of focus
about her, he recalled, grounded in a passionate, unselfconscious
commitment to the ideas. Young recalls a dinner party in the autumn
of 1980 that they both attended, along with all of the graduate students from the philosophy department. A huge thunderstorm blew
in halfway through the evening, and everyone crowded out onto the
apartment balcony to watch. When the first blast of rain arrived,
most people retreated inside, with the exception of Zwicky, Young,
and a few others. She was ecstatic, he recalls, leaning over the railing, water pouring down her face, her whole being lit up as she took
the storm on her nerve endings. "I've seldom seen anyone happier,"
Young said.[35]

Meanwhile another storm was gathering as the pressure to finish her PhD intensified. Zwicky still had no idea how to tackle the
paradox of writing about that which defied the grasp of language
(at one point she thought about handing in a stack of blank pages).
She focused her dissertation on the philosophy of language, writing *A Theory of Ineffability* in a single, mostly sleepless three-week
stretch in 1981. Experiences of an ineffable nature, she argues at
the outset, are often characterized by a non-linear and non-logical
organization of thought, a temporary erasure of a sense of self, and
a sheer inability to render those experiences in words without feeling

as though something utterly vital had melted away in the process.[36] Such experiences, she notes, are common to mystics and artists. They are of life-changing importance to those who are fortunate enough to have them. They should not be dismissed as epiphenomena or as evidence of mental illness. To mount her philosophical defence of ineffability, Zwicky turns to Sigmund Freud, finding in his notion of "primary process" many of the characteristics associated with the ineffable experiences of mystics and artists mentioned above. What Freud got wrong was that he saw primary process as a refusal of reality and as something of a dumping ground for any form of thought, including analogy and metaphor, that took place outside of language-dominated "secondary process" (secondary process, like analysis, relied on a fundamental distinction between self and world, operated according to linear orders of time and space, and was made of logic and language). What Freud got right, Zwicky maintains, is that there is more than one way of knowing, and as she writes in a later essay, "there is coherent, meaningful mental activity that cannot be adequately modeled with standard logical and causal structures."[37] Despite Freud's view to the contrary, were there ways in which primary and secondary processes could come together and complement one another? Zwicky was not sure what to expect at her PhD defence, given the intensity of her private feelings about analytic philosophy; however, her dissertation was not only allowed to pass but also, to her astonishment, commended by her committee.

After graduation, Zwicky spent the following academic year on a post-doctoral scholarship at Waterloo. It was an appointment she took up half-heartedly because she was increasingly uncertain if she had a future in the discipline. Years of pushing against the philosophical mainstream had left her convinced there was no place for her in it. While she had let both her music and acting slide while in Toronto, Zwicky now re-immersed herself in both vocations. She continued to play with the Kitchener-Waterloo Symphony and formed the Austin String Quartet. The group took its name from Zwicky's Austin Mini, the tiny vehicle in which they transported themselves and all of their instruments to gigs (three quartet members rode in the back seat with the viola and two violins in their laps while the cello rode upside down in the front seat). She also acted in a number of theatre productions, getting laughs as a comic actress as well as kudos for her dramatic roles. Her interest in theatre was now sufficiently strong and her commitment to institutionalized philosophy sufficiently weak that Zwicky decided to apply for a place at the prestigious Guildhall School of Music and Drama in London. To her surprise, she was accepted.

The plan to move to England and study acting was derailed when Zwicky got a telephone call out of the blue from the chair of the Department of Philosophy at Princeton University, who offered her a one-year sessional position. He'd talked with her PhD supervisor, who had supplied her name for the job with extraordinary recommendations. She told the chair that she would have to think about his offer – she was, after all, already halfway out the door of academic philosophy. She talked with a number of friends about her dilemma, all of whom advised her that the discomfort she felt with the discipline would evaporate if she went up to the big leagues. She was less certain of this, but in the end heeded their advice.

Before leaving for Princeton, Zwicky finished her first poetry manuscript, *Where Have We Been*, and sent it to Brick Books, where it fell under the editorship of Don McKay. A chronicle of a complicated love affair, the collection follows a calendar-like structure in its close attention to the movements of the seasons. The speaker's perception of the world is heightened in moments of emotional intensity – a snowstorm against the side of a house, the grain in the surface of a table. Love, even when under strain, constitutes a way of knowing, illuminating the deeper nature of beings and things otherwise obscured by routine and the linguistic structures that saturate our senses. Yet language is one of the only tools we have to communicate meaning, even if our words are hopelessly inadequate for the task. So says the speaker of "The Spires of Martinville":

Piecing scratch-marks
into letters, letters into words, arranging these
one way, another, yet another.
Poke poke with the
thumb; mind like some thick unkenny stump[38]

Zwicky remains deeply embarrassed by the poems of *Where Have We Been*, is said to have pulled copies of it off the table at book fairs, and urged me more than once not to read it. While not every poem in it works, the book is successful in conveying a sense of the high hopes, emotional upheavals, poverty, and misery that many twenty-somethings go through almost as a kind of rite of passage. On a deeper level, the process of writing *Where Have We Been* allowed Zwicky to see how poetry could complement and even constitute an alternative to institutionalized philosophy. In a poem, words were allowed to carry both thought and feeling; they could be organized into patterns of sound and meaning that defied linear order; they could make use of the resources of the page in ways that logico-linguistic discourse could not; they could speak to the extra-logical connections active in the world dismissed by the intellect committed to analysis.

Zwicky was treated extremely well for a sessional instructor when she arrived at Princeton in the fall of 1982. She was given Walter Kaufmann's old office, which had "as much space as three of the ordinary university offices I've occupied since" along with an Ivy League view of rolling lawns and trees.[39] Here was a culture of academic philosophy with a perspective on itself far wider than what she'd found in her previous stops. Kaufmann, who'd passed away two years before her arrival, was a philosopher of religion and had published celebrated translations of Nietzsche. She ran tutorials for J.W. Smith, who brought a deep historical perspective to the practice of philosophy. Zwicky realized that she did not have anything approaching a proper philosophical education and was convinced that she had to learn the history of her discipline – a huge and vital shift. Yet Ivy League philosophy was not without significant, even debilitating drawbacks. Many books and journals in the Firestone Library were either missing altogether or had key chapters and articles razored out of them as a result of the intensely competitive atmosphere among graduate students. "It was so bad that the philosophy department had its own unofficial library, made up of books donated by profs," she said.[40] One afternoon, she saw one of the most famous academics of his generation reduced to an emotional wreck upon discovering that a rival philosopher at another school was being paid more than he was. That clinched it for her. Academic philosophy was clearly not connecting with the lives of the people who professed it. The day she handed in the grades for her courses, she packed up and headed for the border.

Zwicky returned to Waterloo in the late spring of 1983, somehow managed to score her old apartment, and resumed the post-doc she'd suspended a year earlier. She was assigned an introductory philosophy course for third-year engineers, and it was there that she finally got an education in the history of philosophy. The students, mostly male and only a few years younger than her, turned out to be stunningly bright and, as it happened, hungry for the kind of philosophical training she herself now wanted. She taught all the big names in the history of European philosophy, sometimes two a night. "In order to do this, of course, I had to learn the stuff – really learn it," Zwicky said. "Unlike a normal class, this one didn't lull me into imagining that I could get away with a rough outline and hand-waving. They were geniuses. They came to class prepared; they'd understood the stuff; they had questions. We ran hot. And so I learned, by reading and having to teach – in a pressure cooker – the history of European philosophy."[41]

Zwicky's core circle of friends came together over a period of several months around her thirtieth birthday. She and Don McKay had first met in the summer of 1982, after the publication of *Where Have We Been*, and met a second time that Christmas when she was back from Princeton visiting friends. They exchanged friendly letters from time to time. In the spring of 1985, some months after McKay's marriage broke up, they became romantically involved. Later that spring, McKay insisted that they attend a reading at Wilfred Laurier University given by Robert Bringhurst, who'd designed *Birding, or desire*. Bringhurst's work, she said, "isn't on the bookshelf; it has been open on the desk of the inner room of my thinking since I first encountered it."[42] Another vitally important friendship began shortly after the Laurier reading, this time with the poet Roo Borson. "I remember, clearly, her coming down a shallow flight of stone steps and 'recognizing' her, although we'd never met."[43] The last major addition to her circle arrived early the following year, when she and Tim Lilburn sat down for lunch at a tiny bistro in Kitchener called Marbles.

Around this time, Zwicky was visiting another friend at the Ontario Institute for Studies in Education (OISE) in downtown Toronto when she commented that what she really wanted to do was write philosophy that was also art. Looking west into the city's maze of concrete and tree canopy, she realized in that moment she'd said something true. "That was what I wanted to do," she said. "I had no idea at the time how to do it."[44] More specifically, she wanted to respond to the "misinterpretation of Wittgenstein's work, the then-current attempt to cram it into a positivist straight-jacket," that had troubled her for several years.[45] While Wittgenstein in the *Tractatus* felt that he had finally hit upon an honest method for bringing what was genuinely precious to people's attention, his stance was completely misconstrued by both his former colleagues and generations of philosophers afterwards. "My British-trained undergraduate professors treated his work with the reverence accorded Plato's and Hume's – that is, not much, but a great deal more than was accorded by most others'," Zwicky writes. "When I encountered him, Wittgenstein had already passed beyond the pale of 'thinking human being': he'd become a classic," and, she adds, "for the wrong reasons."[46] What he was actually saying – that the most important experiences of one's life cannot be accommodated by the analytically conditioned mind – was invisible to them. As a result, Wittgenstein's real views were out of reach to the philosophical mainstream. When discrepancies began to appear between what Wittgenstein actually said and what others wanted him to say, he went from being a figure lionized by the philosophical establishment to one considered intellectual trash. Zwicky writes: "I wanted to draw attention to the unity of Wittgenstein's life and work. I hoped to show how profoundly he experienced the moral dimensions of language's relation to the world. Most importantly, I wanted to argue that his questions pose a fundamental challenge to anyone who wishes to take philosophy seriously."[47]

These were the intentions that Zwicky brought to the writing of *Wittgenstein Elegies* (1986/2015), a five-part long poem that lives up to her exemplar's intuition that "philosophy ought really to be written as a poetic composition."[48] *Wittgenstein Elegies* brings together an ecology of voices, quotations, metaphors, and images inspired by or drawn from Wittgenstein's life. These are placed "side by side to reveal the resonances they bear in each other's presence," her colleague Sue Sinclair notes, allowing "meaning to move between them without proscribing or regulating that movement."[49] In the 1986 version of the poem, shifts in individual voice are indicated with different indents, while the 2015 edition makes use of the margin to distinguish one voice or text from another. In "Philosopher's Stone," Zwicky ventriloquizes him during the First World War, when he wrote the *Tractatus* and dreamed of "an inexpressible, crystalline world of logical relationships" while being shot at on a regular basis.[50] His chaotic circumstances are referred to only obliquely, as "the rolling / piecemeal world."[51] Elsewhere in "Philosopher's Stone," her re-imagined Wittgenstein speaks of the sheer overreach of logico-linguistic analysis, and gestures to another way of knowing:

We will see things
stark and dead if we see only things
themselves and not the pattern that informs them.
What must be understood, not collectivity, not
substance, is the depth of an embrace.[52]

In the second part of the sequence, "The Death of George
Trakl," Zwicky orchestrates something of a thought-fugue between
Wittgenstein and the brilliant young Austrian poet he funded whose
sensitivities were obliterated by the war. As she explains in a note
on the text, Trakl was institutionalized at the very end of his life,
requested help from Wittgenstein, and died "possibly by his own
hand" three days before his benefactor could reach him.[53] Hence
Trakl's final, haunting contribution to this fugue: "*We will never
know / whether it is a strength or a weakness / to have survived
where others could not.*"[54]

"In The Elder Days of Art" explores the "middle period" of
Wittgenstein's development. After quitting academia, he worked
as a schoolteacher, designed a house for his sister, and embarked
on a full-scale reappraisal and renovation of his earlier thought.
Language, he realized, was more complicated than he thought:

Our language is an ancient city, maze of interlocking
streets and squares. To know it, we must
walk it, crawl through sewers, feel our way
by night along the walls

. . . .
Think of tools: a hammer, pliers,
glue-pot, glue, screwdrivers, saw,
nails, rule. So might we see
the purposes of words. Their
uniform appearance though
misleads us, tempts us
into superficial thought, sees
form in stasis rather than in life.[55]

In "Confessions," the fourth part of the sequence, Zwicky orchestrates a two-in-one dialogue between the Wittgenstein of the *Tractatus*
and the Wittgenstein of *Philosophical Investigations*. This philosophically substantial and compassionate "Dialogue of Self and Soul"

builds to a moment of powerful lyric release. "Can we say anything adequate to the unuttering landscape, its mountains, mist and shore?" Sue Sinclair asks. "No, but we can try to speak in a way that makes us available to its silence."[56]

By the spring of 1986, Zwicky had started a new manuscript that looked to explore the poetics of *Wittgenstein Elegies*. She wanted to expand the boundaries of philosophy beyond the narrow concepts of analytic rigour without abandoning analysis or giving up on the need, at least in some circumstances, for rational argument. When Don McKay quipped in conversation, "What decent poet cares about rationality?" she realized that "he was pointing to something important, and that nevertheless I did care."[57] It seemed, though, that she was looking for a mode of organizing her thoughts that didn't exist, a prospect that was confirmed when every effort she made to write the manuscript stalled out after twenty pages. "I had a sense of where I wanted to go," she said, "but I couldn't figure out how to get going."[58]

When Robert Bringhurst came through Ontario early in 1986 and stayed with McKay and Zwicky at their farmhouse in Coldstream, she showed him her work-in-progress. Sitting around the kitchen table, she admitted that she was unable to get beyond the expository introduction. The difficulties she was having were structural in nature. She couldn't figure out how to incorporate the voices of other thinkers into her writing in a satisfying way. She didn't want to use footnotes, which seemed to be a big part of what was so alienating about standard academic style: they enacted the idea that philosophy consisted of monologues in which other voices were dissolved. "You didn't get the sense from such monovocal writing that philosophy was a *living colloquy*," she wrote.[59] What she wanted to do was get their words onto the page at the same time as her own, without containing them or surrounding them with her voice. Bringhurst, fresh off *The Blue Roofs of Japan*, took seriously her desire to structure the manuscript in a way that made room for other people's voices. He told her about a form of medieval commentary whereby an older text was located in the middle of the page or at one side while a newer text wrapped itself around or alongside the older text – usually in a slightly smaller or narrower hand. "I saw in a flash that I didn't want the effect of commentary, but that I did want two texts," Zwicky said. "*Two simultaneous*, parallel *texts*. That was the key. It was like a crystal being dropped in a supersaturated solution. I didn't see every word of the final text in that moment, but I certainly saw how to start putting them together."[60]

Zwicky returned to the fundamental unit of book typography, the codex format or two-page spread, and decided to approach it as a design challenge. She chose to reserve the left-hand side of every page spread for her own short, aphoristic statements while the right-hand side contained quotations from her intellectual ancestors and interlocutors. (As the manuscript evolved, the right-hand entries would come to include, among other things, entire poems, reproductions of paintings, musical scores, entries from dictionaries of etymology, and photographs alongside block quotations.) The left- and right-hand entries might support one another, or openly disagree, or one might amble off in a direction whose relevance only becomes clear as the book unfolds. She writes: "The relation of the two texts to one another is somewhere between counterpoint and harmony, somewhere between a double helix and the allemande of the earth and moon."[61]

Zwicky's double-text approach allowed a dance of thought to arise beyond the standard unit of the two-page spread (Dennis Lee has called these two-page spreads "duons"). Individual page spreads fit with others to form sections (there are twenty-one sections in all, including the Introduction and Coda). These are organized according to a particular musical strategy – "a dance of theme and counter-theme" as Lee puts it – that produces a relatively consistent A-B-A-B-A-B pattern forming the book's intellectual bass line.[62] "In formal terms," Lee writes, "Zwicky is stating her first main subject, with variations; juxtaposing her second main subject, with variations; and then tracing the way the two themes collide and refract. Once this thematic counterpoint becomes apparent, details which had seemed arbitrary assume a coherent place in the orchestration."[63] Such counterpoint can be apprehended in the book's first section, which is composed of six duons organized around the contrast between analytic philosophy and the more integrative mode of knowing she calls "lyric philosophy." If we read the opening section for the pattern implicit between the two-page spreads, we find each entry is linked crosswise to a partner. "The section is a mirror sequence, hinged in the middle," Lee writes. "And it resonates internally, each part with its own counterpart."[64]

Zwicky wrote the left-hand entries to *Lyric Philosophy* in longhand, first drafting reams of material that she would whittle down in

order to find "the one thing I needed, in any given sentence, to say."[65]
Some of the right-hand text arrived before most of the left-hand text,
but a good deal of it came on the heels of whatever left-hand aphorisms she had written. Other chunks seemed to drop out of the sky.
She'd be flipping through the *New York Review of Books*, tired at
the end of the day and with no purpose in mind, when she would
find a reference to a passage or thought that was what the manuscript was calling for. A conversation overheard in the university
cafeteria – she was teaching on a sessional basis at the University of
Western Ontario at the time – would point her to a particular book,
which she'd then track down, flip open, and find by chance a passage exactly and precisely resonant with something in the left-hand
text. "It was a full-blown, extended experience of what Carl Jung
calls synchronicity," she said. "At first I couldn't believe it; I thought
I must be so wrapped up in the project that I was just seeing connections everywhere, and that they'd dissolve in the sober light of
revision. But they held."[66] In conversation she compared the manuscript's structure to that of a spider web – an echo of Wittgenstein's
comment that in his work he felt was trying to repair a torn spider
web with his fingers. "Everything is, sometimes very delicately,
connected to everything else," she said.[67] "In the late stages, it was
difficult to hold the whole thing in my head. But I needed to, because
that's precisely what I was trying to create: a lyric work, a coherent
whole. I was standing in the kitchen late one afternoon, feeling that
I couldn't physically contain my mind anymore, and remembered
that Russell had said that while working on *Principa Mathematica*
he had felt he had worked his intelligence to the limit, had actually
strained it; and I knew what he meant. You feel, somatically, the
activity of your mind, as though it's a muscle; you can tell you can't
think any harder."[68]

Three interlocking ideas are at the heart of *Lyric Philosophy*. The
most important of these – and the most enigmatic – is "lyric." Here,
Zwicky takes that term as it is traditionally understood and turns it
inside out. She divests lyric of its Romantic associations, foremost
among them the "outpouring of subjective emotion" whereby the
artist's charged emotional reflexes are privileged over the lived phe-
nomena that inspired them.[69] When love and attention are directed
back to reality itself, there is now an opening through which the
luminous particularity of other beings and things can reach us.
In certain moments, we might also apprehend, in a flash, full and

complete, an underlying order or pattern to which these beings or things belong. Moreover, it is possible to be *met* by that larger life and reminded that everything has meaning, everything is connected to everything else, and that love really is the governing force of the world. To be informed by such insights and to attempt to live by them is the basis of lyric philosophy. Philosophy assumes lyric form, she proposes, when "thought whose eros is clarity is driven also by profound intuitions of coherence."[70]

Zwicky maintains that we do not get to live inside those experiences on a permanent basis because of who we are as human beings. Our capacity for tool-use gives rise to an experience of the self as phenomenologically distinct from our surroundings. We survive by manipulating our surroundings to meet our needs and wants, and are thus predisposed to overlook the fact that other beings and things have their own existence apart from our uses for them. Language, as a subset of tool-use, shares in such ontological alienation, one to which humankind may be predisposed. "As beings with the capacity for language use, it is our nature to be able to see a thing in a way that obscures presence," she writes.[71]

Domesticity is the name Zwicky gives to the taut middle ground between lyric comprehension and technological domination. It recognizes that we are pulled in competing directions by our desire to forfeit the self in radiant fusion with the earth and our capacity to overwhelm it through technological exploitation. Domesticity involves the realization that there is great power in our technologies, and asks us to take responsibility for that power so that it does not erase the presence of others. It acknowledges the intense ache we feel to join the world, yet accepts the fact that our capacity for language and technology makes such union impossible to sustain. She writes: "it is both the sadness and the strength of thought that it can see beyond what drives it, the sadness and the beauty of human being that it can comprehend the incompatibility of its essence with its most fundamental desire."[72]

Just over two years after her double-text epiphany, Zwicky had a finished manuscript that came in at just under 900 pages, and her friends were instrumental in its completion. She talked through all the major ideas with Don McKay, who was willing to debate them from all sides and who read the manuscript several times over. Tim Lilburn also read the manuscript in draft. During one conversation outside at Coldstream, late one winter day and with a wind rising around them, he urged her to step past epistemology into ontology. No, she said, that was precisely what she couldn't do. "Ontology is *exactly* what lyric insight realizes is beyond language," Zwicky told me. "The point of doing lyric philosophy is to acknowledge what is real but unlanguagable, and to understand language's relations to it."[73] Last but not least was Sam, her enormous Great Dane/Golden Lab cross, who played the part of active and intelligent listener. He would sit very straight with his head cocked as she read swaths of the manuscript out loud to him. "I caught an untold number of mistakes and soft spots that way."[74]

Another four years would pass before *Lyric Philosophy* appeared in print. Many publishers she approached were simply unwilling to take a risk on a manuscript with such an unusual structure. "We do not think the double-text will do," one of them replied.[75] The book eventually found its way to Ron Schoeffel, at University of Toronto Press (UTP), who was not deterred by the manuscript's complexity and who steered it through the press's byzantine publication process, which involved several different editorial boards that met sporadically, sometimes only once a year. Other complications pushed back the date of publication, including difficulties setting the musical scores she included in the right-hand text, and the gargantuan and expensive task of securing permissions for the hundreds of quotations she used. Zwicky's insistence that the book should honour quoted authors' styles of spelling and punctuation was another hard sell with UTP's copy editors. "The dates may give the impression of delays, but there were no unexpected ones, no major fights, no having to persevere in the face of adversity, or having to sustain my confidence on lonely nights when it seemed no one else in the world understood what I was up to," she said. "It was just an enormous, a humungous, undertaking – the sheer volume of it, and its outsized complexity."[76]

There was, however, a massive earthquake in Zwicky's personal life that made the fact of the completion of *Lyric Philosophy* all the more remarkable. In 1987, her father died of cancer at the age of sixty. The poems in *The New Room* (1989) bear intimate witness to his decline, his death, and the immediate aftermath of his death. They count among the most unguarded and unflinching in Zwicky's oeuvre. The trauma associated with a parent's passing opens up a space for the airing of other, older traumas and grievances. A grandmother emerges as a severe, erratic, and willfully cruel presence before whom the young speaker of "Last Steps"

can feel only "bewildered failure."[77] There is a predatory grandfather, who nonetheless is not as toxic as the grandmother. Thus
the speaker of "Grey Whales in Migration," with Herakleitos in
mind, says: "Home is the strung muscle / of back-stretched connection."[78] Several speakers acknowledge the precarity of work
and the alienation and rootlessness that comes with shuffling from
place to place. *The New Room* is an emotionally courageous book;
its publication must have alienated other members of Zwicky's
family and gives us some insight into the burdens this poet has
carried throughout her life.

Zwicky moved to New Brunswick with Don McKay in 1990 after
he took up his position in the Creative Writing program. For her
part, she was offered a sessional gig in philosophy at the university.
She found aspects of their living situation near the CFB Gagetown's
firing range difficult and, in 1992–93, the year *Lyric Philosophy*
was first published, spent a year as a visiting assistant professor in
the Department of Philosophy at the University of Alberta. McKay
joined her in Alberta in 1993–94 while she worked on a new collection of poems with the support of a Canada Council grant. McKay
very much wanted to return to New Brunswick, however, and convinced Zwicky that they should move into Fredericton, split his UNB
position, and both teach part-time. While they negotiated with the
university in an attempt to make the arrangement permanent, she
taught environmental philosophy, creative writing, and the philosophical background to literary theory ("a most unusual course for
the time," her former student Charles Barbour observed, "organized
around a reading of Kant, Hegel, Nietzsche, and Freud").[79] Zwicky's
clarity and engagement in the classroom won her a faculty-wide
teaching award in 1996, even as she found herself less and less
able to imagine herself as a career academic. She supplemented her
income playing with Symphony New Brunswick, the New Brunswick
Chamber Orchestra, and the Bangor Symphony Orchestra in Maine,
which all meant a fair amount of commuting to and from gigs.

On a brilliant spring morning in 1995, Zwicky was riding the
shuttle bus to the Calgary airport from the Banff Centre when
suddenly the idea for the book that would become *Songs for
Relinquishing the Earth* came to her fully formed, "like a bolt from
the blue."[80] With light pouring in the windows and reflecting off the
chrome struts around her, she decided that instead of going with a
traditional publisher, she would make the book herself, on recycled

stock, and sell it for cost. She would use nothing more complicated than a photocopier, needle, and thread. Every poem would be published first in a journal to honour the peer review process. She would use a typeface designed by a woman (Diotima), defy marketing logic by making the cover completely plain, and, instead of promoting the book, would simply let word of mouth do the work, trusting that it would find whomever it was supposed to find.

Zwicky had long been frustrated with the business of publishing poetry in Canada. There was, for starters, the enormous impact it had on the environment. "Why weren't publishing companies – people who could really put some pressure on printers, who could put some pressure on pulp mills – asking for recycled stock? Why were we cutting down old growth to publish stuff that we didn't know was going to stand the test of time? Why were we cutting down old growth to publish anything?"[81] She was particularly troubled by the attempt to put poetry to work within a capitalist framework. As part of Brick Books' editorial collective since 1986, she had already locked horns with the Canada Council, arguing against their policy of treating poetry as a consumer good. Marketing to the literary mainstream through the likes of back-cover blurbs by other authors was not how poetry sold – it relied instead on a very small but rock-solid audience that communicated with itself one conversation at a time. "The injustice, the waste, the distortion of what poetry was drove me nuts," she said.[82] Could the book-as-public-good be brought back into right relationship with the intimacy of the creative act?

A year later, Zwicky began producing handmade copies of *Songs for Relinquishing the Earth*. Once all the materials had been assembled and she was well practiced, it took her just over two hours to make each one. She opted for plain unbleached card stock for the cover on which she pasted the title, cut from a sheet of the same recycled stock on which the text was photocopied. The endpapers were green, slightly ridged, recycled stock, and on what would normally be the dedication page, she pasted a small photo of lavender fields extending to distant mountains. By the fall of 1996, she had made about 120 copies, and there were so many requests coming in that she was having trouble keeping up with the demand.

Meanwhile, things were not working out at UNB. McKay and Zwicky had not been successful in convincing the administration to split the position and hire them both permanently part-time. McKay had told her that if she could spring them, he'd go with her. The

University of Victoria was, at that point, advertising a tenure-stream position with a specialization in environmental philosophy. "I have never been a career academic," she told me. "'Being a professor' has never been a goal for me."[83] But she needed a substantial salary if she was to replace McKay's income, and she didn't want to end up at the age of sixty under a bridge eating cat food. In the early 1990s, she'd designed and marketed courses in environmental philosophy to the University of Alberta and University of New Brunswick. "Putting these courses together and convincing universities that they needed to be taught, and then teaching them, was, for me, activism," she said.[84] She applied for the Victoria job.

For Zwicky, the environmental crisis is fundamentally an epistemological crisis. It begins between our ears, in how we have been taught to know the world. "There was something wrong not just with how we were voting, but with how we were thinking, and academic philosophy was heavily implicated," she said. "It was championing an epistemology that functioned as a hit man for the technocracy."[85] Systematic Enlightenment epistemologies are based on the idea that all beings and things are ontologically separate, or can be isolated and understood in isolation from one another. Proponents of those epistemologies achieve understanding by breaking things down into their component parts, which are themselves considered "independent of and prior to the wholes into which they are combined."[86] "Knowledge" involves analysis, aggregation, and the creation of taxonomic hierarchies – along with the erasure of relationship and context. The point of knowing is to be able to manipulate other beings and things "for comfort, to demonstrate power, for the hell of it" without ever allowing oneself to be vulnerable or energetically available to them.[87] As analytic-system knowers, human beings thus presume to occupy the very top of the hierarchy of life.

Out of these systematic Enlightenment epistemologies evolved the technocracy. Here is how Zwicky defined the term in one of her letters: "The technocracy believes that doing it by machine means doing it better. It believes that to the extent something can't be conceived as a machine, it doesn't exist. It views all things as assemblages of parts. It understands value as monetized profit. Its ideology is profoundly anthropocentric and positivist. There is nothing beyond the reach of language. Contextualization obscures rather than reveals truth."[88] To Zwicky, the technocracy has made its way into every corner of modern life. It exerts enormous pressure on how

we think, feel, and behave. It directly intervenes in our ability to connect to and find nourishment in one another and our surroundings.
Yet for the most part, it remains mostly invisible to us. "The power
of the technocratic worldview," Zwicky writes in a later essay, "is
not fundamentally illustrated by the extent of its achievements, but
rather – as Heidegger thought – by the extent of its ability to disguise
from itself that it is a perspective, a way of viewing the world."[89]
As Heidegger wrote in his "Memorial Address" from *Discourse on
Thinking* (1966), with especial emphasis, "*The meaning pervading
technology hides itself.*"[90]

Zwicky was successful in her application for the position at the
University of Victoria (UVic), and in the summer of 1996, she and
McKay crossed the country yet again. When she began teaching
at the university that fall, she opened her classes by telling students
that the cardinal philosophic virtue was courage – courage to ask
questions that they thought were stupid. Those questions, she maintained, were nearly always the most important ones because they
pointed to assumptions that everyone else was taking for granted.
She wanted her students to understand that philosophy is an activity,
one characterized by an attempt to coordinate intuition with logical,
rational argument. The first aim of this activity was for students to
figure out which of their intuitions crumbled under pressure. Some
of the things we take to be true are really just assumptions we've
inherited from our family or from our culture without properly scru-
tinizing them, and once we do think about them, we find that we don't
accept them anymore. We also discover there are intuitions that hold
even when we ourselves can demonstrate that they have no articulate,
analytic, "scientific" defence. Such intuitions must be respected. This
does not mean regarding them as inviolable; it means seeing them
as challenges. Rationality is not simply to be discarded, for it will
have become obvious how it helps you in finding out what you really
do think, and how at least some parts of the world work. What the
presence of such intuitions suggests is that perhaps there are areas in
which analytic literal-mindedness doesn't give us the whole picture.
The task is to build the capacity for discernment between the intuitive
and the rational, and this we learn only through practice. "It is a long
apprenticeship," she said. "You have to put in years."[91]

With her intellectual integrity and compelling presence – for she
knew that good teaching involves an element of theatre – Zwicky
had an immediate galvanizing impact on campus, both in and out

of the classroom. On the first day of her introductory philosophy class in the fall of 1996, she walked into the room, took out her pocket watch to confirm the time, and then announced: "Philosophy is hard, *really* hard."[92] Using *The Classics of Western History* as her core text, Zwicky helped her students understand just how blinkered the discipline was to its own history. "She noted how little of the text was taken up with philosophy before Descartes, holding that huge paperback textbook up in front of her and flopping it like it was a dead bird," Darren Bifford, who was in the room that fall, told me.[93] She challenged her students at every turn. "Leaving class we'd say that we had been 'Zwicked,' as if we'd been subject to an electric charge," Bifford said. Students routinely trailed her from the lecture hall back to her office, eager to continue the conversation. Before long she had so many of them lined up outside her door she had to institute a fifteen-minute policy.

Zwicky also helped restore a sense of community to a department that had hitherto been something of a professional dormitory, a place to teach and nothing more. "Being committed to a department doesn't come easy to someone like Jan," James O. Young told me. "She went out of her way to make it work."[94] She organized a reading of Plato's *Symposium* in the grad lounge so that students and faculty members could drink wine, and played washtub bass alongside other professors at department parties. Three years after arriving at UVic, Zwicky managed to parlay her job into a part-time position – what she had always hoped to do – and began reclaiming the space she needed to write and play music. Even in her efforts to quietly ease away from the university, her popularity as a professor continued to grow; in 2002, she won a second faculty-wide teaching award at UVic.

Meanwhile, *Songs for Relinquishing the Earth* found more readers after Brick Books published a "facsimile edition" in 1998 – complete with a brown-paper-bag cover and the absence of promotional blurbs – part of an unlikely journey that culminated in a Governor General's Literary Award a year later. Almost half of the poems in the book are rooted in close study of the lives of the great composers, or are direct responses to particular pieces of music, or have borrowed and learned from their structures. "I have more works of music memorized than works of literature," she said, "and even when I don't cue it in a dedication, it's often a musical gesture or insight to which I'm responding."[95] While many poets have looked to Western European classical music for inspiration, very few have done so as professional musicians in their own right. For Zwicky, practising and making music is a way of being in the world and is part of her daily routine. One of her colleagues, Bruce Vogt, head of piano studies at UVic, told me that one of the German words for practising or rehearsing is *probieren*, or to probe into something. Music is a valid mode of inquiring into the world; it can explore what Zwicky described to me in one letter as "various aspects of sonic ontological-emotional geometry."[96] Her poems are not an exaggeration or an echo of the music she loves but an intensification of it, an attempt to capture in her own "soundworld of words," as Vogt put it, what the music is doing. "They are not impressions of a piece of music," he said. "They are about finding words which recreate the mysterious way that music is put together and can say so much and affect us so deeply."[97] Her poem "Beethoven: Op. 95," for example, makes use of key phrases from the composer's own journal entries, sometimes carrying over whole lines intact and in other instances modifying them slightly. In "Kant and Bruckner: Twelve Variations," she explores the unusual biographical overlaps between philosopher and composer by way of a polyphonic play of voices. In "Brahms' Clarinet Quintet in B Minor, Op. 115," she finds in the work of the neo-classicist composer a great emotional range that has been buried under the avalanche of modernity and what Ross Leckie describes as "the harsh rigours of a violent and mechanized century."[98] Zwicky's discipline of listening is evident in the prose poem "Trauermusik," where she crafts a complex meditation on mortality and absence around Paul Hindemith's decision to omit the leading note from the closing cadence of a memorial setting of a well-known hymn – a missing seventh that the untrained ear can sense but cannot name.

In *Songs for Relinquishing the Earth*, Zwicky distinguishes between the losses that come naturally, as part of the order of things, and those generated by runaway technology. Beginning with "Open Strings," the first poem in the book, the speaker wakes up to the unavoidable fact of her own non-being. "Open strings / are ambassadors from the republic of silence. / They are the name of that moment when you realize / clearly, for the first time, / you will die."[99] Staying at her mother's house, the speaker of "Poppies" glances up from the dinner table at a familiar picture hanging from the wall and experiences "the sudden clear presentiment that I would live / to walk into that dining room someday, after / the last death, and find it / waiting for me, the entire past / dangling from a finishing nail."[100] In "Trauermusik," the last poem in the book, the speaker suggests that we only arrive at the end of mourning, the letting go of loss, by accepting that it involves the death of desire; "we must pass through – as through a ghost – that absence in ourselves."[101] In an age of widespread species extinction, Zwicky suggests that we must also face the prospect of the end of nature itself. In "K. 219, Adagio," "the sky above New Mexico / is hazy with Los Angeles."[102] "Five Songs for Relinquishing the Earth" begins out of doors, in a Romantic reverie reminiscent of Gustav Mahler's *Das Lied von der Erde*, before careening swiftly downward with images of burnt Amazonia, oblique calamity, and, finally, a ruined tent and a human heart reduced to nothing. If the ideal at the centre of the Enlightenment project is to secure our lives from loss by rendering the earth heroically knowable, the task now is to acknowledge that this compulsion may have mortally wounded the earth.

Zwicky had just pulled out of her driveway in downtown Victoria when the core insight that became *Wisdom & Metaphor* (2003) arrived in a flash, with everything else sliding and dropping into place in its wake. "It hit me, like an idea from someone else's mind – full, complete – *understanding, all understanding, is seeing-as*."[103] Grasping a metaphor, or recognizing how things *do not* and at the same time *do* resemble one another, was the pure case of the experience of meaning, and not some distorted phenomenon that had to be explained. Things rhymed – faces, landforms, events – quietly affirming the interwoven nature of reality. Analysis, which broke the world down into smaller and smaller parts in order to understand it, had it exactly backwards. "I had to pull the car over," she told me. "I didn't have words, but I got out my notebook and began, in a state of some anxiety, to try to find some."[104]

This time around, there was no question how to build the text. The parallel-text format Zwicky had invented for *Lyric Philosophy* was perfectly suited for an inquiry into the double-jointed nature of metaphor. She wrote out her ideas on the left-hand side of every page spread in the form of aphorisms, some no longer than a sentence or two. The right-hand side of the text, as in that earlier work, made room for quotations from other thinkers and artists, along with poems, gestalt figures, visual proofs from mathematics, song lyrics, and excerpts from musical scores. According to Don McKay, the use of parallel texts allowed Zwicky to incorporate "the semantic operations of metaphorical understanding" in the shape of the work itself.[105] The reader is asked to "be alive not only to the aphorisms on the left and the quotations on the right," he adds, "but to the dance of the mind as it ferries back and forth between them."[106]

A crucial figure who helped her better understand that dance of the mind is Max Wertheimer (1880–1943), the Czech-American psychologist and associate of Albert Einstein. Zwicky came across Wertheimer by happenstance, in the early 1990s. She was at Boston University and had just given a lecture on dreams and reason when a professor in the philosophy department, Robert Cohen, suggested she might find Wertheimer's work of interest. She felt an immediate sense of kinship with the mind behind books like *Productive Thinking* (1959) – the emphasis on pattern, configuration, and holistic structure over piecemeal knowledge – but it wasn't until she found herself grappling with *Wisdom & Metaphor* that Wertheimer's influence truly began asserting itself ("This guy has the golden goose in his mental chicken coop," she remembers thinking).[107]

Wertheimer rejected analytical, brick-by-brick, word-based accounts of thinking because they simply could not explain how we make sense of melody in music or suddenly see structural solutions to problems in mathematics. He argued for the existence of a non-linguistic mode of thinking based on the gestalt, the German word for "form" or "shape." We perceive things as wholes, he proposed, instead of building them up out of parts. We hear the symphony, not *these* notes followed by *those* notes. When we see things through the lens of language, though, we engage in a way of thinking that isolates bits of the world and leaves them isolated. Language conditions us to perceive the world as a collection of objects. And as physiological beings who live in a world we have to take from in order to survive, we actually need language to do this for us – to keep things distinct – so that we can make use of them. What we need to do, Zwicky reasoned, is go beyond language and open up a layer of non-linguistic mental activity. We do this by picking up on the resonance between things – how, for example, the legs of the table I am writing at resemble the trees that hold up the canopy of the forest a short walk from my house. Recognizing the existence of such resonances is a step in the right direction, but we still haven't entered the world as an integrated whole.

Crucial in our efforts to think along with a world of shapes is Wertheimer's notion of the "gestalt shift." This phenomenon is famous from Joseph Jastrow's "duck/rabbit" figure, L.A. Necker's reversible cube, and Edgar Rubin's vase/faces-in-profile, each of which is a visually ambiguous image that can be seen in two different ways. Both are present in the same figure, even though they cannot be grasped at the same time. Yet such figures, which Zwicky relies on extensively in *Wisdom & Metaphor* and elsewhere, have their limitations. They encourage us to think of the gestalt shift in terms of a simple binary – we ping-pong back and forth endlessly between the two faces and the vase – distracting us from the fact that we are talking about a form of thinking that is impossibly open-ended and fluid and capable of reaching out in all directions. Instead, the gestalt shift must be seen as the very engine and dynamo of a non-linguistic thought process that metamorphoses from one "intellectual and emotional complex" to another "in an instant of time," to borrow from Ezra Pound.[108] Language, for its part, cannot keep up with such associative leaps and jumps. It can accommodate them, however imperfectly, by transgressing its own rules, and one of the ways it does this is with metaphor. The gambit of *Wisdom & Metaphor* is that a successful philosophical defence of this seemingly innocuous figure of speech would legitimize an entire order of non-linear, extra-rational thought processes. Accept the validity of metaphor and so much more than just musical thinking gets its foot in the door.

Close to the geometric centre of *Wisdom & Metaphor*, Zwicky introduces the term "*this*ness" as part of her effort to describe the relationship between the individual particular and the larger whole it belongs to. She is referring to the specific constituents of our surroundings – "*this* porch, *this* laundry basket, *this* day."[109] Even just to notice such things, whatever they may be, is to "respond to having been addressed." She writes: "We are addressed all the time, but we don't always notice this."[110] The phrasing here and elsewhere is so quiet we might easily overlook the fact that Zwicky's notion of *this*ness amounts to a primal experience as I have been using that term in this book: the particulars of the world possess the capacity and the agency to reach out and impress themselves upon us. In a complicated paradoxical turn, she suggests that because the *this*ness of something is highlighted by everything it is not, its uniqueness drives into and pierces us all the more. And when we are pierced by something, we can intimate the presence of the larger whole to which that individual belongs. This brings us back to one of the central insights of *Lyric Philosophy*: "The gift of lyric is to see the whole in the particular; and in so doing, to bring the preciousness, which is the loseability, of the world, into clear focus."[111] In an interview with Darren Bifford and Warren Heiti published in *Chamber Music: The Poetry of Jan Zwicky* (2015), Zwicky elaborates on her experience of "the ontology of *this*ness" in more colloquial terms: "What is it like to be available? For me, some being, some action, some scrap of memory, some musical phrase – an emotional/visual/aural/kinaesthetic/intellectual/perceptual complex 'in an instant of time – will stand a little forward in the world, will be haloed with visual or aural light, and suddenly I will have a feeling of terrible responsibility toward it, as though I need to do something – to honour it, to pray in gratitude, to offer due acknowledgement ... If I can stay under long enough, I sense – well, *more*. And it's not until I sense that *more* ... that the haloed image-complex – the 'individual' thing, situation or event – stands stably in my perception. It's when I sense the shape of the *more* that I can *bear* it."[112]

Having run the gauntlet of academic publishing for *Lyric Philosophy*, Zwicky didn't want to try that route with *Wisdom & Metaphor*. She had reconciled herself to the fact that she was unlikely to have a scholarly impact given how conservative the philosophical establishment was – how it lacked the openness to new ideas it so loudly proclaimed to cultivate. Because "all aspects of a lyric gesture are fundamental to its meaning," she wanted to find a publisher who could produce a book whose form didn't undermine its content, or who could make the book's philosophical gestures coherent.[113] She was familiar with Gaspereau Press from Don McKay's experience with *Vis à Vis* and was drawn to their maverick approach to publishing. She admired Gaspereau's life-on-the-line commitment to producing beautiful books despite the fact the press had no capital. She loved their recovery of gorgeous classical designs, their use of hopelessly outdated print technologies that other publishers had taken to the dump long ago, and their refusal to be co-opted by the larger literary culture (this stance was put to the test in 2010, when Johanna Skibsrud's novel *The Sentimentalists* won the Giller Prize, spiking demand beyond the press's abilities to meet it). All this – plus the fact you could tear the back-cover copy right off the books – "warmed the cockles of my prairie farm cum Luddite heart."[114] The final results did not disappoint. Ten years after its publication, Zwicky called the first edition of *Wisdom & Metaphor* "one of the most stunning physical volumes I've ever laid eyes on."[115]

The phenomenon of "seeing-as" is central to *Robinson's Crossing* (2004), one of two poetry collections Zwicky wrote alongside *Wisdom & Metaphor*. That collection is filled with crossings and re-crossings, circular movements that enact the dance of the mind intrinsic to metaphor, and is studded with numerous moments in which the similarities between things point to the underlying lyric structure of the world. The first poem in *Robinson's Crossing*, "Prairie," brings together the memory of the hasp of the underside of her grandparents' farmhouse table with the "rusty weight" in the speaker's chest that gives way to "a slow opening of sky" on her return to the prairies after a long stint in New Brunswick.[116] In the title poem, which spans the book's centre, the speaker is at the family farm and cleaning up after a fallen poplar when she recognizes that the tree's scent is also that of her family. "It was / the body's scent, the one / that's on the inside / of your clothes, the one a dog / picks up."[117] The last poem in the book, "Glenn Gould: Bach's 'Italian' Concerto, BWV 971," features a dramatic leap between a tumultuous sky and the pianist's artistry, allowing the speaker to catch a glimpse of her more authentic self, "always here, right here, / but outside history."[118] Such moments of seeing-as, incandescent as they are, sit uncomfortably within a larger, darker narrative: the collective blindness on the part of non-Indigenous people to recognize and embrace the connectedness of the world.

The idea for *Robinson's Crossing* came to Zwicky one summer in the late 1990s while visiting her mother at the farm. It was the second year of a three-year drought in northwestern Alberta, and the earth had been baked to dust to a depth of two metres. "Sitting there, watching the soil billow and drift, I felt a sick grief. I'd have done almost anything to make it stop; and there was nothing I could do."[119] She realized that she herself had not yet thought critically about the 100-year-old colonial experiment on the prairies but was nonetheless personally implicated. "My deep love for that piece of land was a function of having grown up there," she said. "And my having grown up there had been made possible by colonialism."[120] The very place where Zwicky felt most connected to the earth – the place where the experience of meaning was most readily available – was in fact occupied land, taken by coercion and force.[121] She couldn't think of what to do to make up for the atrocities of colonialism. There seemed to be no plausible recompense. "In such situations," she told me, "I think witness becomes a moral imperative."[122]

The title poem of *Robinson's Crossing* combines fragments of family legend with those of the history of the colonization of Lac Ste Anne County. When settlers began arriving at the end of the nineteenth century, they travelled by rail as far as the Pembina River, waited for the ferry to cross the water, and made the final part of their trip by foot or wagon. Zwicky returns to that moment of waiting, settlers poised to come into the country, and uses it to reflect on both the colonial project and the technocratic culture that followed it. The speaker notes that settlers carried with them a Victorian outlook at its most optimistically parochial, hoping to transform the land from aspen parkland and muskeg into some reflection of the English countryside. In order to maintain their claim to it, they faced the Sisyphean task of converting thirty acres of gumbo-like soil into farmland in three years:

The homestead map shows
maybe two in three men
made it. Several of their wives
jumped from the bridge.[123]

Meanwhile, the Indigenous inhabitants of the region – Treaty 6 identifies the negotiants as Cree and Assiniboine – are glimpsed in the background of a couple of antiquated photographs. Their summer gathering place had long been buried under the town dump, and their presence erased, by the time the speaker came to consciousness. In the second-to-last stanza of the poem, she suggests that the time to renew the kind of intimacy her family felt with the land may have passed. The climate is changing; the water levels on the river are alarmingly low; "the highway's / been twinned; Monsanto / just released another herbicide-resistant / seed."[124] The way of being of the first settlers, which prepared the ground for the emergence of the technocracy, is itself sliding out of awareness.

Technocratic consciousness and its antidote are the subjects of "Metaphysics" and "Epistemology," two poems that face each other across a single page spread of *Robinson's Crossing*. The first poem, she said, "is deeply, heavily ironic, cast in the voice of an ecstatic analytic philosopher, spoken on the brink of the apotheosis of technology that analytic philosophy has aided and abetted."[125] In order to participate in the project of mastering the world, philosophy had to purge itself of those elements that got in the way of that goal, summarized here as "Hume, the Pre-Socratics, and the gaudier / confusions of unbridled sense experience sold off / as kitchen ornaments."[126] What remains is an unswerving, single-minded commitment to objectification, reductionism, and analysis. The poem ends with the world on the brink of collapse, even as those caught up in the delusions of technocratic epistemology celebrate their achievements.

On the other page of the spread, "Epistemology" identifies "where we have to go to get away from positivist metaphysics and its attempt to kill the real world by insisting that only analysis can know it."[127] The speaker gestures to a number of events or insights saturated with meaning, the likes of which the ecstatic philosopher of "Metaphysics" sought to expunge from the human condition altogether. A few representative examples: "Because I've tried hard to forget. / And, without warning, I could tell that I was / seven storeys in the air"; "Because it was a river in my heart, because / it moved like winter underneath my skin. A tree / came into leaf behind my eyes"; "Because my body / was a flock of horned larks and my bones were / bells."[128] When I asked Zwicky about this startling list of impressions, she was hesitant to discuss it. Beyond an explanation of the poem's title and the source of the epigraph from Wittgenstein, she told me, "there's nothing else I can say about it. I'm already treading close to the line in the poem itself. Saying more would be trespassing."[129] For her, the really honest and attentive gesture is not to affix any name or tradition to such experiences. "The affixing of names, the sequestering in traditions, is a way of taming, controlling, making social, what ought to be left untamed and unsocialized," she said.[130] The world is full of sensory brilliance that is incontrovertibly, overwhelmingly real, yet cannot be proved through analysis or rational reconstruction. Wild metaphoric leaps and throws can catch a reflection of its meaning. That is one way in which the world – the real world – can be known.

This helps us understand why Zwicky's favourite book among the ones she has written is *Thirty-seven Small Songs and Thirteen Silences* (2005). There she invites the reader to join her in the world as she knows and experiences it, outside the frameworks of colonialism, globalization, and technology. "Plants mean, stones mean," she told me. "And I believe that humans can tune into that meaning quite easily if they are paying attention."[131] Not just plants and stones, but everything – the entire gamut of reality – including different kinds of

wind, shades of light, household fixtures, emotions, events. A bath-
tub waits calmly for its tired owner. The "iron ribcage" of an old
grate.[132] The "chinchilla skin of night" of the breeze before dawn.[133]
The moon stares at us with its "quartz eye."[134] Darren Bifford
and Warren Heiti describe *Thirty-seven Small Songs and Thirteen
Silences* as "an animist's field guide" that can be read in light of
the pre-Socratic philosopher Thales's observation that "all things are
full of gods."[135] This is the world Zwicky has remained true to all her
life, the one that continues to accompany her and nurture her, even
when so many of her kind are doing their best to destroy it. What
to do when met by these huge forms of meaning that are constantly
trying to communicate with us? The poems of this little book suggest
that we should sing. Here is "Small song for the offshore breeze":

> Sunday, out on my bike,
> I drop down from the hill's brow
> and you come to meet me:
> wing off the water, or two hands
> at arms' length, grasping the shoulders –
> *you're here!*–unlooked for
> plunge into the present:
>   quenching thirst
> when I had not known I was thirsty.[136]

Zwicky's intention was to make music with her surroundings and,
more specifically, to create "the echo of Spanish song in English."[137]
Federico Garcia Lorca's *gacelas* and *canciones* were "startlingly resonant, and achieved huge effects with the most minimal means."[138]
Yet the musical resources of the English language prevented her from
doing certain things that were easy in Spanish. She found inspiration
in a comment by translator Don Paterson in *The Eyes*, a collection
of translations of Antonio Machado, in which he suggested that
Spanish is comparable to a guitar while English is a piano. This
seemed exactly right. "The piano is a percussion instrument," she
told me. "It has great range, and can handle great harmonic complexity, but it can be difficult to make small gestures sing. But that's
what I wanted to do."[139] In order to recreate the simpler resonance
of the guitar, she composed her small songs mostly out of words
with no more than one or two syllables. Many of the poems in the
book are no more than eight to ten lines in length. Set against vast

tracts of blank space, these tiny gestures point to the many-souled "being of the world."[140]

Heriot Ridge made its presence felt not long after Zwicky began dividing her time between Quadra Island and Victoria beginning in 2007. It did so in part through its sounds, including the voices of the rain and of the creek at different times of the year, birdsong, the singing of the frogs. She also felt the ridge as a form of consciousness that drew awareness to itself through her physical body, "the way you're aware of a dog's consciousness when it presses against you," she said. "My experience of the ridge is very much that it has walked towards me. That it has approached me, in a spirit of incredible generosity. It's as though at every turn, when I've been trying to come to terms with the land here, trying to make a real home different from my home in Alberta, the ridge has understood, has supported me, has grasped the difficulties."[141]

Zwicky reciprocated the land's kindness by paying attention to it with all her senses – by listening, looking, smelling, touching, and tasting, by bringing to conscious awareness the sheer depth of her delight. She put in a garden near the frog pond and took over another plot in a community garden down the hill (a large greenhouse with a solar heater would follow some years later). Gardening has always helped her connect to where she lives, in a way that is both incredibly time consuming and deeply comforting. "Plants are beautiful," she said, "and it's often restful to spend time with them just for that reason. They are intelligent and sensitive, but they don't send you e-mails or phone you up when they want something. They make it clear, but they put it quietly."[142] It is important to her to eat food that grows in the earth where she is living. The activities of planting, tending, and preserving make her life continuous with the lives of her ancestors and the larger life of the land. Every shovelful of dirt she moves, every huckleberry she picks, helps and sustains her. "It's all a kind of magic," she said. "Things just grow; and you can eat them. I'm totally amazed by this fact. It's a way of touching the great mysteries of life and death."[143]

Touching those mysteries through dialogue in the service of human excellence is the subject of Zwicky's next book, *Plato as Artist* (2009), reprinted in *Alkibiades' Love* (2015). From her first encounter with Plato as an undergraduate, she had been deeply interested in his moral integrity as a philosopher as well as his abilities as a dramatic writer, and from early on, sensed the connective tissue between the two. "It was an immense relief to me to encounter a thinker whom everyone thought was central to the canon, who was capable of *feeling* as well as thinking," she said.[144] She came back to Plato in the mid-1990s through Tim Lilburn, "who made me look, and look again," and was drawn to a book by the French philosopher Pierre Hadot called *Philosophy as a Way of Life* (1995).[145] Hadot located the Platonic dialogue in the tradition of spiritual exercises, or those techniques a teacher might use to nudge a student into remembering what they saw before being born on earth. Recollection work allows us to recall in ourselves the source of moral beauty so that we might lead a life guided and supported by that source. "Once we have had such an experience, and can reproduce in memory what caused it, our conviction becomes unshakable," Zwicky writes.[146] Yet the teacher cannot do such work for his students. Zwicky devotes *Plato as Artist* to a close reading of *Meno*, and shows just how hard Socrates works in his attempts to bring a particularly dimwitted student to genuine intuition, using every tool at his disposal ("Meno is such damp wood there is no teasing him into even a flicker of interest in reality," she writes).[147] While Socrates is ultimately unsuccessful in kindling a fire in his student, the dialogue is itself a showcase for teaching as a vessel for moral excellence. She writes: "It is clear that good men, like Socrates, draw the desire for goodness to the surface in all of us, their actions reinforce our dim dream-like intuitions and their conversation may even start us on the path to philosophy."[148]

For Zwicky, that path no longer ran through the university. She quit professional philosophy for a second time in 2009, convinced that the conditions required to carry out even a sliver of a Platonic education no longer existed at the university. Class sizes, for a start, had exploded. The first time she taught the senior seminar on Plato in the late 1990s, she had twenty-two students. It had been a considerable challenge to give each of them the kind of attention that Plato's vision of philosophy required. Ten years later, there were two sections of the course, with sixty students each. The pressure to use digital technology had also been growing steadily, strengthening the chokehold the technocratic mindset had on the university. In capitulating to the technocracy's demands for digital protocols in every sector of the institution, the academy had betrayed its origins and was essentially dead from the centre out (in one conversation, she compared it to a stand of poplars that *appeared* to still be living even though the root system they shared had rotted away). She also couldn't help but notice that students who had never known a world without the Internet were different. The analogies that she could think of to make the questions and ideas meaningful to them did not resonate, and she was not willing to convert to digitality to find new ones. It was a grim diagnosis: old-growth human knowledge was off-limits to the technologically adept young people who filled her classes. One night, sitting in front of the fire on Quadra Island, she realized that she had lost her calling, and that it was time to leave. It was a decision she never regretted, even in light of the financial struggles that came with it.

One of the first projects that Zwicky completed after her departure from the academy was *Forge* (2011), her seventh collection of poems and a book whose complicated architecture took her years to build. Early on in the writing process, she noticed that two lengthy poems, "Music and Silence" and "Envoy," not only contained seven sections each but also were structural and thematic variations on one another. She decided to place them at either end of the manuscript. The two sequences written as responses to Bach – "Practising Bach" and "The Art of Fugue" – corresponded with one another and so she positioned them symmetrically as well. They formed the pillars of an arch. Other poems found counterparts, which not only added to that arch but also intensified its emotional resonance. "Nojack," for example, is about a drive on a bright December day and a couple weighed down by grief. "What is it a woman can do for a man, / his grief so deep it's colourless, like sunlight – / her own deeper."[149] "Nojack" is answered by "Autumn Again." There the speaker acknowledges the songs of crickets, ravens, and chickadees around her, then suddenly asks a question that reaches across the centre of the book back to its companion poem: "What is / human happiness?" (it is not for nothing "Autumn Again" is dedicated to Don McKay).[150] The poem that contains the book's title and identifies the source of its resonance and integrity is "If There Were Two Rivers." It sits at the very centre of the arch and identifies its keystone:

If what lay below was light.
If what you could not find was there.
If its hard fire was a golden river.
If the golden river was a forge.
If the forge was rock, and if the rock was shining.
If the forge was love.[151]

Alkibiades' Love: Essays in Philosophy (2015) brings together eleven essays that challenge the technocratic mindset with the alternative approach Zwicky had, in a sense, been formulating all her life. A quick overview of its contents gives us some sense as to where we have been in this chapter. "What Is Lyric Philosophy?" is an introduction to that approach that she compares to a "signposted boardwalk tour of a wetland."[152] Two claims are at the heart of her work: the world exists, and it has meaning. It sponsors what she calls "lyric thought," whose formal properties are resonance and integrity.[153] "For lyric thought, the foundations of meaning lie in the world, and in human experience of the world, unconditioned by language," she writes.[154] Lyric thought is mostly invisible to technocratic consciousness, which understands meaning as "essentially a linguistic phenomenon."[155] Only words that defer to the world's "extra-linguistic plentitude of meaning" can bear its trace.[156] "Some things can be known that cannot be expressed in technocratically acceptable prose."[157] Hence the importance of metaphor as a way of speaking truthfully about the resonant interconnectedness of the world. "We see, simultaneously, similarities and dissimilarities: we experience things as both metaphysically distinct and ontologically connected."[158] Lyric compositions, which are multi-dimensional and polyphonic in nature, can teach us how to recognize the patterns that are constantly forming out of the incidents and events of our own lives, patterns that echo and join in the larger flow of life itself. Wisdom, for its part, ultimately involves living alongside of and accepting overlapping truths. It is a form of what she calls domesticity, in which we cohabit with complexity without flattening it through increasingly powerful forms of technology. There is the distinctness of things; there is underlying connectedness: flashing back and forth between these two gestalts allows us to reach deeper into the world and touch that plentitude of meaning for which we have no words. "Suppose to know is more like to visit or to cohabit than to own," she writes.[159]

While Zwicky acknowledges this summary of lyric philosophy is limited by the fact that it describes instead of embodies its subject matter, it serves as an excellent point of departure for other essays in *Akibiades' Love* that further consolidate her alternative epistemology. In "Why Is Diotima a Woman?" she locates the source of Parmenidean and Platonic philosophy in "a fundamentally feminine province of the mythworld."[160] The identity of that source constitutes the book's warmest surprise, reverberates through Zwicky's entire oeuvre as an artist-thinker, yet is best approached obliquely, with averted eyes. "Addressing a goddess," she notes, "is not unlike saying hi to a grizzly bear."[161] Coming into contact with that source of beauty, says Diotima, Socrates's teacher, facilitates our intellectual birth, which in turn allows us to participate in the good life. One of the reasons why "Imagination and the Good Life" is such an important addition to this book is because it puts extra emphasis on the mental movement intrinsic to gestalt consciousness. This is a mode of thinking in constant motion. It does not merely oscillate back and forth between two gestalts, but morphs from one emotional-intellectual-pictorial complex to the next, capable of expressing what it knows only by acting itself out fully. "When meaning holds still long enough to get its picture taken, it is dead," she writes.[162] Thought that is unable to move will never find the underlying similarities between things, including our own similarities to non-human and human others. Seeing those similarities is the starting point for empathy and compassion. Without the faculty for seeing-as, she argues, we cannot evolve into truly ethical beings.

In the book's title essay, Alkibiades emerges as a figure of paradigmatic importance. He arrives unannounced in the late stages of Plato's *Symposium* and crashes the round of speeches on the subject of love with a desperate and electrifying one of his own. He confesses: "I swear to you, the moment [Socrates] starts to speak, I am beside myself: my heart starts leaping in its chest, the tears come streaming down my face ... like the Sirens, he could make me stay by his side till I die."[163] Philosophy shakes him to the core, and makes him realize that he has to change his life. Observing this moment, Zwicky asks: "Philosophy – *philosophy!* – could do this to a person?"[164] Through Socrates's midwifery, Alkibiades has awakened from his torpor and bushwhacked his way through intellectual fashions and self-centred thought patterns. He has touched the hem of beauty, and will do anything to touch it again and be made whole. For Zwicky, this is philosophy at its most elemental and urgent. "What is this moral beauty that so overwhelms Alkibiades?" she asks. "At first it looks like courage – or at least this is how it strikes me when I encounter it in a student, say, or a friend. A breathtaking honesty – someone stepping right out into the open, without a thought for how they might appear, their gaze held by something that has nothing to do with themselves. They are simultaneously vulnerable and untouchable – singular. It might look like stupidity or clumsiness if it weren't for the sense of intelligence behind the gesture, an intellectual firmness. We sense that they are in some way compelled – not helpless, but acting under the pressure of necessity, responding with great attention to something they perceive to be obvious. Moral beauty is always unselfconsciously resolute."[165] This kind of personal work, she says, asks us to risk everything and go for it. "It is in being able to risk everything that we become free."[166] Scrutiny of our deepest beliefs, convictions, and attachments allows us to identify and release that which has made us unable to recognize the beauty all around us. The kinks in our soul are straightened out. We acknowledge how little we know and in so doing recover an emptiness necessary for resonance, "an egoless availability, the capacity to touch and be touched by what-is, to become replete with meaning."[167] Only by emptying ourselves out and embracing intellectual humility are we made whole. "Realizing how *fundamentally* wrong we've been can, if the lesson goes deep enough, open us to compassion: others are as messed up as we are; they, too, act out of pain, out of blindness, out of self-absorption. They, too, fail to see what is right in front of them. They, too, hold profoundly mistaken beliefs about the world. Who are we to judge?"[168]

Zwicky's ninth collection of poems, *The Long Walk* (2016), takes as its focus the collapse of nature and culture ("the long walk" is a term that Zwicky and Lilburn use in their correspondence to refer to projects of a particularly long duration). "Courage," the opening poem of the book, feels as though it was composed in the immediate aftermath of the election of Donald Trump, even though it was first published in *Brick* months earlier. The pathologies of mind Zwicky has long written against are reaching their zenith; willful ignorance has been wedded to unimaginable technological power; human communities and their host ecologies everywhere are already disintegrating. Any chance to prevent radical climate chaos and avoid levels of displacement and violence unprecedented in human history has now passed. If we can bear it, we might "step closer to the edge" and take in the entire unfolding panorama outside the wealth, distraction, and privilege that may have insulated us from it. "You must look, heart. You must look," the speaker says quietly.[169]

One of the gambits of *The Long Walk* is that acts of witness fully resonate only when shaped by an awareness of the *meaning* of what is being lost or destroyed. Thus everywhere we find evidence of a living, breathing reality and a mode of human consciousness sensitive to its touch. In "Into the Gap," "To the Pass," and "Late Love," we see how places not only absorb memory and emotion but also hold in trust forms of cognition that human beings can stumble into and be trued by. "Meditation Looking West from the Berkeley Hills" and "Europe," for example, both unfurl out of startling moments of seeing-as, reminding us that finding points of connection between two seemingly incompatible gestalts is one way of being moved or pierced by the deep structure of reality. Yet lyric thought is mostly overwhelmed and forgotten in a global culture committed to speed, materialism, and an unquestioning relationship to technology. "Intelligence" holds back nothing in its assessment of the modern mindset and "the terror that we are," from "our confected optimism and / our medicated sleep" to "the cartoon of our harmlessness."[170] However kindly we might see ourselves, we are a force comparable to the hungry ghosts of Tibetan Buddhism, starved for meaning even as we destroy that which provides it.

The book's final poems, which read like a collection of prayers, acknowledge and celebrate the central mystery and beauty of being. In spite of everything, new life continues to unfurl out of death, renewing our capacity to love, and inviting us to see love as a form of hope. To these things the speaker of "Humility" offers "no folded hands, / but joy, relentless / gratitude."[171] In "Above the Falls," she throws herself dangerously off-balance reaching after a bee caught in the gathering current, for what else are we to do when the beauty that mothers the best in us is at risk of gliding over the edge?

When she was younger, Zwicky imagined that she could help her society by addressing the destructive thought patterns at its root. If she brought her ideas to the attention of the academy, perhaps she could have an impact on changing how people were taught to think, preparing younger generations for the transformative work ahead. Now in her mid-sixties, she has become convinced that academic philosophy is just another version of City Hall, and the change she hopes to see will not come in her lifetime. When the academic journal *Common Knowledge* devoted two issues to *Lyric Philosophy* and *Wisdom & Metaphor* in 2014, three commentaries trashed them, another six were less hostile, and only two – by Garry Hayberg and Ronald de Sousa – were in any measure enthusiastic. "I'd say the critical reaction from within the philosophical community has been for the most part uncomprehending and negative, with a few striking exceptions," she told me.[172] Others in the field do not take so dim a view of her contributions, acknowledging that institutional change occurs in a time frame beyond that of an individual life. James O. Young, the former chair of the Department of Philosophy at the University of Victoria, said: "I think there is a much better chance that people will read Jan's work in one hundred years than that they will read the work of almost any living philosopher. Most philosophers work within a paradigm, solving problems that exist in that paradigm. Once the paradigm changes, their work is useless. The important thinkers introduce a new paradigm. This is what Jan has done."[173] She is a big-idea person, he added, the kind of thinker who is at the plate and swinging for the fences while most philosophers are just trying to put the ball in play. When I asked whether or not Zwicky's work might someday become part of the discipline's mainstream, Young said: "The ball is still in the air."[174]

Meanwhile, Zwicky's stock as an independent scholar continues to rise. She is increasingly in demand as a guest lecturer, fielding invitations to speak at a number of prestigious institutions, including Harvard and Stanford universities. New writings are charged with a clear-hearted awareness of our predicament while continuing to affirm the source of the best in us. The most powerful of her recent essays, "A Ship from Delos" from *Learning to Die: Wisdom in the Age of Climate Crisis* (2018), acknowledges that "catastrophic global ecological collapse is on the horizon," accompanied by rising levels of war, disease, and mob violence.[175] She looks to core Socratic virtues – awareness, humility, courage, self-control, justice, compassion – for guidance as to how to live ethically in the midst of breakdown. There is hope in the fact that "the earth is prodigious" and will proliferate after technocratic civilization has fallen, yet as Robert Bringhurst puts it, "this beauty that visits us now will be gone."[176] She writes movingly of contemplative practice and how it can transmute loneliness into solitude, which deepens our sense of gratitude and expands our imaginative reach. "We start to become attuned to the world's resonance," she writes. "I have not met a contemplative who does not experience this attunement as love."[177] The being of the earth is kind and ever-generous, even to those who have betrayed her.

In spite of these and other activities – more invited lectures, a book of essays called *The Experience of Meaning* published in 2019, a new collection of poems called *Fifty-six Ontological Studies* published a year later – Zwicky still thinks of herself first and foremost as a gardener. Writing essays and poems is what she does when she isn't caring for the non-human beings around her. Music also remains a vital and sustaining part of daily life. She has been learning chamber music and commuting to Victoria to play with her string quartet for the last four years, which continues to bring her joy in spite of everything. While she is convinced that ecological breakdown has passed the point of no return – and holds herself personally responsible for being unable to stop or slow it – she continues to put her shoulder to the wheel. She speaks at public hearings regarding pipelines and offshore oil and gas development. She organized against the installation of a cellphone tower on Heriot Ridge. She printed up road signs alerting drivers to newt crossings and pounded them into the ground herself around the island. When I asked why she continued to work so diligently for the earth when she herself thinks the battle is over, she said: "Let's go down singing. It would be disrespectful to being to do otherwise."[178]

5

Tim Lilburn

The Conversationalist

Nose Hill, northwest Calgary, Alberta. Courtesy of Donna Marzolf.

There is a mural-like quality to Tim Lilburn's career-capping 2017 book of essays *The Larger Conversation: Contemplation and Place*, a sweeping historical vision that begins in the cave art of the Upper Paleolithic, touches down at various points in the spiritual history of Europe and the colonization of North America, and ends in the revitalization of Indigenous languages on the West Coast. Everywhere, there is evidence of his central preoccupation with human interiority: how places feed it, wisdom traditions sculpt it, and societies transformed by imperialism and technology flatten it. What compels him most of all is how the descendants of settlers might free themselves from the logic of colonialism; resuscitate a richer, more expansive sense of self; and join others in the creation of a larger body of kind that encompasses all of life.

Lilburn felt the absence of a meaningful relationship with place in adolescence, an experience so asphyxiating it nearly killed him. He was drawn to Christian mysticism in his early twenties, which coincided with a spiritual breakthrough and precipitated his entry into the Jesuit order. It wasn't until his late thirties that he thought to apply the lessons of the spiritual masters he had been reading to the landscapes around him. Close study of Plato, a number of visits to China, and a lengthy apprenticeship to Cree elder Joe Cardinal added to the mélange of places and people inside him. These all blurred together in an every-which-way mode of consciousness that he sensed was worldwide in distribution, trailed back to the religious practices of the Upper Paleolithic, and was illuminated by something beyond itself. On the other side of a lengthy period of illness that followed a move to Victoria, British Columbia, in 2004, Lilburn began sketching out the protocols for a "larger conversation" inclusive of all beings, things, ancestors, and landforms, the centerpiece of a political project that could prepare non-Indigenous Canadians for a genuine dialogue with both First Nations cultural authorities and a rapidly changing climate.

Familiarity with the arc of Lilburn's life and its fascinations is a useful point of entry into the poetry, which with the publication of *The House of Charlemagne* (2018) now includes eleven books. Much is to be gained from reading his poems in linear and literal fashion – we can examine his word choices, isolate and identify his various influences, and look to his biography to access some of the hidden drawers built into his work (knowing who Huaizhao is, for example, is crucial to a deeper engagement with *To The River*). To limit ourselves to such a piecemeal approach, though, is to miss what makes his poetry unique and not simply a curiosity.[1] If we tilt Lilburn's poetry on its side and approach it slantwise, the intellect engaged but kept in its proper place, everything changes. It acquires a new dimension, like a stereogram, and springs to life in the theatre of our interiority. We are able to see through its wild leaps and throws to the fecundity it seeks to honour, celebrate, and emulate, the deeper gestalt that lies at the heart of Lilburn's work and of all the exemplars and teachers he is drawn to. His poetry is defiantly incomplete, joining in a world in continuous birth, opening outward, giving us everything.

Tim Lilburn's forebears on his father's side emigrated from farm country near Dromore, Northern Ireland, to Canada. His maternal grandfather, John Blaylock, came from one of the poorest districts in Birmingham, England, and had a homestead near Gooseberry Lake in southern Saskatchewan prior to the Depression. Lilburn's parents, Walter Lilburn and Winnifred (Wyn) Blaylock, met at a dance in the summer of 1939. They had to conduct much of their courtship through the post when war broke out that fall, writing to each other every day for the six years while Walter served in Europe. Wyn served as a corporal in the air force while Walter was a sergeant assigned to a mounted gun, "a kind of tank without a cover."[2] He lived through some of the fiercest fighting of the war in Italy and Holland but did not talk much about it, sharing "maybe two and a half stories combined" with his family after the war.[3] Walter found work as a mailman in Regina while Wyn got a job as a clerk in a dress shop.

Tim Lilburn was born on 27 June 1950. The family lived in one of the only permanent houses on Alexandra Street, part of a working-class neighbourhood in the city's northwest end. They grew much of their own produce in the backyard, storing it in a root cellar they dug themselves. The CN line into southern Saskatchewan ran right past the front of the house, bringing, among other things, the circus train into town – a spectacle so magical that Lilburn's enthralled younger brother waved it down one year, stranding its performers, exotic animals, and equally exotic mechanical rides right outside their front gate.

Across the railroad tracks, a number of other veterans lived in one-room shacks, drawing water from a communal tap. Their children,

Lilburn's friends, lived in a world awash with artifacts liberated from their fathers' war troves – helmets, backpacks, belts, dispatch shoulder carriers – and made use of these things on their own expeditions and sorties along Wascana Creek. Lilburn had a paper route, and composed funny little limericks for his own amusement as he walked the streets. He loved football, played hockey, and was a rink rat at Regina Pats junior hockey games. He sometimes attended the United Church with his mother, where the rhythms of the poetry and prose of the King James Bible became part of his early world. He and his younger brother also spent a few weeks every summer on a farm near Windthorst in southeastern Saskatchewan owned by Wyn's older sister, Marjorie, where his uncle Soren would give the children a calf to take care of, and sometimes ride.

Northwest Regina in the late 1950s and early 1960s was not so idyllic. Lilburn was equal parts terrified of and fascinated by the dangerous, larger-than-life rogue males that patrolled the streets, including one who robbed his younger brother at knifepoint outside a corner store; another who liked to flick a shortened straight razor at people; and yet another who was rumoured to have killed a hit man from Detroit, stored a Thompson submachine gun in his cousin's porch freezer, and beaten to a pulp someone who had stuck a knife into his stomach at a party (these and other characters play prominent roles in his 2016 collection of poems *The Names*). Lilburn willingly entered their world and, well before entering high school, was already drinking, engaging in petty crime, and getting into fights.

Looking to insulate themselves from gang life, Lilburn and his brother decided to enrol at Luther College, a private school in northwest Regina, paying the tuition from their paper routes. Luther, he said, "cold-turkeyed" him out of the thrill of the crime world so many of his peers had fallen into, and, by his mid-teens, he was putting all his energy into sports.[4] He was named an all-star in his last year of midget hockey and was invited to try out for the Regina Pats at sixteen, which he turned down when he realized that playing against farm boys would be more dangerous than life in a gang. He was equally passionate about football, having graduated from childhood pickup games to the position of linebacker in high school. A knee injury during a game put an end to any prospect of a career in sports.

It was shortly after his invitation to try out for the Pats that Lilburn began to feel an unexplained panic and anxiety. He had always been "aggressively interested" in conversation as a mode of inquiry, but that impulse soon boiled over into regular clashes with authority figures at Luther College.⁵ Not long after the start of grade 12, he committed an act of vandalism on school property that got him expelled. He was sent to a number of specialists for poking and prodding, but no one – including he himself – could explain his disruptive behaviour. He felt asphyxiated, he said in retrospect, as though there wasn't enough in the culture to sustain him. He could see no opportunities for personal growth in the church, in school, or in the society around him. The sense of spiritual poverty he felt was overwhelming, and his response to it, he said, was "breakdown and dissipation."⁶

Hoping to somehow settle Lilburn down, Wyn's minister recommended that he head west to the Okanagan and enrol in Winter Session at the Naramata Centre, a four-month-long program of study in spiritual formation and youth leadership established by the United Church after the Second World War. At this point, Lilburn was carrying paper and pen with him wherever he went, having been encouraged to write in grade 11 by a good English teacher; the process and the experience of writing some stories and a long poem felt "emotionally different" than anything else he was doing at the time.⁷ At Winter Session, the poetry he composed was influenced by the music of Bob Dylan, Gordon Lightfoot, and Leonard Cohen. When participants organized a show to tour around the valley, Lilburn wrote much of it (the quality of his writing, he said, was "poop").⁸ He still didn't see himself as a writer – no one coming out of working-class Regina would have had the audacity to aspire to such a thing – and throughout his travels remained dimly aware of the land as an eloquent presence. He was, at the time, "looking for something, full of appetite, but in free fall."⁹

Lilburn made his way back to Regina in the spring of 1968 and, as *persona non grata*, returned to Luther College for prom on the arm of a friend of his high school sweetheart. He drank too much, did too much acid, and in late 1969 ended up in Munroe Wing, the psychiatric ward of the Regina General Hospital. "My razor was taken from me, and I was kept under a twenty-four-hour watch, initially in a segregated room."¹⁰ After more therapy, more drugs, and more fights with his father, he spent a year at the Regina campus of the University of Saskatchewan before transferring to Campion College, where he took classes in philosophy and English, and got a job emptying septic tanks.

Other odd jobs followed, and it was while working with a company contracted by the post office to pick up mail that Lilburn experienced something of a spiritual breakthrough. He was reading between split shifts and had found his way to a book by P.D. Ouspensky called *In Search of the Miraculous*, about the European spiritualist George Gurdjieff ("an odd fellow," he said).[11] There he came across a reference to a form of Christian monastic practice on the Greek island of Mount Athos. Lilburn didn't even know that such a thing existed, and so he "started to dig with the intellectual equivalent of a toothbrush sharpened at one end."[12] He read his way through Evelyn Underhill's massive compendium *Mysticism* and from there to Thomas Merton, Teresa of Avila, *The Cloud of Unknowing*, and St John of the Cross. He understood very little of what was going on ("maybe twenty-five per cent"), but before he knew it, he had burrowed his way into the mystical landscape of medieval Europe.[13] This tradition had everything in it he was looking for. It had sustained and deepened many lives, accommodating those who had felt the same need he did.

It was during this period of initial reading that Lilburn broke through to an experience he described as "definitely Christian" in nature, "fairly quick and utterly complete."[14] Here was "a visit from some rushing form of beauty that filled me and filled me with rising surges of love that went on so long and at such a pitch, that, weeping, saying thank you, thank you, I almost asked it to end."[15] In the days and weeks afterwards, he stumbled around in a glad happy haze. "It was like I was drunk and in love with everything," he told me.[16] He insisted that he did not set out to have a Christian experience, but added: "What else is there to do after an encounter with such beauty but follow it?"[17]

Looking to build on his breakthrough, Lilburn recalled a reference in Merton's writing to a Trappist monastery in Manitoba, got out a map of the province, and looked for any place with a Catholic-sounding name south of Winnipeg. Out of sheer luckless desperation he wrote to these communities, asking if they might know where this monastery was. It was a long hitchhike from Regina to Our Lady of the Prairies in St Norbert – more than 600 kilometres – followed by a lonely trek through the suburbs and finally a walk down the monastery's long laneway. "The first monk I met after the gatekeeper was Fr Ambrose Davidson, the guestmaster, and his brilliant, gentle, expansive listening was a pool I dove into," Lilburn recalls. "He told me the worth of what I had experienced; he advised me, as well, to patch things up with my father and finish my degree."[18] Lilburn was fascinated by everything he saw during his first week-long visit. He participated in *ora et labora*, the ritual cycle of prayer and work that began every morning at two with prayers, singing, and meditation. The celebration of the Mass came at four a.m., followed by another two hours of prayer, song, and reading – all of this before a light breakfast of bread and coffee at seven. Daylight hours were spent in periods of prayer and song structured around whatever manual or intellectual tasks one had been assigned by his superiors. Lilburn made a second visit to the monastery that winter, arriving late at night in minus-thirty temperatures; instead of waking the monks, he curled up and went to sleep in the milk room, the only building that was unlocked and heated. While his introduction to Cistercian thought, in particular the Rule of Saint Benedict, made a lasting impression on him, he wasn't at home in this highly structured daily life for reasons that he could not put his finger on. Instead of taking up permanent residence at the monastery as a postulant, he decided to move on.

In 1974, having completing a bachelor's degree and a year of teacher training in Regina, Lilburn took a teaching position in rural Nigeria with CUSO. His deep hope was that he might be able to recapture the magic of his mystical breakthrough by going some-place completely alien. The magic, however, did not show itself, and what followed was "a bit of a drop-off" and "a very import-ant failure."[19] He lived in a school compound between two small towns on the Adamawa Highlands, and taught African and English literature at Government Secondary School in Yola. *MacBeth* was a huge hit among his students. They recognized in Shakespeare a feudal system similar to the one they lived in. Local politics revolved around a tribal leader, the emir of the area, who enjoyed a status comparable to a sultan and rode around with a horse and guard; his retainers wore chain mail that had been ripped from the bodies of Crusaders centuries earlier. Lilburn spent two years there, endured several bouts of malaria, and made a number of forays into the Nigerian-Cameroonian borderlands, allowing himself to be "pulled here, pulled there."[20] Highlights included a trip through the Atlantika Mountains with a small company of travellers where only the colour of his skin saved him from the bandits patrolling the mountain passes. He visited the Trappist monastery at Mbengwi in Cameroon, a bone-rattling trek by public transport over the Mambilla Plateau that included a wild ride through the Taraba River in a jeep, and

managed to get himself kicked out of the prestigious Yola Club
(a fixture among British colonial institutions) with a lifetime ban
when an evening of drinking and rowdiness with friends ended with
them serving themselves from the bar.

While Lilburn found no great spiritual boon in Nigeria, he discovered an important early exemplar in Christopher Okigbo
(1932–1967), "the best poet of twentieth-century Africa."[21] Raised
in a time when the Igbo culture of his ancestors had not been fully
displaced by colonization and modernization, Okigbo had from an
early age helped his uncle perform seasonal rituals in honour of
Idoto, the river goddess and "mother of the community" who dominated the mythic landscape around his village and who installed
herself as the central figure, even the spiritual anchor, of his imagination. He wrote: "Before you, mother Idoto, / naked I stand; / before
your watery presence, / a prodigal // leaning on an oilbean, / lost in
your legend."[22] He witnessed the alienation and anxiety that resulted
when cultures that existed under the protection of such beings were
displaced by impoverished interpretations of reality not of their
making. He was passionate in his support for the establishment of
the Republic of Biafra, which seceded from Nigeria in May 1967
less than a decade after the end of British rule. When a catastrophic
civil war broke out three months after Biafra declared its independence, he drove straight to the front, gave himself the rank of Major,
quickly earned the adoration of his fellow-soldiers for his fearlessness, and was killed two months later trying to throw a grenade into
an armoured car during a hopeless rout of Biafran forces. He was
thirty-five years old, and the poetry he left behind – or what wasn't
destroyed in the war – amounted to a little over 100 pages. Lilburn
became deeply fascinated with the life and work of this man, who
less than a decade after his death had already grown into something
of a legend and martyr. He made a number of pilgrimages to visit
the landmarks of Okigbo's life, poking around the library at the
University of Nigeria, Nsukka that Okigbo spent two years building,
visiting the open-air market where he shopped, and stopping in at
the huge Catholic church he attended, which still had shell marks
on the walls from the civil war.

Lilburn's discovery of African literature galvanized him. After
returning to Regina in 1976, he thought about going back to Nigeria,
learning Hausa, and somehow making a life for himself there. He
sensed a number of parallels between the upwelling of Canadian

literature in the late 1960s and that of post-colonial African literature. He grasped how a truly autonomous nation depended on a flowering of local genius and wrote an essay on the subject that was published in *The Sphinx*, a short-lived literary journal out of the University of Regina. He applied to study African literature at the University of Texas at Austin with renowned scholar Bernth Lindfors and was admitted into grad school. Only after the prospect of returning to Africa went from pipe dream to an actual possibility did Lilburn realize that this course of action would be a dead end. Whatever role Nigeria played in his life had concluded.

After a couple of years in construction, including one summer as a roofer, Lilburn found his way into the left-leaning flank of the Roman Catholic Church, which in the wake of Vatican II was deeply engaged with liberation theology and social justice issues – boycotting banks that supported the apartheid movement in South Africa; advocating for land rights. He worked with the Archdiocese of Regina, organizing "learning suppers" that brought together Cree and non-Indigenous families from one of the ghetto areas for potlucks.[23] These suppers, staged at the Wickiup, the church-run cultural centre, were opportunities for shared conversation and community-building in an otherwise racially tense part of the city. Other outreach projects he was involved in included visiting with Cree people on the Piapot reserve north of the city, spending time at the Piapot high school, and working with the Regina Native Women's Association to help organize a cultural learning camp. During this time, Lilburn also managed to reconcile with his father, who was ill with colon cancer. The two had long, intimate conversations on a range of subjects, talking about everything including what they dreamed at night. Walter Lilburn died in 1976. His son was twenty-six years old.

Lilburn joined the Jesuit order in 1978. For much of the first two years of his training, the novitiate stage, he was placed with ten other aspirants on a farm near Guelph. The founder of the order, Saint Ignatius of Loyola, a former soldier and nobleman, had conceived the novitiate as a trial period in which novices could discern for themselves the subtle presence of God in their lives, and confirm or reject their calling. Lilburn and his fellow novices worked in various posts alongside people in severe pain and distress, including prisons, hospitals, and downtown drop-in centres. They spent time each day engaged in a number of menial tasks to develop their sense of humility. They took a number of classes in theology; undertook a forty-day silent retreat; and spent a month on pilgrimage, where they were dispatched from the farm with little money and had to rely on the kindness of strangers. Lilburn found the novitiate stage deeply grounding. He thrived on all the time set aside for private prayer and interior reflection. He loved the emphasis on intensive conversation, became close with his fellow-novices, and enjoyed a sense of belonging and conviviality he had never known, so much so that after the novitiate phase it seemed only natural for him to take his vows of poverty, chastity, and obedience.

For the next phase of his training, Lilburn went to Gonzaga University in Spokane, Washington, to study philosophy for two years. He worked with a brilliant Hegelian scholar who walked him through the *Philosophy of Right* and taught him the beginnings of *lectio divina* – the practice of close, attentive, selfless reading through which a text reveals its hidden layers. He also became interested in Karl Marx's critique of normative consciousness and how it buries and hides class relations and systems of power. Lilburn wondered whether Marxism and Christianity could intermingle, and wrote his master's thesis on the neo-Thomist Bernard Lonergan, Marx, and human development. He made friends with people on the fringes of society, moved freely through skid row, and spent one day a week cleaning out the rooms of its most notorious hotels where, he said, "you would find and deal with all sorts of things."[24]

For his fifth year in the order, the "Regency" phase, Lilburn was supposed to take up a teaching position. However, because he already had experience from his work in Africa, he was sent instead to the Farm Community (or Ignatius Farm) near Guelph, right across the road from where he spent his novitiate. A cousin of Jean Vanier's L'Arche project, the Farm Community was a place where people recently out of jail could be restored by working with and being around animals. The Farm was run out of an old farmhouse, with five bedrooms, a big kitchen, a dining room, and a parlour. Residents tapped maple trees; worked with cattle, goats, horses, and chickens; and played with the farmhouse's black Lab. Lilburn loved the physicality of the work. He learned how to weld, feed the animals, and keep them clean. He found the calving process "deeply dramatic," especially during breech births when he and his associates had to push calves, their legs splayed, all the way back into the womb so that they could turn themselves around.[25]

The cattle barn was also the site of one of Lilburn's primal experiences. One afternoon, after finishing a round of chores that included lining the stalls with fresh bedding and putting in a last feeding of grain and stalky first-cut hay, he was walking out of the barn when, with no forethought, he reached out and touched the flank of the cow nearest him. "It was like touching a live wire," he said. "The cow seemed virtually human. All of a sudden it possessed a centre normally reserved for human beings."[26] He didn't just feel the life force in that one cow. The whole barn came alive. Moreover, it was as if he could feel every cow, in every barn, for miles around.

While at the Farm, Lilburn was making small but significant strides as a writer. He had always been attracted to words and the way they could hang together to form little energy systems. He sent a handful of early poems written in Nigeria to Chinua Achebe, the legendary author of *Things Fall Apart* and a close colleague of Christopher Okigbo. Achebe was living in exile in Massachusetts at the time, where, among other things, he edited the African literary journal *Okike*. Lilburn was stunned when he opened his mail one day to find a cheque signed by Achebe, who had liked his work and decided to publish it. It was crucial validation from a literary giant, and Lilburn was so thrilled he never cashed the cheque.

Lilburn initially hoped to write philosophical essays while at the Farm, yet sharing a bedroom with a troubled and lovable character prone to fits of rage was not a space for deep, athletic thinking. Circumstances were pushing him to a smaller, more compact form. One of his best-known early poems came about when Lilburn was put in charge of a scheme to generate income by growing pumpkins to sell by the side of the road. He was given an acre of land beside the house for a hundred or so plants. Following the example of yam farmers he had seen in Nigeria, he mounded the earth and set about tending his new charges. He quickly developed an attachment to them. Pumpkins were always doing something new in terms of their phases of growth, often with great comic flair – for example, how on a young fruit, the stem of a pumpkin looks like the hat of a bishop. "They put on a great show," he said.[27] He would visit them at all hours, in all conditions, even under the moon; he would often lie down with them, gaze at them close up, do whatever he could to experience them from as many different angles as possible. While the scheme didn't produce any money for the Farm, it did produce one of Lilburn's most exuberant early poems, "Pumpkins."

Oompah Oompah Oompah, fattening
on the stem, tuba girthed, puffing like perorating parliamentarians,
Boompa Boompah Boompah,
earth hogs slurping swill from the sun,
jowels burp fat with photons, bigger, bigger, garden elephants,
mirthed like St. Francis, dancing (thud), dancing (thud,
brümpht, thud, brümpht) with the Buddha-bellied sun,
dolphin-sweet, theatrical as suburban
children, yahooing a yellow
which whallops air. Pure. They are Socratically
ugly, God's jokes. O jongleurs, O belly laughs
quaking the matted patch, O my blimpish Prussian
generals, O garden sausages, golden zeppelins. How do?
How do? How do?[28]

In spite of such effervescent play, Lilburn was developing a serious "wobble" in his spiritual apprenticeship.[29] After the intense camaraderie and fellowship of the novitiate phase, he was lonely and having a difficult time making new friends. Some of his confreres began to back away, as though his doubts about religious life might somehow be contagious. Complicating matters was the fact that the political milieu of the order was shifting under his feet, its left-leaning flank increasingly scrutinized and its emphasis on social justice slowly being forced out. After the Regency phase of his training, he was supposed to do another two years of theology but was sent to Brampton to work in two prisons instead, offering company and a sympathetic ear to whomever wanted it, including a number of violent offenders.

Shortly thereafter, Lilburn decided to spend several months in residential therapy at Southdown, a care facility for the religious and clergy north of Toronto. He recounts this period of his life in "Breakdown As School," an essay published in the Catholic journal *Grail* in 1990. Spiritual development, he proposes, moves back and forth between deprivation and breakthrough. Personal breakdown occurs when old ways of understanding the self and relating to the world no longer work. The "dark fruit of the spirit" that breakdown offers is "passage from a less to a more inclusive understanding."[30] Going through trauma, he writes, is "perhaps the only way you could tear yourself from whom you once were."[31] Lilburn illustrates his "mystical theology of collapse" with an account of a memorable

group therapy session he experienced at Southdown in which he
restaged an encounter with his father and ended up paralyzed on the
floor, "too tired, too fed up to summon the energy to mount the fiction of being alive."[32] Some sort of "mock death" had occurred, and
later, at the request of his therapist, Lilburn delivered his own eulogy
"in which I stated that the sole attribute of 'the deceased' was that he
had tried to love."[33] Some ancient aquifer of grief had been tapped;
the "great fatigue" began to lift. "I look back on that hour when I lay
on the floor, 'dead,' as the moment I began to live again."[34] Lilburn
expands on this theology of collapse and rebirth by making recourse
to Lakota spirituality and the trials of the vision quest. Yet in one of
our conversations, he looked back on this turn to Indigenous spirituality with some misgivings. "The way that guy borrowed from
Lakota spirituality gives me pause," he said, referring to his younger
self in the third person. "It comes pretty close to spiritual tourism."
He was, at the time, still trying to work things out, "halfway out in
the ocean and grabbing on to whatever was still floating," with no
sense of what could be brought over from Christianity.[35]

Lilburn takes up that challenge in "thoughts towards a christian
poetics," a pivotal early essay written at Southdown and published
in *Brick* magazine in 1987. He begins by distancing himself from
the Aristotelian view, shared by Thomas Aquinas, that all beings
and things possess a common form or an essence shared among all
members of its kind. A tree is a tree because it participates in "tree-
ness"; a stone in "stoniness"; a deer in "deerness." Common form
elevates essence over specificity, erasing the individual by reducing it
to a universal set of traits or attributes. It cultivates an intelligence
divorced from the realities of the body and its phenomenological
experiences in the world. A Christian poetics based on Thomism,
Lilburn suggests, would only rub away the grain of detail in things
and drive "sensibility to angelism," up and away from the world we
actually live in.[36]

In place of Thomist abstraction, Lilburn looks to the medieval
theologian John Duns Scotus (1266–1308), who proposed that in
addition to common form, there is a second form, unique to every
individual, that he called *haecceitas*. "It's like the thing welling up in
itself and saying 'me,'" Lilburn explained in a later lecture.[37] He was
not the first to find nourishment in Scotus's work. Martin Heidegger
wrote his post-doctoral habilitation thesis on Scotus, and later
used the term *aletheia* to refer to such moments of self-disclosure

or "unconcealment." The nineteenth-century Jesuit poet Gerard Manley Hopkins, to whom Lilburn was often compared in early career, used the word "inscape" to refer to the dynamic individual identity of something, and "instress" to the human capacity to apprehend it. For Lilburn, things call out to us with a certain flair. They put on a show. He writes of *haecceitas* as "a charm, a theatricality, a seduction, a personality, a loneliness communicated by things."[38] When we are caught by something, a kind of relational knowing can occur, one that Lilburn likens to a form of symbiosis. "Rather than thinking of *haecceitas* as a 'thing' or force within, say, an apple tree, it is more helpful, I think, to consider it a relation between the apple tree and other things, specifically between the apple tree and a conscious human being," he writes. "The tree as it exists in relation with its loving observer, the tree-known-in-love, is greater than the tree in isolation."[39]

Lilburn left Southdown with enough poems for a manuscript, and set out to find a home for them. He shared his work with the poet, anthologist, and publisher Gary Geddes, who was so enthusiastic about it that he said he'd either find a press for it or go back into publishing and do it himself. *Names of God* (1986), published by Ron Smith at Oolichan Books in 1986, is a confident and boisterous debut, a kaleidoscopic interweaving of historical personalities, human calamities, holy beings, and numinous landscapes. The book begins in a riot of praise-poems and hymns for a god who can be experienced directly on our nerve ends:

Salamu, my Lord. Salamu alaikum.
You are here
for my synapses whip and sparkle
like lightninged willows,
are in tumoured air storm's throbbing,
are wind's ululation to my steel-shod nerves
dancing them as dust-spooked stallions.[40]

Such experiences are a recovery and a continuation of a relationship that began before the womb, Lilburn's reconstituted Pseudo-Dionysius says in a face-to-face encounter with God, who "tugs / your cowl to its mouth and breathes / into brown fabric a breath moisture flax-flower blue."[41] Elsewhere he describes how human beings alienated from the divine grow "suspicious as Hutterites / in the small towns of our hearts," isolating themselves spiritually from the rest of creation while at the same time brutalizing it.[42] A human interiority divorced from the living source manifests itself on a mass scale through industrialization; its most devastating expression is the nuclear fireball. The poem "Living As If Only The Culture Existed" looks at the Cuban Missile Crisis from the perspective of a twelve-year-old boy, suggesting that in modernity we exist in a state of permanent trauma, wounded by a never-ending succession of disasters and near-calamities and catastrophic, world-ending threats. Meanwhile, the other beings in the Garden have not forgotten their original instructions. What we might do, the speaker of "Waking From Newton's Sleep" suggests, is give up this quest for control and domination, and learn once again the songs "imprisoned / in stone, beaver, pine, one /another."[43]

Lilburn took a leave of absence from the Jesuit order the same year that *Names of God* was published. His goals were to continue to write, work on farms, and teach. He taught English at Conestoga College and got a part-time job on a goat dairy near Elora run by a retired psychology professor from the University of Guelph. From Saturday to Monday night, he worked as a herdsman, arriving at six-thirty in the morning after first milking. His tasks included trimming hooves, administering inoculations, and seeding and harvesting the hay the goats ate. Goats, he found, were highly comical creatures – as risible as pumpkins – easy to push around and tease and befriend. He had lugged his library to the farm, so it was an ideal place to read between shifts. It was here the poems of his next collection, *Tourist to Ecstasy* (1989), began to take shape.

Lilburn finally left the Jesuit order in 1987 at the age of thirty-seven. He found work on a commercial cattle dairy, where he spent a lot of time looking after the Holsteins and dodging the notoriously violent resident bull; the best way to neutralize an animal that big, he learned, was to squeeze it between the nostrils as hard as he could. He upgraded from Conestoga College to Wilfred Laurier University, where he taught one day a week in the religion and culture stream (one of his courses was on the subject of love, and the other on evil). He became romantically involved with a visual artist named Susan Shantz, collaborating with her on *From The Great Above She Opened Her Ear To The Great Below* (1988), a collection of poems and artworks that explore and celebrate Inanna, the Mesopotamian earth goddess who makes a perilous descent to and return from the Sumerian underworld.

The prospect of making a life in poetry – at one point utterly unthinkable – became more real when Lilburn introduced himself to Don McKay at a reading the latter gave at the Princess Theatre in Kitchener. The one-time Jesuit trainee and the birdwatching academic hit it off swimmingly, and in late 1988, Lilburn accepted an invitation from his new friend to serve as the writer-in-residence at the University of Western Ontario for the 1989 winter semester. He moved in with McKay and Jan Zwicky at their farmhouse near Ilderton, a half-hour north of London. Before long, the three poets were talking continuously about poetry and philosophy, engaging in "mammoth conversations" that would start over breakfast and sometimes go into lunch.[44] Lilburn noticed how these conversations were sympathetic to everyone's intentions yet not identical or reducible to any one position. They seemed to have cognitive powers of their own. He began to suspect that the three of them were making a case for poetry as a mode of philosophical thinking. He became aware of other pockets of conversation taking place across the country among poets with similar concerns. Dennis Lee and Robert Bringhurst, for example, had been in correspondence since the mid-1970s; Bringhurst and Zwicky, since 1986. This network of conversations went beyond the five of them and included a number of other writers, including Roo Borson, Stan Dragland, Kim Maltman, Anne Michaels, Jane Munro, Peter Sanger, John Steffler, and others. "There was an extraordinary level of talk going on."[45]

Shortly after his stint at Western ended, Lilburn and Shantz, who'd just finished an MFA at York University, joined McKay and Zwicky for a ten-day hiking trip to Pukaskwa National Park on the eastern shore of Lake Superior. They travelled first by boat down the shoreline, stopping halfway to leave a cache of food for the way back. The trail itself was something of a scramble, unspooling across beaches filled with ankle-twisting boulders or up and down over rain-slicked tree roots. McKay's extraordinary sense of direction and advanced woodcraft – including his nose for a good campsite on difficult terrain – were constantly pressed into service. At one point, Lilburn fell in the water and had to hike for part of a day in his long johns. He also carried with him a jar of strawberry jam, which he referred to in near-liturgical tones as "consolation." They came across great beauty on the trail, as well as a number of places with a hard-to-explain spooky feel that unnerved them all

("No one says Wendigo," McKay writes in "Black Spruce"[46]). They talked continuously about philosophy when the trail allowed it, and drank straight from the lake.

Lake Superior left a profound impression on Lilburn and Shantz, and the couple returned later that summer looking for a place to hole up for a while. Not far from Sault Ste Marie, they discovered a property owned by a Finnish family on a tiny peninsula on Batchawana Bay. A collection of lodges and outbuildings, the property hosted mostly visitors from Michigan who would come up for ice fishing. Lilburn and Shantz got a deal on their accommodation largely because he offered to help with snow removal come winter; he got more than he bargained for when snowfall that year topped an incredible twelve feet. It was a magical setting – short days and long winter nights, the sweet yellow warmth of their cabin, the sauna, everything crowded in by enormous trees.

That winter, Lilburn began a full-fledged exploration of Christian mystical theology. He returned to a number of writers whose work he had first encountered in his early twenties, including St John of the Cross and Bernard of Clairvaux. He also had with him a selection of writings by Maximus the Confessor, whose ideas he'd come across a few years earlier in Lars Thunberg's book *Man and the Cosmos* (1985), which he'd found while browsing the stacks in the basement library at St Peter's College in Muenster, Saskatchewan, during a writer's retreat. He went back to these authors hard this time, digging around, taking notes, trying to find in their writings a framework for understanding his own experiences. He sensed in their works a "ravenous appetite" that wasn't explicitly sexual, a reach from within the self for some greater beauty.[47] This was *eros*, "that boarded-up tradition in the West" or "Western treasure" that had been turned into a distorted and debauched version of itself.[48] While *eros* in modernity has been conflated solely with sexual desire, Lilburn discovered that it could start in a number of different places and misfire in a number of different directions. Sexual energy was one possible source of *eros*, but only one; it might originate there, but not culminate in it (sexual fulfillment, he told me, "is actually a dissipation, a fleeing").[49] He compared *eros* to an acetylene torch, the likes of which he learned to use in his welding activities at the Farm Community. "You want the force of the fire," he said, but must learn how to "adjust the ferocity of the flame."[50]

According to those mystics and theologians associated with Christian Neoplatonism, the tradition Lilburn was nibbling his way into, it is by cultivating an awareness of these interior movements that we know ourselves to be wooed by something at the very centre of Creation. "Here was the source of a vivifying erotic essence, the origin of the foundational self," he writes.[51] This "goodness beyond all," as he called it in conversation, is infinitely durable, always reaching, "simultaneously full and incomplete."[52] Something inside us "lifts its head above water" when we come into contact with or are approached by that energy emanating from the heart of the world.[53] Some "non-empirical innerness" is charged and vivified in these encounters.[54] Good teachers and exemplars are essential in helping us negotiate and make sense of these instances of energetic intermingling, though not all of them have to be human.

At Batchawana Bay, contemplation and place came together. Lilburn went everywhere in snowshoes that winter, crisscrossing the peninsula. He was practising what the Desert Fathers of fourth-century Egypt called *otium sanctum*, "holy leisure," wasting his time within the natural world, drifting about with a certain deliberate idleness, trying to look at things in a way that vivified both subject and object.[55] He was looking without the impulse to know and master, waiting to be caught by things, drawn into that peculiar form of mutual thinking Scotus called *haecceitas*. Turquoise ice dunes piled high far beyond the mouth of the bay, fox tracks, the branch of a birch tree: beyond what his cultural upbringing told him, what were these things? He felt a profound desire to know them completely but not with the epistemological tools he'd inherited as a modern. If he stayed in that place of desperate looking and did not try to assuage it, something had room to step forward and reveal itself in all its strangeness. Lilburn writes: "The contemplative must be disciplinedly poor: you must stand before your subject, attention straining, convinced that you know nothing. You do not presume to name, define; the task is simply to look in 'perfect' puzzlement."[56] This discipline of looking led to awe, which is how "the world links itself to us," and through that awe a "super-apt gestalt" could be apprehended, however momentarily.[57]

Lilburn thought it was only fitting to celebrate the weirdness of things with extravagant, over-the-top language. But because "the deepest truth in all things is numinous," it felt equally appropriate to retract all those words because none of them could capture that truth – nor should they try.[58] "You don't want to build something rough about this in language," he told me. "So you draw a line, refute it, pull back."[59] Apophatic language, or "language used against itself," keens desperately after something, throws all its resources at it, admits defeat, climbs back to its feet, and tries again. "None of the names is as true as the rhythm of naming then cancelling the name in quest of a further aptness that woos the mind with even more insistence," he writes.[60] Apophasis participates in that "goodness beyond all," mimicking the movements of the enormous web that is continually expanding and contracting, growing and dying, beyond all our names and concepts for it.

When Susan Shantz took a tenure-track position in art and art history at the University of Saskatchewan in 1990, Lilburn found himself back on the prairies after many years away. He spent some time visiting his mother and reacquainting himself with his home city. One memorable afternoon, while standing on the steps of the Regina Public Library, he experienced a moment of perceptual vertigo in which the buildings around him all seemed to be floating over the land, as if airlifted in from above, their loyalties and allegiances pointing somewhere else. He realized in a flash that he did not know anything about the land beneath his home city and, more shockingly, had no idea how to live with it in a respectful way. He was floored by the fact that his own culture has left him so utterly cut off from the land, in a state of near-complete impoverishment. He was embarrassed that he had not done anything on his own to correct such a lack of decorum. "I had done nothing to educate myself to be someone who could live with facility, familiarity, where he was born," Lilburn said.[61] In the weeks and months that followed, he felt the onset of what he calls a "panic-struck hermeneutics" that left him no way of translating to himself his own dilemma.[62] Nothing in the instruments he was holding, culturally and philosophically speaking, was of help in locating himself – nothing in philosophy as he understood it; nothing in psychology; nothing in orthodox Christianity; nothing in politics, at least as it existed on the surface of this culture. "It was like trying to build a snowmobile when all you have are kitchen parts," he said.[63] A question began to crystallize in his mind: how to be here?

Lilburn put this question to the test when he and Shantz bought a home in the hilly terrain southwest of Saskatoon, an old trailer that had once been used at a military tracking station. Sitting on forty acres of land, with an endless supply of blown-down poplars to heat the Vermont Castings stove in the basement, the trailer proved to be a cozy place to hole up. Lilburn got a job as a sessional instructor at St Peter's College about an hour away, teaching first-year English literature and composition. He also worked one day a week on a medium-sized ranch not far from his new home, tending to the animals, cleaning out pens, putting in fences. He was still left with a lot of time for reading, writing, and, most of all, looking and exploring this foreign landscape. The land had never been farmed on account of the enormous sand deposits left by the glaciers as they receded north; in fact, it seemed as though the land hadn't been paved over by the colonial mind at all. "It didn't even have a layer of thinking on it, let alone a layer of cultivation," he said.[64] His initial reaction to it was one of profound unease. "I kept wanting to possess it somehow. I kept wanting to have it in language, or in my affections. I wanted it to be closer to me and to stay still. And it would never do that."[65]

During that first winter in Saskatchewan, and in the face of some panic and confusion, Lilburn began fumbling for the epistemological materials he'd been gathering for nearly two decades. What would happen, he found himself wondering, if he laid Christian mystical theology on its side in this particular landscape, and tried to see it through desert eyes? It beggared belief to think that a two-thousand-year-old tradition might have something to offer him in this predicament, but he was willing to try anything. The crucial interior shift, he realized, was to reverse the Western impulse to somehow consume the land and take it into the self, an impulse that preserved the centrality of the self. Would it be possible to give himself over to that place and be ravished by it?

Lilburn entered into what he described as a "liminal state," scouting the land with his dog, hoping to be taken in by the "good graces" of the place.[66] "I felt like my work was to walk and to look."[67] The previous owner had cut a broad fireguard near the house after a particularly bad wildfire, and he began studying how the plants were re-establishing themselves in that great gash. He gradually began to permit them their differentiation without turning away or rushing to close the gap with unearned familiarity. "At the very edge of contemplation, there are no guides, no words, there's no structures, nothing's going to help you out," he said. "And you just go into this night, this night of the infinite, this cloud."[68] He came across piles of buffalo bones and traces of worked stone. He wondered at kill sites. It became important to him to lie down on the land, taking its measure with his whole body. He became aware that there were deer everywhere. They practised their own form of social distancing, shifting the patterns of their movements to avoid human beings, retreating into the far coulees, and leaving only the saucer-like depressions in the ground where they'd lain. He learned to read the land for signs of their comings and goings, noting that some beds were only visible when the sun was low in the sky, its light coming in slantwise to reveal tracks and shapes otherwise washed out at the height of day. Back at the trailer, he discovered a large store of grain that the last tenant had left behind. He began making offerings of a sort, leaving grain out in order to draw the deer closer to the house. As he started to recognize individuals as well as families, the more he became convinced of their utter strangeness. They were simply untranslatable into human terms; his desire to know the deer and their ability to be known did not intersect. Moreover, he realized in these moments of *haecceitas* that he was as strange to them as they were to him. When they looked at him, they planted him inside the fact of his own strangeness, the human merely one odd form among a myriad of others.

Lilburn found a stabilizing influence in the figure of James Gray, a monk who lived in a tiny shack at the edge of the poplar forest south of the abbey at St Peter's. He first met the man who called himself "the Bush Dweller" in the library under Severin Hall, where a casual conversation in the stacks turned into a friendship that lasted until Gray's death twenty years later. Gray demonstrated what it meant to cultivate a relationship to the land through a Christian framework. He had given his home place an intimate name, "Maranatha" ("Come, our Lord" or "God approaches"), and, tasked with looking after the nearby orchard, had structured his days around a number of private rituals. These included cutting and arranging dead trees on the ground in patterns that held deep meaning for him. He took the time to get to know the birds in his forest, his pockets full of shelled peanuts for the chickadees and nuthatches that would encircle him "like mosquitoes."[69] For his human visitors, he offered tea, single malt Scotch, and the gift of conversation. Gray and Lilburn discussed the great lights of mystical theology – John Cassian, Teresa of Avila, Bernard Clairvaux, Aelred of Rievaulx and others – and commiserated over the Catholic Church's neo-conservative turn and the demise of its left-leaning social activism. When Lilburn brought Don McKay and Jan Zwicky over to meet Gray for the first time, the monk was standing in his garden, surrounded by sweet peas and raspberries, and looking into the late afternoon sun. When they asked him how he was, the monk replied, without missing a beat, "I'm awe-full!" He then laughed at his own joke. Zwicky later commented: "There was no irony or apology... Nor was there any false innocence. This man was utterly delighted to be alive in the sunshine."[70]

As his own land apprenticeship progressed, Lilburn started to diversify his activities. He wondered what would happen if he started sleeping directly on the land, away from the house and the structures of thought and feeling it imposed on him. He headed out with tent and sleeping bag, making camp wherever he felt compelled to do so. He started recording his dreams, training himself to wake up and transcribe them before they were buried by more sleep or burned away in the glare of daylight consciousness. He said: "My idea of sleeping out there was that the land would give me dreams. And it in fact did give me dreams, but they were uninterpretable. I had no idea what these dreams were about. I dreamed once about bears, running in grass, and my running past them. There was no clarity. It gave me none of the confidence I was used to having as a Western man."[71] In the summer of 1991, when his desire to be taken in and digested by the land was at its peak, Lilburn started digging a root cellar in the hillside behind the house. He didn't stop until the first frost, and had no idea what drove him. "There was only a helplessness to it, an asking," he said.[72] At six feet into the earth, he found strangely shaped stones and ancient deer bones; at nine feet he poured a concrete foundation, put in walls, and buried the entire structure under a thick layer of earth. It was the mirror opposite of the buildings he had sensed, a couple of summers earlier, hovering over Regina and a desperate attempt to insert himself into the earth so that some part of him might die there and be reborn. "I used to sleep in the buried house on hot nights through the following summer; I was looking for dreams; it was a place to wait."[73]

Meanwhile, Lilburn remained aware of the network of conversations among his colleagues. In early June 1992, he and Shantz drove west to the Banff Centre, where Don McKay and Jan Zwicky were staying after the former had just finished a stint teaching in the Writing Studio. They made their way through the Rockies to

Kokanee Glacier Provincial Park, not far from Nelson in eastern British Columbia. Their trip was a reprise of sorts of their earlier ten-day hike, though this time they stayed close to home base – no major undertakings, just day scrambles, returning to camp in the late afternoon. They talked, as before, of philosophy and poetry, yet this time they were acutely aware of the absence of other people who were now a part of their larger conversation – Robert Bringhurst, Roo Borson, Dennis Lee, Kim Maltman, and others. Early one morning they were sitting around the picnic table, the campground utterly deserted because of the cold. The air was filled with big wet flakes of snow; water for coffee was boiling on a butane stove; a fire was already going. With the small roar of the stove in the background, Lilburn floated a couple of questions to his friends, not in the nature of a program but in the spirit of an *essai* or a tentative probing: what was poetry and how did it know? And was it worth writing to other poets about these questions, and getting a collection of thoughts together?

Lilburn had no ready answer to the first of those questions, as he was deeply uncomfortable with the tone and speed of his new poems. The spontaneity and jubilation of earlier collections had given way to a voice that was oracular and gnomic, filling him with a sense of hopelessness. "This is what the end of writing feels like," he remembered thinking, appalled; at the same time, he felt like he had no choice but to press on.[74] "You write the poem as it presents itself," he said.[75] "Contemplation Is Mourning" enacts this leap into darkness. Here is the first stanza:

You lie down in the deer's bed.
It is bright with the undersides of grass revealed by her weight
    during the
length of her sleep. No one comes here; grass hums
because the body's touched it. Aspen leaves below you sour like
    horses after a run. There are snowberries, fescue.
This is the edge of the known world and the beginning of
    philosophy.[76]

The poem begins in exquisite observation of local particulars. The speaker has found a depression in the grass left by a sleeping deer, lies down in it, and discerns her presence in the way the grass is still coiled, spring-like, from her weight. He realizes that to take a step in the direction of the home that she has made in the world is the beginning of real philosophy, or that journey that leads beyond what we know and into the heart of the world.

> Looking takes you so far on a leash of delight, then removes it
>   and says
> the price of admission to further is your name. Either the desert
>   and winter
> of what the deer is in herself or a palace life disturbed by itches
>   and sounds felt through the gigantic walls. Choose.[77]

In order to travel beyond the "known world" – made up of the web of names, categories, and associations within which we enmesh things – the speaker suggests we must slender ourselves. Two vastly different possibilities are presented. The first requires extreme solitude and namelessness, an erasure of the old life in the manner of the ascetic monastic practices of the Desert Fathers. In the "palace life" of modern culture, one lives in a soporific, cozied, appeased state, prodded in one's quiet moments by intimations of some larger unlived life. This was a dilemma that Lilburn had to face head-on. "I had to pick the first," he told me.[78] Yet the path of ascetic monasticism offers little consolation:

> The deer cannot be known. She is the Atlantic, she is Egypt,
>   she is
> the night where her names go missing, to walk into her
>   oddness is
>   to feel severed, sick, darkened, ashamed.[79]

Faced by the overwhelming strangeness of the deer, the speaker feels useless and small. If one chooses the desert over the palace, there is no welcome party, no seduction, no reward. There are no guarantees of anything except the constant fact of deprivation: "Her body is a border crossing, a wall and a perfume and past this / she is infinite. And it is terrible to enter this."[80] How far outside of this culture is the speaker willing to go? Could he live there? And would he be able to come back if he went? To abandon one's home culture, Lilburn told me, is to commit a kind of treason. Why risk such charges in order to go into a place that eludes cognition? Why reach for infinity? The poem leaves that question unanswered, protecting the integrity of the inquiry. "You lie down in the deer's bed, in the green martyrion, the place where / language buries itself, waiting place, weem."[81] There are two references to early Celtic monasticism here. "Green martyrion" refers to how the giving up of selfhood was seen by the Celtic teachers as a kind of martyrdom, while the second – the "weem" – is the cave used by seekers within that tradition. Lilburn uses a word like "weem" as a kind of signal flare: the reader he has in mind will notice how it stands out and make the effort to discover what it means. In the poem's final lines, the speaker does not resolve the sense of weirdness he encounters in resisting the easy move from beauty into epiphany and celebration characteristic of his earlier poetry:

> You will wait. You will lean into the darkness of her absent
> body. You will be shaved and narrowed by the barren
>   strangeness of the
> deer, the wastes of her oddness. Snow is coming. Light is cool,
> nearly drinkable; from grass protrudes the hard, lost
> smell of last year's melted snow.[82]

As more and more poems like "Contemplation Is Mourning" arrived, the shape of a larger manuscript began to reveal itself. Lilburn called it *Moosewood Sandhills*, after a name he found on an old surveyor's map of the region. He told me that upon finishing the manuscript, his first thought was actually not to publish it at all. It was such a product of that particular piece of land, he said, and so strange and gnarly, that he thought he might design a box for it and simply bury it somewhere in the hills. Instead, he found a committed publisher in McClelland & Stewart, who sent him on a rousing book tour through southern Ontario with Christopher Dewdney and Olive Senior, and would go on to publish his next five collections of poems.

Lilburn felt empty in the wake of *Moosewood Sandhills*, as though he had been orphaned by the book. Not knowing what else to do with himself, he decided to return to academia and dedicate himself to a close study of Plato. He first encountered the philosopher he called "the great nourisher" while an undergraduate student at Campion College, sitting through uninspired discussions of the *Republic* and the *Gorgias* before setting him aside.[83] When Dennis Lee came to read at St Peter's and at St Thomas More College in Saskatoon in the early 1990s, he suggested that Lilburn might enjoy

Plato's Political Philosophy (1991), a book by his colleague Zdravko Planinc (Lee also recommended George Grant's writings to Lilburn, which changed his life). Arguing against long-established academic orthodoxy, Planinc claimed that Plato was not, in fact, the father of dualistic interpretations of reality or the chief proponent of two-world theories in which the account of the second world is the subject of occult fascination. There was only one world for Plato, made up of a continuity of all beings and things that encompassed everything, including the gods. Plato, Planinc was suggesting, had been wildly and even willfully misunderstood – "a name to conjure with in the service of some other project."[84] Lilburn didn't just read Planinc's book that winter while sitting beside the wood stove in the basement of his trailer in what he now called the Moosewood Sandhills. He devoured it. *Plato's Political Philosophy* demonstrated that mystical theology was not confined to medieval Europe but reached back to the very beginnings of Western philosophy. Lilburn sensed that the entire edifice of his thinking had been torn down and a new one erected in its place. He phoned Planinc from the trailer, and by the end of the conversation, they mutually agreed that he should move out to Hamilton and start a PhD.

Lilburn did not transition easily into life as a mature student. He simply ignored the bureaucratic requirements of the McMaster University PhD program that were imposed on him, following his own plan of study wherever it led (Planinc described Lilburn to me as "the most difficult student I ever had, in the best possible sense").[85] His personal life was also in turmoil: he and Shantz had separated not long after he arrived. In the period of disorientation that followed, he found a source of good company in Planinc, who was three years younger and with a couple of children under the age of five at home. Planinc, Lilburn said, was a model of the teaching life – a professor who was generous with his time and willing to talk philosophy outside of the seminar room, preferably over good food and wine. Lilburn became a frequent visitor to the Planinc household that winter, growing beyond the role of student and into that of family friend. It was the authenticity of their exchanges that struck Lilburn, a vital reminder that "deep conversation is a form of sustenance" – a fact not lost on the author of the dialogues himself.[86]

Plato's dialogues, at first glance, can come across as a weighty, sprawling mass of voices, ideas, ever-shifting positions, and speeches-within-speeches that don't form a coherent whole ("Plato's endless concern with frame and posture, and his addiction to debate, not only dazzle me; they exhaust me," Bringhurst said).[87] In his graduate seminar on Plato, Planinc looked to clear a path through this confusion by having his students read the dialogues out of order, as part of a dramatic sequence that led up to the death of Socrates. In contrast with most philosophy departments where Plato is interpreted as something of an "inept systematic philosopher," Planinc helped Lilburn see that the old master was pointing to what philosophy was really about: following the fragrance of meaning to its source.[88]

During his year at McMaster, Lilburn took an active role in shepherding the conversation-in-progress he'd identified among his peers to the next stage of its development. Most of the poets he'd contacted a year earlier responded enthusiastically to his queries about poetry and knowing (only Daphne Marlatt and Christopher Dewdney decided not to participate). He made several trips into Toronto for pizza nights with other poets, including Roo Borson and Kim Maltman. This wave of activity crested with the "Poetry and Knowing" gathering held in March 1994 at Trent University. Poetry and Knowing wasn't so much a symposium or a conference as "an event," Lilburn said, that drew a number of poets and academics.[89] Seven of the ten poets he had written to after the trip to Kokanee Glacier Park managed to make it out, including Borson, Dennis Lee, Maltman, Jan Zwicky, John Steffler, Anne Michaels, and Patrick Friesen. Don McKay could not attend due to illness. Robert Bringhurst, who had been at Trent since January of that year as the Ashley Fellow, also took part. Panel discussions were open to the broader university community and held in a large lecture theatre. Momentum stalled at times because of challenges from the floor that smacked of what Zwicky called "post-structuralist evangelism" in their questioning as to whether or not there really even was a reality that could be known outside of language.[90] Some effort was made to put together an informal session between poets and Trent mathematicians, with the latter group initially sticking to the opposite side of the room like "Grade Nine boys at their first dance."[91] Throughout it all, Lilburn remembered looking around and feeling as though he was right at the centre of something. "Nowhere else could you find a conversation like this among poets, expressed in essays, poems, and letters, not even in the hothouse of twentieth-century American poetry," he said. "I thought there was something historic and important that I was witnessing in these conversations, and I wanted to take a snapshot of it."[92]

For *Poetry and Knowing*, the anthology that came out of the Trent gathering, Lilburn brought together a dozen essays by his colleagues, laying out their central concern in the book's preface. "A style of knowing shapes the world technology has wrought; the ghost of Descartes hovers over the waste dump, the clear cut," he writes. "Is there another way to look at things, something more benign?"[93] He engages with this question in "How To Be Here," his contribution to *Poetry and Knowing* and the opening essay of *Living in the World as if It Were Home* (1999). In what counts as one of the most memorable passages in all his writing, "How To Be Here?" begins with a face-to-face encounter with deer he had behind his house in the Moosewood Sandhills. "Their bodies are dense with strangeness and are weightless, brief electric arcs on the eye, eloquent, two does faring well this winter, bow-sided, v-faced, coming down the slope through low willow and wild rose that holds the last of light."[94] To presume that we might be able to capture their wild particularity in language constitutes a fundamental lack of decorum on our part. What we can offer, and what poetry offers, are words humbled by a sense of their own limits. Apophatic speech yearns after the "withinness of things," but knows it cannot do them justice. "Language asserts and cancels itself, names the world then erases the name, and in this restlessness one glimpses the aptness of confusion before the ungraspable diversity of here," he writes.[95] Poetry is language enlivened *and* undercut by awe, empowered *and* diminished in service to it. This constitutes not only a schooling of language but also the beginnings of a re-positioning of the human presence on earth – "a slendering of self" so that we might find a home "in the garden of otherness."[96] To engage with the world courteously is to allow ourselves to be held in the gaze of another being so much so that the tendency to think of ourselves as somehow standing apart from and superior to the world is lost. "Let the deer's stare seep deeply into you," he writes, "and you lose your name."[97]

At the end of his second semester at McMaster, Lilburn dropped out of the PhD program and returned to Saskatchewan (Plato, he said, came with him, having already installed himself as the "base floor" for all future thinking).[98] He couldn't go back to the home he had shared with Shantz in the Moosewood Sandhills – everything would be charged with memory after their breakup – so he took an apartment in Saskatoon instead. He picked up where he had left off in his teaching at St Peter's. His course load was bumped up to include a

first-year philosophy class ("your job description is to have fun," his
dean told him), and he helped put together the college's writing program.[99] He began patrolling the land again, making long, seemingly
random peregrinations from his apartment to see what might catch his
eye. There was the landscape as colonization had transformed it – the
low-lying city straddling opposite banks of the South Saskatchewan
River – and then what lay beneath it, overwhelmed and buried but
still present, the place as settlers never learned to apprehend it. It
soon became clear that if anything might hold up under the weight
of the contemplative look, it was the South Saskatchewan River itself.
It was the only thing that felt substantial in that built environment; it
had not been entirely contained within and subdued by the colonial
imagination. "Of course this is what a person would look at," Lilburn
remembered thinking.[100] He followed the South Saskatchewan north
to Batoche – where the Métis resistance had been stamped out in the
battle that ended the North-West Rebellion of 1885 – and then south
to the ruins of an old Métis winter camp. He explored the river by
canoe with friends in summer and watched it recede inside a domicile
of ice in winter. He couldn't sleep by the river, as he had slept in the
Moosewood Sandhills – the place was still too public and anybody
might happen upon him, and then, he said, "I would have to translate
what I was doing."[101] Having been caught by the stare of the river,
Lilburn began reaching for some sort of poetic response. How would
English, his mother tongue and the language of colonizers, have to
contort itself in order to move with this great presence? How might
he woo the river so that some small part of it might roll into words?

   Meanwhile, Lilburn had embarked on a major new romance – with
a person, a city, and an entire imaginary – that had a substantial impact
on the texture of his next collection of poems. While at McMaster,
he'd met a writer and journalist from Beijing named Huaizhao Liu,
who was writing a thesis on women in Taoist monasticism. After he
returned to Saskatoon and she to Beijing, Lilburn would wait for a
break in the school year at St Peter's – sometimes leaving the day after
exams – in order to cross the Pacific to stay with her for a month or
so at a time. Beijing in winter was beautiful, he said, "like a village
that happened to have twelve million people in it."[102] The massacre at
Tiananmen Square had taken place only five years before his first visit,
and Huaizhao had been part of the generation who had occupied, and
subsequently lost, that idealistic moment in the square (she was getting
a lift across the city on the back of a watermelon cart when she heard

the shooting begin). Occasionally at parties, she and her friends would bring out photos of themselves in the square during the protests, and the energy in the room would shift. Like the Biafra uprising and the Métis rebellion, something absolutely alive to its particular time and place had been overwhelmed by "blunt force" and quickly buried.[103]

It was through Huizhao that Lilburn came into contact with Beijing's thriving poetry scene. When people began to speak out against the Communist government after the end of the Cultural Revolution, in the early years of Deng Xiaoping, one of their chief means of doing so was poetry. The so-called "Misty" or *Menglongshi* school of Chinese poets came of age during the clearinghouse years of the Revolution, many of them having been "sent down youths" dispersed to remote rural areas for re-education.[104] A number of them enrolled at Beijing University (or Beida), on their return, a beautiful old campus established by American Presbyterians in the 1890s and described to Lilburn as the "soul of the nation" by one farmer he met in the hills north of the city.[105] After Tiananmen, the new, post-Misty generation went underground (when Lilburn, who was scheduled to speak at the university, tried to approach Beida, the guards wouldn't even let him set foot on campus). Poetry now lived in tiny, dimly lit *danwei* apartments and around night-market sidewalk tables over great spreads of food and beer. Poets like Xiangzi ("Acorn") and Xi Chuan ("West Stream") were familiar with some of the giants of twentieth-century poetry that Lilburn himself had been reading – Jorge Luis Borges, Paul Celan, Zbigniew Herbert, Pablo Neruda, and Tomas Tranströmer – having encountered their works in translation, and argued over their meanings in heated Mandarin (Xi Chuan's notion of "bad poetry," based on a refusal of lyric beauty, a hard-to-follow voice, and a co-optation of the poem as "private cultural museum," affirmed for Lilburn his own *sui generis* approach to poetry). The post-Misty poets also wondered if China might retrieve something from its own past as a matter of cultural survival, beyond "a few couplets from the poets of the T'ang Dynasty"; at their most guardedly optimistic, they asked whether intellectuals and poets had a role to play in post-Tiananmen China.[106] Perhaps they could provide the country with a philosophical core after the "traditional cultural stabilizers" in Taoism, Buddhism, and Confucianism had been destroyed or pushed to the margins.[107] Lilburn felt a profound sympathy for these writers and the slivers of hope they still carried; for their desperate, life-on-the-line commitment to poetry; for their impossible task of thinking inside a civilization whose totalitarian government was bearing down on human interiority with all its might. "I felt I'd stumbled onto one of the great poetic generations," he writes, "comparable to the one that grew up around The Stray Dog cabaret in St Petersburg in the early 1900s, Mandelstam, Akhmatova, Gumilev and others."[108]

Lilburn drew extensively on his experiences in China and his knowledge of Chinese culture and history for *To the River*, his fifth collection of poems published in 1999. *To The River*, though, is not a book about China. It is to Lilburn what *The Blue Roofs of Japan* is to Robert Bringhurst: an early, rudimentary effort at enacting a kind of polyphonic consciousness on the page. Instead of interpenetrating voices, Lilburn brings together Taoist and Christian mystical imaginaries and layers them on top of the South Saskatchewan River so that he might approach it from a perspective beyond the colonial. The book is dedicated to Huaizhao, who is a constant presence in *To The River* beginning with the dedication in Chinese characters. From her very first appearance, which coincides with the first stirrings of spring, she is described in ways that suggest she is an emanation of her surroundings. Some examples: "her waist is a crane-coloured path, / a hawk-coloured path"; "The flexed tree of her looking"; her "apricot breasts"; "Poplar luff of her belly, / dragonfly of her belly"; the "clay light" of her skin; "Her berry-dark neck."[109] She may be the embodiment of what Laozi called "the subtle and profound female," a spirit being associated with the land and the Tao itself; something in her depiction in *To The River* also evokes what Taoist poets and thinkers called *tzu-jan*, "self-ablaze" or "occurrence appearing of itself."[110] David Hinton, whose translations of the rivers-and-mountains poets of Ancient China Lilburn was reading, explains: "The vision of *tzu-jan* recognizes earth to be a boundless generative organism, and this vision gives rise to a very different experience of the world. Rather than the metaphysics of time and space, it knows the world as an all-encompassing present, a constant burgeoning forth that includes everything we think of as past and future. It also allows no fundamental distinction between subjective and objective realms, for it includes all that we call mental, all that appears in the mind."[111] In "Poverty," this primal cosmology, which does not seem at odds with Neoplatonism, collides violently with twentieth-century Chinese social reality as a darker force imposes itself on the land:

Her leafy hands are part of a choral attention
that includes the flute of evening, its flamingo,
pepper-sauce light and the secret wheat,
the blue hump of the hill in its milky air
and the prisons west of the city
under beating stars where canola
dawns and dawns, floating out against the smoky
                    reptile weight of the prisons.
Out there black motes of the absolute muster
in the pod. The prisons' salt tents huff and clench
against stakes of bone. The hills there are dead animals.[112]

Here Lilburn immures into the wall of his poem a memory of a trip
he and Huaizhao took by train to the Tibetan plateau, two and a
half days from Beijing. There they found small communities of people who still followed traditional pastoral-life ways, living in open
tents and compounds, along with massive state-run prison farms
with their adjacent fields of canola. "Anytime you see canola," he
was told, "look for the prison."[113]

By the late 1990s, the "moveable discussion" among the poets
of this book entered into a period of robust growth, stimulated in
part by a number of gatherings organized by one combination or
another of Lilburn, Don McKay, and Jan Zwicky. "Contemplation
and Ecology," the first of these, was held in 1999. Participants at
"Conversation and Silence," a ten-day nature-writing workshop
held in June 2001 at St Peter's, alternated between days of intense,
complex conversation and days spent entirely in silence, the quietude
punctuated only by prepared readings offered at mealtimes ("We
resorted to making faces at each other across the table at dinner,"
Adam Dickinson remembers).[114] A number of writers attended,
from those new to the craft to more seasoned voices, including Sheri
Benning, Degan Davis, Maureen Scott Harris, Ross Leckie, Jeanette
Lynes, Alison Pick, and Anne Simpson. Conversation and Silence
inspired "In The Field," a one-to-two year program modelled after
some of the low-residency writing programs offered in the United
States. Consisting of ten days in residence followed by a year or
more of study and correspondence with a mentor figure, In The Field
was also based out of St Peter's. Intensive discussions took place at
the college and in one of three hermitages located at the end of a
contemplative walk just inside the woods. Some of the writers got

to meet and spend time with James Gray. The naturalist and writer
Trevor Herriot took participants on a nature walk. At supper, people.
reported on the birds they'd seen. There were baseball games and
charades in the evenings (no one had any problem guessing *penthos*).
The overall atmosphere, Maureen Scott Harris told me, was fun and
harmonious, and had the feel of "an anti-capitalist enclave."[115] In
The Field ran for three years and ended in 2005.

One morning over breakfast in Victoria, Lilburn suggested to
McKay and Zwicky that there was "more to be said" in the wake of
Poetry and Knowing, and perhaps it was time to consider a second
anthology.[116] He winnowed the list of contributors from twelve to
five (six including Brian Bartlett, who wrote the introduction), solic-
ited from them new and previously published essays, and framed
the results in the spirit of dialogue, echoing what Zwicky described
as "his moral commitment to conviviality as part of the process
of understanding."[117] Like its predecessor, *Thinking and Singing:
Poetry and the Practice of Philosophy* (2002) is oriented around
specific questions, and these are listed on the book jacket: "Is poetry
an appropriate medium for philosophy? Is philosophy the subject
of poetry? How do these two disciplines connect, intersect, relate?"

Lilburn has always maintained that what brings these five poets
together, distinguishing them from other out-riding members of the
group, is a conscious commitment to exploring and developing an
alternative epistemology that expresses itself through musical thinking.
"What I understand knowing to be," he said, "determines the nature
of the world I perceive and my understanding of how I should be
in it."[118] With *Thinking and Singing*, though, Lilburn was reaching
beyond thought processes as we experience them as individuals to
thought processes as we experience them at the community level. In
the book's tiny preface, he makes no effort to paper over points of dis-
agreement among his colleagues for the sake of "unraveling a single
thought" or asserting an ideological conformity that does not exist.[119]
The book's very structure points to something lightweight, flexible,
and polyphonic that defies description even as we are invited to enter
it. "You are welcome to join in," Lilburn writes. "Pull up a chair, lean
back from the table. Where were we?"[120] In our very first conversation,
when I asked Lilburn what brought these poets together, he paused,
looked up from his meal, and said, "a shared shape of thought."[121]
What an electrifying idea: their respective projects *think together*. He
wrote: "from Robert I took the translations, Dōgen; from Dennis,

Grant and a sense of striving's beauty; from Don, the trail, Charles Wright, and Levinas; from Jan, Plato, the pre-Socratics. From all came a sense of a community of thought. And it has been a deeply human thinking, not in the least academic – everything is in."[122] The notion of a "community of thought" – of people putting their minds together without surrendering their mental autonomy – transcends the individualism we find at the centre of modern epistemology. We are invited to enter an entirely different order of interior activity, one that integrates the head and heart as surely as it brings together people in all their diverse ways of experiencing the world. Beyond terms like "consensus building" and "mutual thinking," this higher level of human activity has no name. In her book *Small Arcs of Larger Circles: Framing through Other Patterns* (2016), Nora Bateson asks, "Why don't we have a word for those bodies, families, forests, and other buzzing hives of communication – and for the mutual learning that takes place within those living contexts?"[123] Bateson coins the term "symmathesy" (learning together) for such ecologies, and makes it clear that what emerges from their patterns of interdependency is a *living being* in its own right, "an entity formed over time by contextual mutual learning through interaction."[124] All this raises a fascinating question. What do these larger bodies of thought know that lies beyond the abilities of the solitary thinker?

Up until this point in his development as a poet, Lilburn had been engaging with Western Canadian landscapes through wisdom traditions imported from elsewhere, outmanoeuvring colonial ideology by perceiving the Moosewood Sandhills through desert eyes or the South Saskatchewan River through a Taoist lens. That changed when he came into contact with Cree elder Joe Cardinal (1921–2003). His invitation to Cardinal's camp came by way of the renowned Cree poet Louise Bernice Halfe, who had studied with Lilburn at the Senior Poetry Colloquium at Sage Hill in 1993. The two had remained friends, connecting on a regular basis "to talk about poetry and interior matters feeding poetry."[125] Over coffee one afternoon in early 1997, Halfe and Lilburn got to talking about the fast, "a three to four-day period you pass in silence, in the bush, with no food or water, under the guidance and protection of an elder."[126] When Halfe explained what the fast really was – a preparation for death – Lilburn felt the pang of inner affirmation. He writes of that moment: "I'd heard that phrase before; it came from the mouth of Socrates. This was philosophy's work."[127]

Joe Cardinal grew up in a world without ceremony. Born on a trapline between Fort McMurray and Fort Chipewyan in 1921, he spent seven of his formative years in residential school, which filled him with anger for his parents and for whatever traces of their culture remained. As a young man, he was forbidden to leave the reserve without a pass from the Indian agent or even to buy a trapline to feed himself because of ongoing efforts on the part of the Canadian government to convert the Cree into farmers. According to Ross Hoffman, who attended camp with Lilburn and wrote his doctoral dissertation on Cardinal, it wasn't until the outbreak of the Second World War, when Cardinal enlisted in the Canadian military and joined an anti-tank regiment, that he finally enjoyed a modicum of freedom; during the invasion at Normandy on D-Day, he realized that non-Indigenous people were just as capable of suffering as anyone else. When he reached his thirties, the stories, songs, dances, gatherings, and ceremonies still alive in his grandparents' time had either disappeared or gone underground because of the federal government's ban on traditional gatherings that began in 1884 and lasted until 1951. He had no idea of the value of what had been lost, and no idea either of who he was. After years of confusion, Cardinal found his way to Raymond Harris, an Arapaho elder who lived on the Wind River Indian Reservation in central Wyoming (when Harris asked him who he was, Cardinal took out his Indian status card and showed it to him). Harris introduced him and other spiritually displaced people to a repertoire of ceremonies, including prayer sweats, doctoring sweats, and the night lodge. Cardinal brought these back to Alberta, blended them with Cree practices, and made them available to First Nations and non-Indigenous people alike, establishing Saddle Lake as a crucial node in the larger resurgence of indigeneity in western Canada.[128]

When Lilburn arrived at camp in May 1997, he talked with Cardinal at length, stating his hopes and goals for the fast as humbly as he could. He then set about building his lodge in the woods, cutting willow saplings with Peter Butt, Halfe's husband, and Francis Whiskeyjack. At one point, Lilburn laid down inside it as the structure was taking form, looked up at the trees overhead, and realized with a start that he had been working toward that place for twenty years or more. He was utterly astonished by the events of his first fast, despite having gone in with no expectations, even a kind of "craven skepticism."[129] "All kinds of relationships started that weekend," he told me, "and not all of them with human beings."[130] Cree ceremony confirmed for him what he had long suspected – that the "philosophy of erotic interiority" he'd read in Plato and various Christian mystical thinkers was not limited to the Western tradition.[131]

Between 1997 and 2002, Lilburn made six trips out to Cardinal's spring camp to participate in ceremony in the wooded hills and poplar groves on the Saddle Lake reserve northeast of Edmonton. At first, and in keeping with the profound sense of affirmation he felt in ceremony, he shared the good news with anyone who would listen. Such generosity, however, quickly left him feeling somewhat "debauched"; when he admitted as much to Louise Halfe, she told him bluntly: "So don't talk about it!"[132] Lilburn came around to this advice, changed course, and closed his mouth. The truth of those experiences, he told me after six years of gentle inquiry on my part, is both very powerful and very frail. It exists in a kind of brine, or "sustaining substance of behaviour," one source of which is ceremony. Separated from this source, truth withers.[133]

Yet there did remain one place where Lilburn could talk about his experiences in ceremony, albeit from an oblique angle. They might be simultaneously invoked in and protected by what Xi Chuan called "bad poetry," their energy embedded in long oracular utterances, unwieldy word-collisions, strange imagistic bundles, zigzagging patterns of sense. Cue the poems of *Kill-site* (2003), Lilburn's sixth and perhaps most furtive collection. There, he enacts on the page an every-which-way, all-at-once, multi-dimensional interior state that resembles the movements of ceremonial consciousness. The poems of *Kill-site* form an extended reverie that takes place in the faster's mind, spreading around and returning to a singular encounter described on the first and last pages of the book. Here are the opening lines of *Kill-site*:

Corn-coloured, stroked movement, a dark brown of choosing
sailing it forward, the animal came near the round-roofed willow
hut, bees stabbing along the pollen-knuckled dome;
the animal curved to the place that breathed apart, on its own,
                          its breath circling it like a moon,
and lodged itself in the deep water of wintered-over leaves,
                where an ear scouted, spinning the leaves with a
                throaty blue light.[134]

The "round-roofed willow hut" and "pollen-knuckled dome" likely refer to Lilburn's fasting lodge, while the arrival of the "corn-coloured" animal may suggest a visitation that occurred during his first ceremony. As we move deeper and deeper into *Kill-site*, other guests make appearances in the theatre of the speaker's interiority, including teachers from different moments in the Christian mystical tradition, family and friends, scenes from his travels in Western China with Huaizhao (including a memorable encounter with three elderly Taoist nuns on the side of a mountain), and even passers-by whose presence registered in his consciousness in some way, however inconsequential the encounter might have seemed at the time. In this state of being, the constituents of one's life slip their moorings, drift, bump, and sometimes pass clean through one another like voices in a motet. Human beings from across time and space shake hands with one another; landscapes morph in and out of each other like the changing settings of a dream.

> Plato is talking with John Scotus Eriugena; a young woman,
>   asleep in her
> back of the throat body, from a class in advanced poetry; Julian
>   of Norwich,
> with her neck-bell of blood; Isaac of Stella and *The Cloud of
>   Unknowing*;
> they've come in off the range for the night and are under the
>   ground,
> whickering orange-winged grasshoppers around them,
> dust, an angry stray dog, a buffalo-scented, mudfooted moon.[135]

"It is strange that we are startled when we see this kind of thinking," Lilburn told me. "This is how we are. This is how the *Homo sapien* mind works."[136] Everything blends together in a way that confounds chronological order and makes a mockery of any arbitrary distinction between head and heart, thinking and singing. Over the last few years, he has begun to call this mode of thinking "triple-ply consciousness," describing it in one of our conversations as the overlapping of the past, the mythological, and the now as they come together inside us. The animating force behind this "pure and generous phenomenology" is the land itself.[137] It speaks to us through a vocabulary of our own making, drawing on, rearranging, and projecting against the screen of our conscious awareness those events, experiences, and points of reference that accrue over a lifetime. "When the world approaches you," he said memorably, "it walks towards you as yourself."[138]

Kill-site went on to win a Governor General's Literary Award in 2003. It was Lilburn's first major prize. Suddenly the relationship between contemplation and place was being talked about on CBC Radio, and Lilburn was no longer hiding in plain sight. A handful of younger critics, including Carmine Starnino and Zachariah Wells, did not warm to what Lilburn called the "maieutic complicity between writer and reader," and attacked his poetry on the grounds of inscrutability.[139] "Tim's poems are like a kind of space," Maureen Scott Harris told me. "If you stay in them for a while, they become habitable. You can walk around in them."[140] Another perceptive piece of literary criticism on *Kill-site* came from a Cree woman Lilburn met on the grounds of St Peter's before one of his readings. She was a residential school survivor who had been incarcerated there decades earlier, and on this day had driven herself out to the school on a whim, "testing the wound," as Lilburn said, curious and wary.[141] He accompanied her around campus, took her to James Gray's orchard, and gave her a handful of birdseed. The chickadees and nuthatches did not disappoint, coming down from the branches to feed from her hand. The sight, Lilburn told me, was "radiant."[142] She stayed on to attend Lilburn's poetry reading later that evening and listened to him read the poems of *Kill-site*. She came up to him afterwards and said that hearing his poetry reminded her of listening to people speak the old Cree language. In certain moments, she said, you can feel an enormous shape open up beneath and through their words.

The success of *Kill-site* helped Lilburn win a competition for a tenure-track position in the Department of Writing at the University of Victoria in 2004. Now fifty-four, he finally had financial security after decades of piecemeal work. He and his new partner, artist and curator Helen Marzolf, found a house on the bend of a quiet street that backed out onto the lower slopes of Mount Tolmie, a rocky outcropping in the north end of the city. Don McKay and Jan Zwicky were a short drive away, and the university was within walking distance. In an attempt to sensitize himself to his new surroundings, Lilburn began walking everywhere, field guide in hand, learning the names of things as a form of courtesy. The place, however, stymied him. "There is nothing here," he said when I checked in with him a year after his arrival, a fresh coat of paint still drying on the walls of the tiny A-frame shed beside the house that he had taken for his writing studio.[143] He told me he felt even more helpless than before – like a two-year-old – because he had yet to find any openings that led behind the stage set of colonial reality. "I didn't know how to breathe or act or name things outside the old place," he writes.[144]

Lilburn's disorientation cut to the root of his being. Six weeks into his first semester at UVic, he developed a mysterious autoimmune disorder that attacked his body's core. He had never been seriously ill in his life, yet now was swept up in a medical nightmare that lasted three years. He was subjected to multiple surgeries, contracted various superbugs while attempting to recover from those procedures, fought through numerous other complications and infections, suffered a frightening relapse while at the Muskwa-Kechika Artist Camp and had to be helicoptered off the top of a mountain, and faced the very real possibility of optic nerve damage and blindness. During one particularly intense crisis, Lilburn had been all but abandoned by hospital staff when Don McKay arrived and used his enormous wingspan to physically corral a doctor to his bedside. This long period of illness, Lilburn writes, "took off the first couple of feet of soil in me. Everything now seems more urgent."[145]

Published in 2008, *Orphic Politics*, Lilburn's seventh collection of poems, is about illness and the transformation of subjectivity it can invite. The book follows the speaker into a place where consciousness goes into a disintegrative, feverish free fall, only occasionally ricocheting off quotidian reality:

> I hold this up to what I am doing, lying on the divan, haven't
>   pissed
> or shit in days, infection's horse's rider lashes back and forth
> with his black flag. Two winter stars with dessert plate heads
> two months ago were nailed at either edge of my groin.
> I've been pensioned a shield of bees
> below my chin, under earliest skin, a bridge, a sleeve of industry.
> The MRI tech asked if I like country or classical.[146]

Throughout *Orphic Politics*, Lilburn includes passages from a number of ancient texts that give structure to this state of siege. Entering into his work for the first time are the spiritual landscapes of Suhrawardi and Ibn Arabi', two exemplars of Islamic Neoplatonism he encountered through the writings of French scholar Henry

Corbin (Corbin's book *Creative Imagination in the Sufism of Ibn Arabi'*, which Lilburn discovered in the UVic library in the early 2000s, was as important to him in his fifties as Lars Thunberg's *Man and the Cosmos* had been to him in his thirties). Other passages suggest a complicated exchange between interiority, community, and ecology in which illness plays a regulatory role. There are forms of madness sent by the gods, Socrates tells us in the first prose excerpt from Plato's *Phaedrus*, and these can cleanse families and communities of the psychic residue of past crimes and wrongdoings. Warren Heiti, reviewing *Orphic Politics* in *The Fiddlehead*, suggests that for Lilburn, such purification in a Canadian context must also involve resolving "the atrocities of colonialism."[147] The descendants of settlers cannot help but absorb under their skin the violence and staggering loss of life their culture has inflicted on its surroundings and on its original inhabitants. They lack the tools to clear away this interior wreckage, and until they do, they will be unable to perceive the land outside intellectual and spiritual categories that distort it.

Lilburn begins the essay collection *Going Home* (2008) with George Grant's assertion that non-Indigenous Canadians do not know how to be "fed by place" or nourished spiritually by the land, "because of our diminished capacity for the practice of attentiveness."[148] While Grant believed that the absence of a contemplative tradition meant permanent spiritual exile for settlers, Lilburn proposes that such a tradition can be retrieved and rehabilitated. In *Going Home*, he gathers together under "a single skin" a number of texts that constitute the forgotten erotic masterpieces of the Western contemplative tradition – among them the *Odyssey, Phaedrus, Symposium, Conferences, The Mystical Theology*, and *The Cloud of Unknowing* – and proposes that a certain kind of reading can activate in us the erotic life they describe.[149] "When you read, you have to *listen*," he would tell his students at UVic, writing the words out on the blackboard. "But listen with *alacrity*! You have to be *trans-fixed*!"[150] The core texts of the Western contemplative tradition are psychagogic in nature, containing hidden levels of meaning that offer certain readers a more nourishing and vivifying experience of "what draws but cannot be said."[151] These are books meant to be read over and over again so that we can release the energetic shapes they contain. These go to work on our disposition and reorder our sense of virtue and relationship. "The psalm becomes the mind, and the mind goes ahead of comprehension," Lilburn writes. "Then one's inner postures become one's own teachers."[152] This is reading as *lectio divina*, as direct participation in a transformative hiddenness the likes of which can shift a life on its axis. In the book's final essay, "Getting into the Cabri Lake Area," he enacts the contemplative stance in a remote corner of western Saskatchewan that stands in for the desert landscapes of the early Church Fathers. "Being in a place demands a practice," he writes, circling back to the book's core concern.[153] Engage with books that will make the body inside your body sit up and rub the sleep from its eyes; push past "the wall of fear" and put yourself out on a piece of land; walk around in a state of energetic availability, presuming nothing about your surroundings.[154] "As you walk, you are already as there as you're going to get, though you hardly feel this: the reeling, toppling condition of always wanting is as close as anyone gets to grace."[155]

The interior life of Lilburn's next collection of poems, *Assiniboia* (2012), is audaciously expansive. "Assiniboia" was the name used by the provisional government of Louis Riel for the lands purchased by Canada from the Hudson's Bay Company in 1869 (Lilburn describes this sale as "closer to your local Tim Horton's [*sic*] franchise selling your neighbourhood to China or the State of Washington than we care to think").[156] "Assiniboia" was also the name for the Métis homeland that manifested as a nation-state for a few short months in the winter of 1869–70 and again during the NorthWest Rebellion of 1885 before being "destroyed by armies from central Canada."[157] The gambit of *Assiniboia* is that the visionary polis founded by Louis Riel in Western Canada did not dissolve after his death by hanging in 1885, but simply receded to an order of reality untouched by colonialism where it is "still available for imaginative re-occupation."[158] His poems are an attempt to find a way into that imaginary state, "where everything has franchise, including land forms, the dead, animals, plants, wished-for presences."[159] Here is "Bull's Forehead Hill":

Two-thousand-pound hill with a gigantic cock. Times
A few hundred thousand. Teeming, dolphin
Necked, patched with a sand saddle, deuce of rivers
Cable link into each other's rattler's jaws in front
Of it, runaway
Current sand slab downshifting against the bluff,
Then mooching east. A heron works
The dusk, crackle of shadows.
Antelope.[160]

This is a Western Canada that has been freed from the suffocating grip of a "single-ply consciousness" that reduces all beings and things to natural resources. It is helpful to think of this book and the polyphonic reality it articulates as a form of medicine offered by Lilburn to his younger self who was nearly asphyxiated by that ontology. The importance of landscape in the formation of the soul is thus among the book's chief concerns. For Lilburn, it is a topic of central importance should First Nations and the descendants of settlers ever sit down together for a serious conversation about "the deep structure of being and different cosmological and ontological accounts."[161]

The final poem in the book, "Antiphon," points to a passage from Plato's *Timaeus* that might be relevant to such a conversation. There, the maker of things mashes together the human soul and all the constituents of the world in the same bowl. There exists a continuity between human interiority and other beings and things, this excerpt suggests, because we are all made of the same stuff. The soul wasn't created out of nothing, Lilburn said, but "is the cousin of physicality."[162] This insight, deeply chthonic in nature, is at the centre of the Platonic contemplative tradition, yet in modernity can only be found on its fringes. The characters in "Antiphon" have a scrappy hold on this truth; Democritus, for example, overheard it in the Quiney, the bar in Campbell River where Don McKay hung out while writer-in-residence at the Haig-Brown House. The real life is to be found in marginal places; in menial labour and illness; among outcasts, rebels, and half-crazy visionaries; or wherever the human imagination, flirting with its own destruction and bare-knuckling its way beyond modern ideology, can reach out and meet the land as it is. There is terrific creative violence toward the end of "Antiphon" as the demi-urge unleashes huge Plotinean emanations of every possible type, the violence in the mixing bowl echoed in the violence of the ocean (one of the poem's touches of humour is that the ocean, in all its relentless rocking, speaks like someone with OCD). The speaker throws everything he can at this immense process, language piling on top of itself. The human soul, for its part, is made out of whatever junk parts are left over. "Stuck to the edge, electron mucus, / Not the best, lunks, locks, a bit of tooth, could have been, maybe, / A cracked button from a ceremonial coat."[163] *Assiniboia* ends with the image of the soul, coughing and weak, emerging into a world unmoved by the arrival of human beings.

Lilburn spent a dozen years writing and revising the essays of *The Larger Conversation: Contemplation and Place*, which was published in 2017 and completes his "three-part manifesto" that began with *Living in the World as if It Were Home* (another collection of poems, *The Names*, came out in 2016, and burrows after the roots of his preoccupations with beauty and *eros*). He describes *The Larger Conversation* as "a ragged beginning at a personal attempt at decolonization," which would "undo forms of thought and behaviour implanted by colonialism."[164] The book is thus Lilburn's "visionary recital," "the soul's own story" as Henry Corbin called it. The major set pieces of his life are all accounted for here, layered on top of one another in the manner of multi-ply realism. These include his ancestors' homesteading experiences near Gooseberry Lake in southern Saskatchewan; his torturous coming of age in working-class Regina; his encounter with the underground poetry scene in Beijing; Joe Cardinal's fasting camps; the long period of illness he went through after moving away from the prairies; and his apprenticeship to West Coast landscapes. Packed in around these autobiographical passages are excerpts from Lilburn's spiritual exemplars, along with fragmented accounts of their lives. We are asked to engage in a different kind of reading, one in which we jump back and forth and attempt to trace the connections between seemingly disparate materials. "The book's heterogeneity," he writes, "is not diffusion: the entire work has a single focus that possesses both a psychic and political arm."[165] Two obsolete definitions of the word "conversation" can help us understand that focus: "the place where one lives or dwells" and "a manner of conducting oneself in the world." How to be here, as human beings, on this earth?

Lilburn first rehearsed the notion of a "larger conversation" in "Walking out of Silence," the autobiographical essay at the end of *Desire Never Leaves: The Poetry of Tim Lilburn* (2007). He writes: "I suspect a conversation will take place at some point in Western Canada between Crees who have lifted themselves out of the wreckage of the last two hundred years and a small band of white people who have gone down the steep stairs of their own tradition and brought out what is truly worthy."[166] Such a conversation asks non-Indigenous people to take seriously the epistemological and ontological claims of their hosts (this gathering should take place on Cree land). Lilburn is suggesting that anyone who embarks on a rapprochement with the land must at some point engage with First Nations cultural authorities in the context of actual, lived relationships. He stresses that non-Indigenous people should not come empty-handed to that conversation, but bring with them those teachings and practices from their own culture that have either been lost or buried over the last several centuries (in Anishinaabe territory, this act of cultural retrieval and restoration is associated with "the Seventh Fire," and urged upon all peoples as the prerequisite for an imaginable future). The dead are welcome to join this conversation, he adds, and extends an invitation to some of his most important spiritual ancestors: "I'd bring George Grant, Simone Weil and my uncle Jack; I'd set a piece of cut log on end for Evagrius to sit and another for Teresa of Avila. We'd settle down and build a fire; Eriugena would turn up and we'd break out some food."[167] Those familiar with Indigenous diplomacy will recognize what Lilburn is doing here: quietly following proper nation-to-nation protocol, and "waiting in the woods" to be properly received by one's hosts.[168] The essay ends with the arrival of the Cree and the prospect of meaningful conversation between the nations, however late the hour.

In *The Larger Conversation*, Lilburn dramatically expands the scope of this project. It is now "pan-ontological and multi-temporal," extending outward to include "the non-human and, of course, the dead."[169] In other words, everyone and everything is in. To help the descendants of settlers prepare for this dialogue, he proposes four activities. The first of these is the recovery and re-engagement with the erotic masterpieces of the West. "There's much in our intellectual tradition that's been jettisoned or misplaced that needs to be retrieved," Lilburn writes.[170] His pocket summaries of the lives and works of Marguerite Porete and Teresa of Avila, for example, have much to say about the mental reciprocity at the core of the relationship between contemplation and place. Educating ourselves on the nature of desire is important so that we are not made monstrous through those attachments and addictions that twist our interior selves out of shape. Secondly, Lilburn calls for a renewed engagement with ritual and ceremony. He cites Christian liturgy and the sweat lodge, both of which "teach decorum and yearning" and a sense of our connectedness to the material world.[171] "I believe that the physical things in these rituals – fire, water, bread, stone – are not dead, inert, but contain something close to what I contain, so that I can be moved and formed by them," he told me.[172] Poetry is the third activity included in the course of remedial work the descendants of settlers might undertake, for it implicates the reader in a kinship of presence "by which human beings are lifted and altered, made, that is, more richly human."[173] The last activity, building off the previous three, involves restoring convivial relationships with specific locales, or making friends with places. Here Lilburn describes how places take us in, doctor us, and help us think. "Standing, sitting, lying in or walking through locations like these, either actually or imaginatively, can be as reviving as taking a long drink of water," he writes. "The experience of dwelling in these places is restful, vitalizing; they can make us feel lodged in ourselves. They calm us, inform us concerning essence, allow us to feel undispersed, gathered. It can seem that we belong to them, as Coast Salish peoples say of certain salmon rivers and certain families, not the other way around. There is a particular be-friending or fostering going on with these places; here we are taken in, at home, and, oddly, this at-homeness feels like being seen."[174]

Lilburn also identifies a fifth activity, not listed with the others but of direct relevance if we wish to move into the outer reaches of the larger conversation. For more than a decade, he has been learning the SENĆOŦEN language, the "primal language" of the Saanich peninsula, from W̱SÁNEĆ poet Kevin Paul.[175] The two met in the Department of Writing at the University of Victoria, where Paul was Lilburn's student (Paul's collection *Little Hunger*, nominated for a Governor General's Literary Award in 2009, began as a manuscript in the writing program). In a fascinating role reversal, Paul is now Lilburn's teacher, directing the course of his learning. "It became quickly apparent to me that the language would only be the skin of what he would learn," Paul said. "The muscles, the bones and the organs of it all would be the land the language rose from and, subsequently, the culture that once found itself in need of expressing."[176] Lilburn started with the names of birds, fish, and non-human animals, and from there proceeded to place-names and specific phrases. As his vocabulary slowly expanded through their weekly meetings, he found that approaching the land through the SENĆOŦEN language has changed or even *charged* his perception of it. "The language seems to me to be a living being, instructor, trail-sharer, friend, source of companionable beauty, a larger, autonomous, communicating mind," he writes. "And Kevin's instruction has given me the true names for landforms I look at and walk in: P,KOLS (white tip mountain), TENEN̠ (stirred, moved, slope), T̠IQENEN̠ (place of blessing). By these names, I believe I have been introduced to some of the presences within this land, so that a relationship can enter its earliest stages."[177] The extraordinary collaboration between Paul and Lilburn continues to this day, both in their private lessons and in the university classroom, where they team-teach a course called "Writing a Sense of Place."

Where to begin the difficult work of living in the world as if it were home? I put this question to Lilburn on a hike up to the top of P,KOLS (Mount Douglas), a low-lying mountain Don McKay had first introduced him to in 2001. With the grid of the city below us and the snow-capped coastal mountains in the distance, he suggested that simply going outside and spending time in a so-called "green space" was already a huge accomplishment. "See if you can come with less willfulness," he said. "Anger, fear, anxiety, worry – all of these are okay. They are all openings or portals."[178] Whether we realize it or not, he said, something is getting inside us when we are on the land, going to work on us even if on a conscious level we do not think anything is happening. He compared the process by which the land takes someone in to a bus stop filled with people. "They will just shuffle aside and make room for you." The experience, he added, is somatic in nature. It involves the intellect but goes beyond it, and thus can't be imagined or anticipated in advance. It is something you feel. "There is quintessential joy," Lilburn said. "You get the gestalt. You just see the wealth. What more could there possibly be?"[179]

Personal Coda

Anything can become a door into deeper worlds.

Stephen Harrod Buhner[1]

This book took a long time to write. The process was equal parts crocodile death roll and homecoming. It was worth doing because the central claim these poets make is true: a whole other world is hidden in plain sight all around us. They offer five different paths to that world, and I tested them with my life so that I could confirm their validity. In this coda, I'd like to talk about a few of the primals that emerged over the course of the writing of this book. This isn't another story about the transformative power of literature, but about the transformative power that can reach *through* literature to change the shape of one's soul.

I came across *Thinking and Singing: Poetry and the Practice of Philosophy* in the winter of 2003. I was in my first year of the Canadian Studies doctoral program at Trent University and looking for something to do. That tiny book immediately intrigued me, even if I was familiar with only two of the five names listed on the cover. I'd read Robert Bringhurst's *A Story as Sharp as a Knife* in the fall of 2001 and Don McKay's collection *Another Gravity* six months later. Both books reminded me of a larger, richer world the likes of which I'd glimpsed out of the corner of my eye on other occasions in my life, including a pair of memorable stints in rural Indonesia prior to grad school. I took *Thinking and Singing* home and spent about a week going over the essays by Bringhurst, McKay, Dennis Lee, Tim Lilburn, and Jan Zwicky. I didn't understand everything I read, but that didn't matter. The book seemed lit from within. Certain passages glowed with the promise of meaning. With only that glimmer of inner confirmation to go on – which, in retrospect, was all I really needed – I decided to make these poets the subjects of my doctoral research.

A few weeks later, I went to the launch of Dennis Lee's *Un* – and wondered what I had gotten myself into. I hadn't grown up with Lee's children's poetry, wasn't familiar with his poems and essays for adults, and didn't have the literary background to contextualize the *Un* poems within nearly a century of modernist writing. I was entering Lee's project at its densest and weirdest point, with no tools to interpret what I heard. There was something almost archetypal about the event and the sleepless night that followed: an adventure embarked on in naïveté that unravels immediately into fiasco. While it is fair to say I understood almost nothing that night, it would be unfair to say I *felt* nothing. Certain words seemed charged with meaning, however opaque: *flin-/tinlyexcaliburlockjut*. A suggestion from my PhD supervisor, Sean Kane, helped me find my feet. Think of Lee's poems as responding to, and being melted by, some white-hot source of meaning outside language, he said. This image shifted my attention from Lee's word-wrecks to what they were pointing to, putting me back in a productive frame of mind.

In the spring of 2003, I wrote to the poets of *Thinking and Singing* and asked them for the names of texts that had been influential in their own development ("It makes sense to read what they read," Kane said.[2]). They wrote me back immediately, with suggestions that were all over the map. Lee's list featured, for example, German poets, mystics, and philosophers; Abstract Expressionist painters; early rock 'n' rollers and R & B singers; Van Morrison's *Astral Weeks* and Bob Dylan's "Visions of Johanna." Zwicky recommended that I familiarize myself with the Western classical music tradition, including "everything by Bach."[3] McKay's list included, among others, Stephen Jay Gould, Seamus Heaney, and Zhuangzi. Lilburn suggested I read Plato's middle dialogues as well as Christian students of Plato, and then rattled off some names I'd never heard of: John Cassian, Evagrius, Pseudo-Dionysius, the anonymous author of *The Cloud of Unknowing*, and John Scotus Eriugena. Bringhurst threw out a few titles – *Conversations with Ogotemmêli* by Marcel Griaule, *Thinking Animals* by Paul Shepard, and *Steps to an Ecology of Mind* by Gregory Bateson – before upending my expectations altogether and telling me that the text I needed to learn was the land. Hence the field guides to the mammals, plants, and birds of the Pacific Northwest he included on his list, along with the admonition that I get out of the library and go outside. "Remember what kind of texts come first," he wrote.[4]

I cobbled together their suggestions, submitted that list for my comprehensive field exams, and settled in for two years of reading, listening, and looking. I brought some of their texts with me to the park not far from where I rented a room, a long ribbon of forest on either side of a creek that snaked into the city from the surrounding countryside. Daisetz Suzuki and a willow hanging over the water; Anaximander and a round granite boulder a step from the bank; Mary Oliver and an old silver birch: certain authors will always be associated with the places where I encountered them for the first time. I occasionally read their words out loud to my surroundings, dimly aware of the rightness of the act.

Because many of the texts on my reading list had been transcribed from oral sources, I got in touch with Vern Douglas, cultural advisor in the Department of Indigenous Studies at Trent, for guidance. Bringhurst's Haida translations were still a hot topic on campus, and it felt like a lapse in decorum to study those texts without consulting faculty who were familiar with such controversies. I wasn't a stranger to racial tensions in Canada – I had grown up under the same roof as the children of residential school survivors and, at thirteen, had spent an intense afternoon with Jeannette Armstrong in the wake of the publication of her novel *Slash*. Before long, I was participating in workshops and attending gatherings led by some of the finest of a generation of elders and teachers, including Ernie Benedict, James Dumont, Jan Longboat, Josephine Mandamin, Edna Manitowabi, Tom Porter, Michael Thrasher, Doug Williams, and Shirley Williams. It was a relief to once again find myself someplace where meaningful experiences with the land were talked about openly, seen as legitimate, and recognized as the key to human character formation. In Timor and Sumatra, I had lived and worked alongside people who were still on intimate terms with their surroundings, and I missed the inexplicable frisson of those conversations. When I began participating in ceremony – first in the maple forest behind Doug Williams's house on Curve Lake First Nation and later up at Petroglyphs Provincial Park – I saw that my hosts were not content to simply talk *about* the land but, rather, directly *to* it. A different kind of education was beginning, one that closely shadowed my research on the poets and came to inform every corner of it.

After my comprehensive exams were done, I knew that I wanted to meet and talk face to face with the five poets. I wanted to see how they rooted themselves in their home places, regardless of whether that was midtown Toronto or an island off the BC coast. It seemed obvious that I should approach their work in the context of their lives, even though I could not explain why. I would allow my relationships with them to direct my understanding – to a certain point. Everything would be done live, through in situ visits and backed up by telephone calls, letters, e-mails, and consultations with their friends, colleagues, former students, and critics.

The first of these visits took place in June 2005, when I intercepted Bringhurst in the Clearwater Valley of interior BC where he was staying with friends. Our first substantial conversation took place during a hike up Trophy Mountain in Wells Gray Provincial Park, in which I posed questions to him about his coming of age, and struggled to keep up in order to hear his answers (as his friend Michael Peglau observed, hiking with Bringhurst is like walking behind a tractor). On the edge of a cliff high over a glacier lake, I tested Bringhurst's tolerance of biographers by asking him about the Haida controversy and whether or not he would have done anything differently. A week later, I joined him on Quadra Island for what amounted to a sprawling private seminar on living poetically. I asked him every question I could possibly think of and, on the fourth day, ran out of questions. "Now it's my turn," he said. He talked about some of his lesser-known influences, including Robinson Jeffers and Wallace Stevens, and introduced me to some of the music he loved. Throughout these proceedings, he remained acutely aware of, and interested in, everything happening around us. A conversation over a meal went into suspended animation when a black squirrel appeared on the other side of the sliding glass door. He silenced his table saw out of respect when a doe and two fawns passed within sight of his workshop. More than once he remarked on the central fact of the sun, and how all life would cease if it went out. After supper one night, we drove down to Rebecca Spit, where he emptied a bag of frozen fish skins he'd saved from our meals onto the rising tide. "It probably doesn't accomplish very much," he said, "but it just seems like the right thing to do."[5] When I finally made my way to the ferry terminal eight days after my arrival, I felt like I had passed my brain through his, and was leaving some overlooked corner of the old, ancient universe.

My meetings with Lilburn and Zwicky in Victoria were much more preliminary and tentative. Lilburn and I had supper in the Cook Street Village, our conversation continuing back at the

A-frame behind his house that he was busy converting into a writing studio. There was an awkward moment when he described his manuscript-in-progress, *Going Home*, as "an exegesis of ascetic monasticism."[6] I nodded along but had no idea what he meant, and he noticed, and something hardened in his face as a result. I met with Zwicky over a couple of afternoons in folksy cafés of her choosing; at our first meeting, she gave me a tutorial about ontology using nothing more than a saucer and a coffee mug. The morning of our second visit, I happened to open the newspaper to find a glowing review of *Thirty-seven Small Songs and Thirteen Silences*, and later that afternoon I could see the lift it gave her. My visit to Loss Creek with McKay, recounted earlier in this book, took place at the end of this first West Coast swing. I remember how impressed he was when I said I had no agenda that day other than to see what had caught his eye. On the drive back to Victoria, he turned to me and without any prompting began talking about his coming of age as a poet. It was a rare disclosure.

I wrapped up my "listening tour" the following February, when Lee and I met for a beer in his favourite pub on Bloor Street in Toronto. He was friendly, funny, and engaging, and immediately put me at ease. I was especially captivated by his stories of visiting the paleolithic cave complexes of Europe. He shared with me his most startling find – a child's handprint, high overhead – and talked about the moment when he realized how it must have gotten there. The following morning, when we reconvened for brunch not far from his house, he gestured to our surroundings and said: "The music of being is all around us. It's just our antennae that are screwed up."[7]

Meeting the poets in person was richly informative beyond the academic. I lived and breathed differently around them, and in certain moments perceived my surroundings differently too. I saw how they negotiated a space for themselves in a culture indifferent and sometimes hostile to their efforts. I realized how keenly aware they were of one another's intellectual and artistic presence, even if years had passed since their last face-to-face encounter or they hadn't read each other's most recent publications. It became clear to me that they disagreed passionately on several topics, even if they kept their differences mostly to themselves (for example: Bringhurst and McKay on metaphor; Lee and Zwicky on when to speak and when to remain silent, or more specifically where the line between the two lay). They talked about their intellectual, artistic, and spiritual ancestors as if they were in the next room, even if they had been dead for millennia. Seemingly tiny moments spoke volumes about how they positioned themselves vis à vis the non-human world: Bringhurst's excitement seeing otter pups gamboling in the waves near Quathiaski Cove, Lilburn unobtrusively cupping a stalk of lavender on our way to supper, McKay leaning subtly but perceptibly toward an American Dipper on Loss Creek, his body as taut as a television antenna – and then the look he gave me after it flew away.

I spent the next fourteen months writing my dissertation, "Notes to a Poetics of Earth," which I defended on a cold, rainy afternoon in April 2007. Stan Dragland, who had written the foreword to *Poetry and Knowing* and was held in high regard by the poets of *Thinking and Singing*, was my external examiner. Lee was also present as a special examiner. Roughly half the people in the audience were elders, teachers, and friends from the Department of Indigenous Studies. Missing from the occasion was the glow of meaning that had initially attracted me to these poets. Some of the other examiners (there were seven in all) chose to drill down into the minutiae of my dissertation; on three separate occasions, they debated amongst themselves the use of the preposition "to" in my title. Was this all that "thinking" amounted to in the academy? Or was there some other possibility we overlooked that afternoon, one that did not reject the rational but complemented it with other modes of knowing? Lee, for his part, said very little, kept his head down, and admitted to me the next day that he'd seen the life he could have led as an academic flash before his eyes.

I had no work and no funding after graduation, yet for reasons I could not put my finger on, I never seriously contemplated dropping this project. I was caught by something that remained stubbornly out of focus. Lee's support was crucial during this time. I saw plenty of evidence of his legendary commitment to other writers, his willingness to help them back to their feet when they found themselves overwhelmed by manuscripts that seemed beyond their capacity to write. He talked about the "double mind" we write with, distinguishing between the "analytical, plan-ahead mind" and the "intuitive mole and groper."[8] Books that endure, he wrote, are the result of the interplay between the two, even if it means long periods of time in which we have only sporadic inklings of what we're doing. Over and over again, he urged me to trust the process, to believe in those private hunches and insights that I might otherwise dismiss as inconsequential or unworthy. He suggested that I go back to the poets and ask them for more stories and anecdotes around which a different manuscript could be written, one not so indentured to the academic voice.

I was, by now, well and truly outside the academy. Which may have been a prerequisite for what happened next. Sometime in the winter of 2008 – I can't be sure of the exact date – the dog and I were on a long walk through the cedar forest. It was a Saturday, late morning. I had nowhere else to be and nothing on my mind. At one point, I happened to glance up at the sight of the sun shining across the snow. In a flash, I understood what it meant. It was a deceptively simple realization: I had some inkling of what the sun *really meant*, beyond all my ideas and conceptions of it. Bringhurst, of course, had prepared me for this moment back on Quadra. Yet if this was a primal moment in the writing of this book, it was a remarkably quiet one. It was just business as usual, apprehended from an unusual angle – no burning bushes or supernatural reveries. The realization stood out because of the way it seemed to *push* itself into the centre of my awareness. There was also something vaguely familiar about the experience. It seemed to me that there had been a time in my life when I had known, in a bodily way, that certain places could make me think and feel certain things. The land used to make me happy. Could that have been true?

Something was slowly climbing back into conscious awareness. Lilburn gave whatever it was a boost almost a year to the day of my dissertation defence when I met with him in a crowded bistro on Queen Street West in Toronto. During the course of our conversation, he kept bringing up the term "interiority," and for some reason it stuck. A word I'd heard a number of times *without truly understanding what it meant* suddenly made sense on a visceral level. A body within the body sits up straight whenever we come into contact with genuine beauty. We awaken to a hunger so powerful it can make a mess of our lives. This may be why Lilburn's words also gave me pause. My own coming of age had been marred not by a lack of sensitivities but by an excess of them, and after a while I went numb to the core. It was only when I went to Timor and Sumatra and lived in a place where close attention to one's surroundings was considered important that something inside me began to thaw. What Lilburn helped me understand was that there was also a tradition in the West in which an energetic availability to otherness was not a

classifiable disorder or pathology but the beginning of true philosophy. I left our brunch meeting in high spirits, and carried the gift of
good feeling through all my subsequent visits with the other poets
that year – Bringhurst and Zwicky on Quadra in August, Lee in
Toronto in September, and McKay in St John's in October.

I learned something equally important – by negative example –
when I flew through the drizzle, rain, and fog to Newfoundland that
fall. Once again, McKay was a courteous and generous guide. He
showed me around his adopted city, took me on a pair of hikes
on either side of the easternmost phalange of the Avalon Peninsula,
and put me in touch with a colleague from the Edge of Avalon
Interpretive Center who led me to the Ediacaran fossil beds. On that
shelf of rock sticking out into the North Atlantic Ocean, the waves
crashing just below us, my interpreter passed over a pair of surgical
slippers, a magnifying glass, and a laminated identification sheet,
and gave me exactly fifteen minutes with the fossils. Needless to
say, the Ediacarans refused to come to life, and I left with a mild
appreciation of but no connection to the place. I wondered what the
experience would have been like if I gone there with McKay, who
tried to approach everything with both sides of his brain. Certain
people, it seemed, could do more than simply provide us with a set
of facts about a place. They could use their words and thoughts to
bring us to a point of intersection with the land, opening up a space
where it might reach through and meet us.

The absence of such spaces in colonial culture was one of the
themes of the Toronto theatre company Soulpepper's adaptation of
Civil Elegies, which I drove down to see in December 2009. I had
been following the development of the show for about a year and a
half, sitting in on a cabaret performance of some of the songs Mike
Ross had fashioned out of Lee's verse, joining Lee in the cheap seats
to watch Ross perform an early version of the script, and interview-
ing members of the company about the production. None of that,
though, prepared me for what I saw that night. The Soulpepper version of *Civil Elegies* seamlessly integrated passages from Lee's long
poem with some of his children's verse, the philosophical density
of the former illuminated by the emotional directness of the latter.
This feat of thinking and singing laid bare the sheer tragedy of being
Canadian. We live in a civilization based on the outrageous theft of
the land and the persecution of those closest to it. We converted the
emotional and intellectual genius of the land into natural resources

and sold those resources off before we had a chance to be made into our fullest selves. Anyone who comes of age in this culture has to commit an act of self-betrayal in order to fit in: they must deny "the funny tug of otherness" and refuse the promise of a more meaningful life.[9] I too had turned my back on the land before I scarcely knew what it was, caught up in the over-amplified concerns of adolescence, chasing the desperate desire to belong at the expense of my connection to the only place I ever did. My own transgression required appropriate redress – not just on an intellectual level, but in the very way I lived.

I was now dimly aware of the existence of a set of rules or protocols that I had to follow in order to draw closer to the land. Yet if I was being led, I couldn't see my hand in front of my face. In June 2010, a whirlwind of events culminated in my partner and me buying a ramshackle house on a quiet street next to the cedar forest we'd been visiting since arriving in Peterborough. We had finally decided to stay put after years of what Lee jokingly called our "geographic promiscuity."[10] When I thought about it, though, I realized that this pattern of rootlessness, of living lightly and moving from unit to unit and place to place, went all the way back to my beginnings. By the time I was thirteen, my family had moved six times around British Columbia, and one move in particular wounded me unlike anything else up to that point. But now, as we settled into our new house and started to make ourselves at home, something began to mend, almost imperceptibly, at the core of who I was.

I was no longer alone when I approached that point of intersection with the land. The poets of *Thinking and Singing* and the First Nations elders and cultural authorities I was learning from were with me, as if my head and heart had become a site for that larger conversation Lilburn talked about. When I decided that I would like to have a sitting spot in the park – some place I might go to check in with the world – the choice was obvious: the willow by the creek where I'd first read Daisetz Suzuki. The beginnings of a daily practice began to take shape. I made a conscious effort to walk slower out to my spot, and when I did, trees and rocks and landforms I'd never noticed started to stand out. McKay had always spoken of the importance of defamiliarization, so I took off my glasses, let things become indistinct, and noticed how the land seemed to come closer. I paid new-found attention to everything because everything mattered – the coming and going of birds and insects and mammals, the rise and fall of the wind, changes in the light, the phases of the moon, and, most of all, the arrival of unexpected insights and feelings. I tried not to approach the land empty-handed, and found that the simple act of giving, regardless of what I gave, shifted something inside me and, in turn, made me more approachable. I also came to see the wisdom in McKay's suggestion that such acts are best done in private.

I continued to correspond with the poets, calling on them in their home places and visiting important landmarks in their lives. I had a chance to spend time with Bringhurst in Toronto and Montreal, and saw for myself how the energy of large cities fried his nerve endings and filled him with premonitions of doom. I went to Cornwall to look for signs of McKay's coming of age, walked along the old canal to the Moses-Saunders Power Dam, and was intercepted by a security detail upon reaching the facility's perimeter fence. On my first of two visits with Lilburn in Victoria, and after six years of me asking, he finally talked openly about his relationship with Joe Cardinal. On my second visit, we talked around the clock and climbed to the top of P,KOLS. It was there I came to understand that he went to the "Land inside land," as he called it, whenever he could.[11] Over tea on Quadra Island, the night breeze lifting and settling around us, Zwicky implored me to continue to seek out the non-linguistic meaning all around me. "Everything is right in front of you," she said.[12] We met a year later at the Leacock Literary Festival in Orillia. I saw what a dynamic performer she was, and how she could lift up and carry along an entire room in her voice. We went for a quiet walk along the shore of Lake Simcoe, and there I felt the stirrings of genuine friendship. When I gave her a progress report on the book over supper, she nodded in encouragement and said, "Oh, you're *there* now!"[13]

These visits coincided with an extraordinary period of loss. There were long, drawn-out illnesses and the deaths of several family members. A searing professional disappointment and a long spell of unemployment. The approval of a plan to put an expressway through the cedar forest, just steps from my sitting spot, despite massive public opposition. The subject of loss in the works of the *Thinking and Singing* poets had been something of an abstraction to me until I reached middle age, but now I was beginning to understand what Zwicky meant when she called it "the ultimate philosophical problem."[14] Overlaying this narrative, though, were a handful of gains that were like lodestars to us. Marriage. The birth of our daughter.

An unexpected professional affirmation. A rare grassroots victory that halted the expressway project. New life continued to bud at the centre of it all even as old life crumbled away around the edges.

The years ticked by. I continued to reflect on the work of these poets at my sitting spot and on long walks through the cedars. Twelve years after first setting foot in the park, I saw my first owl. Fifteen years on, a deer walked right by me at my sitting spot. I was becoming increasingly secure in my own conviction that the life of the mind and relationship to place could be one and the same. I began to think poetically. I started to notice how different incidents and events in my own life *rhymed* with one another. They formed little ecologies of meaning. Even the mistakes, deep disappointments, and failures were integral, as difficult as that was to accept. "I have never felt there were switchbacks or dead-ends," Zwicky told me. "Every day, every experience, everything I've done or read or listened to has been key."[16] The task, I realized, wasn't only to learn to read the land, as Bringhurst had suggested back in 2003, but to let the land read me. To be vulnerable before it, to presume nothing about it, and to actively invite it into my interior processes so that it might help me make sense of things. To recognize the patterns of meaning at work in my own life has been one of the great rewards in the writing of this book.

I have concluded that the world these poets have found knows far more than we do. It is also far more generous and forgiving than we can imagine. Places have the capacity to reach deep into our personal histories, and know exactly what memories, images, and ideas to push toward us. Hold the ground a bit longer and they rearrange these things into meaningful sequences that play out in the theatre of our interiority like poems of the soul. These sequences follow a recognizable arc that is consistent with the teachings of wisdom traditions elsewhere in the world. There are difficult reckonings as we come to terms with how we have treated others and how they have treated us, followed by insights as to how we might repair, restore, or even put to rest those relationships. There are moments of profound emotional catharsis as we feel the knots in our lives loosen and give way. Those moments allow for direct experiences of that richer reality many of us once intuited was there and whose absence most of us can still sense. Places do this for the simple reason that when we love them they love us back. "Knowing that you love the earth changes you, activates you to defend and protect and celebrate," writes Robin Wall Kimmerer. "But when you feel that the earth loves you in return, that feeling transforms the relationship from a one-way street into a sacred bond."[17] As that bond strengthens, the place reveals deeper iterations of itself, giving a lie to George Grant's conviction that the gods of North American landscapes will not show themselves to the descendants of settlers because of the sins of colonial history. Honkabeests are real. Everything has a face and can look back at us. More than one being can occupy the same place at the same time. Landscapes think and sing. A larger goodness moves behind and through the world as we know it.

From the moment I picked up *Thinking and Singing* nearly twenty years ago, I knew what I was holding in my hands. I knew what it meant, even if it took my mind many years to catch up, and many years after that to figure out what to say. Could the beauty of being be glimpsed through the page? Ultimately, what allowed me to finish at all was the realization that it could not be compelled to appear and has probably been gently laughing at me this whole time. "Point and hope," Zwicky writes succinctly.[18] It is the essence of the poetic life to know that words are not enough but, all the same, to go on trying to find some. It is also important to know when to stop. What remains is a kind of prayer, incomplete by nature but not, in my experience, unanswered.

Acknowledgements

I owe what is an essentially unrepayable debt to the five poets of this book, who took time away from their own important tasks, again and again and again, to answer what must have felt like an endless stream of questions. This book simply would not exist without their generosity, collegiality, and friendship.

This book spent the first five years of its life as a doctoral dissertation-in-the-making at Trent University. Sean Kane, my PhD supervisor, taught me how to read Skaay and Ghandl, encouraged me to go and visit these poets in situ, and steered this project through the requirements and obstacles of a young doctoral program with aplomb. I still remember the question Gordon Johnston posed to me at my dissertation defence, and I offer this book as my final answer. John Wadland has been a steadfast friend from the beginning, and somehow looked past the stolen-boat episode. Stan Dragland, my external examiner, read the entire manuscript, offered excellent feedback, and alerted me to the existence of the other Don McKay. Jonathan Bordo and Michéle Lacombe offered input at key moments.

Conversation and correspondence with the following individuals gave me much insight into the lives of these poets. An incomplete list includes Madhur Anand, Daniel Baird, Brian Bartlett, Nancy Batty, Roo Borson, Nicholas Bradley, Marc Côté, Ewa Czaykowska-Higgins, Amanda Di Battista, Crispin Elsted, Rick Fehr, Graeme Gibson, Nora Gould, Tim Green, David Greenwood, Warren Heiti, Iain Higgins, Jane Hirshfield, Nancy Holmes, Ishmael Hope, Karen Houle, Donna Kane, Owen Kane, Kate Kennedy, Kitty Lewis, John Marris, Travis Mason, Scott McIntyre, W.S. Merwin, Woody Morrison, Alayna Munce, Michael Nicholl Yahgulanaas, Christopher Pannell, Michael

Peglau, Susan Perly, Michael Peterman, Anna Porter, John Porter, Carolyn Richardson, Laurie Ricou, Robyn Sarah, Maureen Scott Harris, Bryan Sentes, Kelly Shepherd, Sue Sinclair, Gary Snyder, Andrew Steeves, Steve Stephenson, Paul Vermeersch, Bruce Vogt, Wendy Wickwire, and James O. Young. Trevor Goward and Curtis Bjork generously hosted me for three days at Edgewood Blue, and gave me something of a crash course in enlichenment, deer-path consciousness, and "man-gentling." It was an honour to correspond with the linguist Ron Scollon about Athabaskan oral literature in the months leading up to his passing in January 2009. I owe a creative debt to Mike Ross and Lorenzo Savoini of Soulpepper Theatre for letting me eavesdrop on their stage adaptation of *Civil Elegies* and showing me how to engage with a complex work without getting bogged down in Heidegger. Colleagues on the conference circuit who made a place for me include Pamela Banting, Franca Bellarsi, Jenny Kerber, Cate Sandilands, and Angela Waldie. Alanna Bondar remains in my thoughts.

André Audet introduced me to geology near Baie St Paul in what was literally a touchstone experience. Chris Shepherd helped me understand the magic of birdwatching. Joe Sheridan realized the necessity of epistemological reconciliation with First Nations peoples twenty-five years ahead of everyone else, and doled out his wisdom, and the grappa, in generous helpings. David Reibetanz probably has no idea what he set in motion when he lent me his copy of *Another Gravity* on the south shore of the St Lawrence twenty years ago. Adam Dickinson's review of *Thinking and Singing* – and his sense of collegiality and generosity – was an important early trail marker. Taarini Chopra, Brent Wood, and Kirsten Addis rehearsed polyphonic poetry with me and helped bring it to life. Tina Northrup, who wrote her own doctoral dissertation on the *Thinking and Singing* poets, made me look, and look again. Philip Benmore taught me a word. Sarah Gauntlett found me a word. François de Montigny gave me three words. Scott Cecchin went for a walk. Holly Barclay offered valuable feedback on parts of this book, and remains a trusted listener in its inner room. Kim Wilson helped keep the fire. Jeff Brankley's shoes have holes in them. Rosie Macadam went from student to friend to family. Christopher Malcolm took some great photographs of The Archer, and shared his startlingly original understanding of Canadian history with me. Won Jeon is fighting the good fight. Trudy Erin Elmore is the real thing. Gabe

Masewich knocked me unconscious with the trailer he put together for this book.

Charles Foran read the entire manuscript eight years ago, pronounced it "basically done," and then watched with dismay as I pulled the whole thing apart and started over again. Richard Gwyn gave me a dose of excellent writerly advice and was refreshingly honest and forthcoming about the difficult nature of the craft. Brent Wood read the manuscript three years ago, offered numerous insights, and encouraged me to abandon the admittedly unreadable polyphonic structure I had devised for it. Darren Bifford provided more than a decade's worth of selfless, edifying feedback and a late-stage dose of moral courage. Clare Goulet got me out of a tight spot more than once, and her literary and editorial talents remain vastly underappreciated. Hire her! Andrew Forbes: don't make me come over there. Tom Bristow and Patrick Curry have been a source of long-distance support from early days. Zdravko Planinc and I got lost in the woods at his own university, but he made up for it with fifteen years of sparkling correspondence. Alex Strachan, who has done more than anyone I know to share the genius of the French River, helped me realize that in spite of Canada's deeply troubled history, I would rather work to reform its flaws than promote a radicalism naïve about its own implications. Erica Wagner's kindness. David Abram with a grin.

Laurie D. Graham befriended this book when it really needed a friend. Among her many contributions, she suggested the form the afterword might take, and in so doing gave me permission to inhabit my own voice. J. Mark Smith went beyond the call of collegiality in reading this manuscript twice with a scrupulous ear and providing me with a generous list of corrections.

It has been an honour to know a number of First Nations academics, elders, and cultural authorities whose guidance and support amounted to a second, parallel education alongside my work with the *Thinking and Singing* poets. Deborah McGregor arranged my introduction to the land in Ontario. John Mohawk, Simon Ortiz, Judy Good Sky, and Gregory Cajete offered early words of encouragement and a much-appreciated thumbs-up. Vern Douglas, former cultural advisor in the Department of Indigenous Studies at Trent, has provided nearly twenty years of counsel and good cheer – even if we disagree about the Rolling Stones. David Newhouse gave me my first teaching opportunity; that, coupled with his fondness for gentle trickery, transformed how I approach the classroom. Dan Longboat's kindness still surprises me in spite of long periods between sightings. Doug Williams's words of support, his reminder about goosebumps, and the look he gave me after I came back from the woods continue to resonate. I am still learning. *Nii'kinaaganaa.*

I thank Zengetsu Myokyo, abbess of Enpuku-ji, for introducing me to Rinzai Zen Buddhist practice and for including me in the Montreal Zen Poetry Festival. My thanks to Mark Riddell for guiding me to that round hut among the pines. A debt of gratitude to Owen and Sergei for the different circles they hold, for rescuing me from space lizards, and for friendship in the dark. I travelled the world looking for a teacher and then, to my surprise, found one just up the road in Barbara Clark. "We make our journey in the grace of flight."

A small grant from the Symons Trust Fund for Canadian Studies allowed me to visit the poets of this book for the first time in 2005. Getting to know Tom Symons, who made the study of Canadian civilization one of the pillars of Trent University, has been an honour. My sincere gratitude to Heather Nichol, director of the School for the Study of Canada at Trent, for opening up a space for true inter-disciplinarity and many-sided conversation, and for inviting me to play in that space.

Mark Abley, my editor at McGill-Queen's University Press, deserves some sort of medal for letting me hand in this manuscript seven years after I said I would. He recognized long ago that this book was about more than scholarship – that I deeply cared for its subjects – and gave me the gift of time to do what I needed to do. A true gentleman of letters. I also had the good fortune of working with Kathleen Fraser at MQUP, who handled her duties with grace; among her gifts to this book was assigning Eleanor Gasparik to copy-edit it. The last stretch was the hardest, and Eleanor was exactly the right person to walk both me and this manuscript across the finish line. Neil Erickson waved his wand and turned this manuscript into a real book.

Close to home, Nick Ragaz did his best to keep me in passable shape, listened patiently to my travails on the trail, and came through with last-minute tech support that saved this manuscript from the shoals. Larry Mallach teaches me something new every time we are fortunate enough to add to our garden, and because of him, I have a deeper understanding of who I am and where I am from. I couldn't have written this book without the steadfast support of Tim Leduc, who has accompanied me on innumerable adventures and more than once reached into the darkness to pull me out. Leelah came into this world just before my dissertation defence and left it as this project entered its denouement; in some other corner of time and space, we are still walking the trails together, and I am following your lead. There is a candle in the forest for Lisa Anne Miller-Pond. Jim Handyside, my father-in-law, became a stand-in for the grand-father I never knew, lavished me with his friendship, and believed in this project, but did not live to see it brought to completion. "If you bet against the Canucks, you'll never lose money." My father, Gary Dickinson, tracked down a copy of *The Rhyme of the Ancient Mariner* for me forty years ago, and I am grateful that the albatross is no longer around my neck. My mother, Barbara Dickinson, led me by the hand into the non-human world and knew well enough to let the world take care of the rest. Amy Handyside, my *wijiwaggin*, carried this burden for as long as I did, suffered through endless "Canadian Primal updates" at the kitchen table, helped me back to my feet innumerable times, did not lose her dignity or poise in the face of her own hardships, and has brightened my days with a kindness and cheer I am not always sure I deserve. We have indeed arrived together. My daughter Fern is the most important person in my life and the person for whom this book is written. As Hannah Arendt wrote, "the birth of a child is the miracle that saves the world." May she someday know the extent to which she saved me. It is my sincere hope that she and others of her generation will find the strength in themselves – and in their surroundings – to carry the light through an uncertain time, and that the ideas in this book might contribute in some small way to their efforts.

Notes

PREFACE

1 Dragland, interview with the author, 4 July 2008.
2 Lawren Harris, quoted in Nancy Lang and Peter Raymont, *Where the Universe Sings*.
3 Atwood, *Survival*, 62.
4 Zwicky, "Lyric Realism," 87.
5 Merleau-Ponty, *Sense and Non-Sense*, 20.
6 Grant, *Technology and Empire*, 9.
7 Lee, *Heart Residence*, 49.
8 Abram, *Spell of the Sensuous*, 49.
9 Gregory Bateson, quoted in Nora Bateson, *Ecology of Mind*.
10 Bateson, *Small Arcs of Larger Circles*, 169.
11 Simpson, "Foreword," 7.
12 McKay, *Angular Unconformity*, 445.

CHAPTER ONE

1 Atwood, *Moving Targets*, 16.
2 Lee, e-mail to author, 10 April 2008.
3 Ibid.
4 McKay, *Angular Unconformity*, 418.
5 Lee, *Heart Residence*, 68.
6 Lee, quoted in Mount, *Arrival*, 147.
7 Lee, 10 April 2008.
8 Ibid.
9 Ibid.

10 Ibid.
11 Lee, interview with author, 22 February 2006.
12 Lee, e-mail to author, 17 March 2018.
13 Lee, e-mail to author, 12 March 2018.
14 Lee, 10 April 2008.
15 Lee, e-mail to author, 18 March 2018.
16 Lee, e-mail to author, 18 July 2018.
17 Lee, e-mail to author, 11 July 2019.
18 Fox, *Meditations with Meister Eckhart*, 117.
19 Lee, e-mail to author, 12 July 2019.
20 Ibid.
21 Lee, e-mail to author, 31 July 2008.
22 Lee, letter to author, 27 June 2003.
23 Hölderlin quoted in Michael Hoffman, "The Unquenchable Spirit."
24 Lee, *Body Music*, 221.
25 Bringhurst, "Editor's Foreword," 4.
26 Lee, e-mail to author, 19 March 2018.
27 Lee, "Principles of Ekstatic Form," 69.
28 Pound, *Selected Poems*, 35.
29 Lee, 19 March 2018.
30 Ibid.
31 Lee, *Heart Residence*, 27.
32 Lee, e-mail to author, 9 March 2018.
33 Lee, e-mail to author, 12 July 2018.
34 Lee, e-mail to author, 7 July 2018.
35 Lee, *Kingdom of Absence*, 13.
36 Lee, *Body Music*, 29.
37 Lee, e-mail to author, 10 March 2019.
38 Lee, 9 March 2018.
39 Lee, 27 June 2003.
40 Lee, *Body Music*, 14.
41 I am grateful to Trudy Erin Elmore for this insight.
42 Roy MacSkimming quoted in Beattie, "Modernism Has Come to Canada."
43 Lee, 9 March 2018.
44 Lee, 18 July 2018.
45 Lee, 9 March 2018.
46 Lee, *Regreening the Undermusic*, 4–5.
47 Lee, *Body Music*, 9.
48 Lee, *Heart Residence*, 39–40.
49 Ibid., 28.

50 Ibid., 35.
51 Ibid., unpaginated.
52 Lee quoted in Christian, *George Grant*, 276.
53 Grant quoted in Christian, *George Grant*, 87.
54 Grant, *Philosophy in the Mass Age*, 27.
55 Grant, *Technology and Empire*, 77.
56 Ibid., 13.
57 Ibid., 14.
58 Ibid., 7.
59 Ibid., 128.
60 Ibid.
61 Ibid.
62 Lee, *Heart Residence*, 262.
63 Lee, *Heart Residence*, 263.
64 There were also some noteworthy on-the-ground achievements, including a health clinic, child care centre, a radio and television station, a newspaper, a library, an Indigenous education institute, a range of food services, and a boost to the city's cultural life by way of Coach House Press, Theatre Passe Muraille, Buddies in Bad Times Theatre, the Toronto Actors Lab, and other creations that outlived the college.
65 Lee, *Body Music*, 114.
66 Ibid.
67 Lee, 5 August 2014.
68 Barton, *Seminal*, 21.
69 Atwood, *Moving Targets*, 15.
70 Lee, *Body Music*, 9.
71 Lee quoted in Lecker, *Cadence of Civil Elegies*, 30.
72 Lee, 5 August 2014.
73 Lee, 9 March 2018.
74 Lee, *Heart Residence*, 35–6.
75 Ibid., 49.
76 Ibid., 51.
77 Mount, *Arrival*, 105.
78 Lee, *Body Music*, 3.
79 Ibid., 4.
80 Ibid.
81 Lee, 15 March 2018.
82 Ibid.
83 Lee, *Body Music*, 17.
84 Ibid., 18.

85 Ibid.
86 Ibid., 21.
87 Ibid., 23.
88 Ibid.
89 Bringhurst, "At Home in the Difficult World," 71.
90 Lee, 9 March 2018.
91 Lee, *Heart Residence*, 265–6.
92 Ibid.
93 Lee, e-mail to author, 22 September 2009.
94 Lee, *Body Music*, 34.
95 Ibid., 28.
96 Ibid.
97 Ibid., 30.
98 Lee, e-mail to author, 11 March 2018.
99 Lee, *Heart Residence*, 132.
100 Lee, *Body Music*, 41.
101 Lee, *Heart Residence*, 141.
102 Bringhurst, interview with the author, 18 July 2016.
103 Lee, *Heart Residence*, 85.
104 Ibid., 89.
105 Ibid., 90.
106 Ibid.
107 Ibid., 93.
108 Lee, 12 July 2018.
109 Lee, *Body Music*, 55–6.
110 Lee, *Heart Residence*, 86–7.
111 Ibid., 98.
112 Ibid., 104.
113 Lee, *Savage Fields*, 11; e-mail to author, 10 March 2019.
114 Heidegger, *Discourse on Thinking*, 50.
115 Lee, 11 March 2019.
116 Lee, 10 February 2019.
117 Ibid.
118 Lee, *Heart Residence*, 275.
119 Ibid., 275–6.
120 Ibid., 275.
121 Ibid., 277.
122 Lee, *Body Music*, 54.
123 Ibid., 60.
124 Lee, 19 July 2018.

125 Lee, *Body Music*, 69.

126 Lee, e-mail to author, 15 February 2012.

127 Lee, e-mail to Won Jeon, 28 January 2016.

128 Lee, *Labyrinth*, unpaginated.

129 Smith, "A Genre that Isn't just for Kids," *National Post*, 23 August 2018.

130 Lee, e-mail to author, 16 March 2018.

131 Lee, 22 February 2006.

132 Lee, 18 March 2018.

133 Ibid.

134 Ibid.

135 Lee, *Body Music*, 189–90.

136 Ibid., 192.

137 Ibid.

138 Lee, 10 March 2019.

139 Lee, *Body Music*, 190.

140 Ibid., 195.

141 Yeats, *The Winding Stair*.

142 Lee, 19 June 2012.

143 Ibid.

144 Lee, 17 March 2018.

145 Lee, *Regreening the Undermusic*, 9.

146 Lee, *Heart Residence*, 316.

147 Ibid.

148 Lee, *Body Music*, viii.

149 Ibid., 157.

150 Ibid., 227.

151 Lee, 12 April 2019.

152 Lee, *Body Music*, 157.

153 Lee, 12 April 2019.

154 Lee, *Body Music*, 227.

155 Lee, *Regreening the Undermusic*, 14.

156 Lee, *Heart Residence*, 327.

157 Lee, *Regreening the Undermusic*, 14.

158 Ibid., 16.

159 Lee, 12 April 2019.

160 Lee, *Heart Residence*, 337.

161 Lee, 12 March 2018.

162 Ibid.

163 Lee, *Heart Residence*, 282.

164 Ibid., 286.

165 Ibid., 287.
166 Lee, interview with author, 19 October 2018.

CHAPTER TWO

1   Oughton, "Lord of the Wings," 35.
2   McKay, letter to the author, 25 November 2014.
3   McKay's poem "Lost Sisters" eulogizes two siblings who died in infancy. His youngest brother is the respected scholar Ian McKay, author of *The Quest for the Folk*. His sister, Kitty Lewis, was general manager of Brick Books for nearly thirty years.
4   McKay, letter to the author, 29 October 2014.
5   Ibid.
6   McKay, letter to the author, 24 July 2012.
7   McKay, 29 October 2014.
8   Ibid.
9   Ibid.
10 Jasen, *Wild Things*, 61.
11 McKay, letter to the author, 6 November 2009.
12 McKay, *Angular Uncomformity*, 202.
13 McKay, *Shell of the Tortoise*, 148.
14 McKay, quoted in Babstock, "Appropriate Gesture," 170.
15 McKay, 29 October 2014.
16 Ibid.
17 Ibid.
18 Ibid.
19 Ibid.
20 Ibid.
21 Ibid.
22 Thomas, quoted in Ackerman, *A Dylan Thomas Companion*, 16.
23 McKay, 25 November 2014.
24 Ibid.
25 McKay, letter to the author, 30 March 2015.
26 McKay, 25 November 2014.
27 McKay, 29 October 2014.
28 McKay, letter to the author, 3 December 2018.
29 Baggett, "An Experiment in Poetry."
30 Avison, "Snow."
31 Avison, *I Am Here and Not Not-There*, 187.
32 McKay, *Air Occupies Space*, unpaginated.

33 Dragland, "Who Is Don McKay?" r2.
34 McKay, *Air Occupies Space*, unpaginated.
35 McKay, letter to the author, 6 November 2009.
36 Capra, *Web of Life*, 86–9.
37 McKay, quoted in mclennan, "Boiling Down to Stone."
38 McKay, *Angular Uncomformity*, 14.
39 Ibid., 17.
40 Ibid.
41 Ibid., 20.
42 Ibid., 35.
43 Ibid., 39.
44 Ibid., 43.
45 Ibid., 44.
46 Dragland, interview with the author, 23 July 2009.
47 McKay, 29 October 2014.
48 McKay, interview with the author, 17 February 2005.
49 McKay, 29 October 2014.
50 McKay, "Why Poetry?"
51 McKay, quoted in Bringhurst, *Everywhere Being is Dancing*, 41.
52 McKay, quoted in Babstock, "Appropriate Gesture," 171–2.
53 Lee, e-mail to the author, 31 January 2008.
54 Ibid.
55 McKay, *Angular Uncomformity*, 154.
56 Lee, *The New Canadian Poets*, xliii–xliv.
57 McKay, letter to the author, 6 November 2009.
58 McKay, "It Won't Work."
59 McKay, *Angular Uncomformity*, 200.
60 Ibid., 203.
61 McKay, "Common Sense and Magic," 235.
62 Graham, *Disputers of the Tao*, 203.
63 Ibid.
64 McKay, "Reflection on Sleeping Places," 49.
65 McKay, 30 March 2015.
66 McKay, "Some Remarks on Poetry and Poetic Attention," 206.
67 Ibid., 207.
68 Ibid., 207–8.
69 Ibid., 208.
70 McKay, 30 March 2015.
71 Ibid.
72 Goulet, e-mail to the author, 21 October 2018.

73 McKay, 15 October 2008.

74 McKay, 30 March 2015.

75 Ibid.

76 Ibid.

77 Ibid.

78 Ibid.

79 Ibid.

80 McKay, *Vis à Vis*, 23.

81 Ibid., 21.

82 Ibid., 31.

83 Ibid., 32.

84 Bondar, "that every feather is a pen, but living," 17.

85 Neruda, quoted in Jan Zwicky, *Lyric Philosophy*, RH136.

86 McKay, *Angular Uncomformity*, 372.

87 McKay, *Vis à Vis*, 20.

88 Goulet, 21 October 2018.

89 McKay, *Vis à Vis*, 55.

90 Ibid., 69.

91 Ibid., 69–70.

92 Dragland, 23 July 2009.

93 McKay, 3 December 2018.

94 Steeves, interview with the author, 2 July 2009.

95 McKay, 8 December 2009.

96 Levinas, *Entre Nous*, 94.

97 Levinas, "From Being to the Other," 100.

98 McKay, interview with the author, 8 July 2005.

99 McKay, *Vis à Vis*, 99.

100 Ibid., 101.

101 Weber, *Biology of Wonder*, 30.

102 McKay, *Angular Unconformity*, 25.

103 Ibid.

104 McKay, quoted in Babstock, "Appropriate Gesture," 178.

105 McKay, interview with the author, 8 July 2005.

106 McKay, *Shell of the Tortoise*, 119.

107 McKay, "Holy Ground," 3.

108 McKay, *Deactivated West 100*, 16.

109 Ibid., 50.

110 Ibid.

111 Ibid., 50–1.

112 Steeves, 2 July 2009.
113 McKay, *Deactivated West 100*, 116.
114 McKay, 29 October 2014.
115 Ibid.
116 Harris, interview with the author, 30 July 2013.
117 Miller, review of *Ornithologies of Desire*, 105.
118 McKay, quoted in Harris, "Dancing in the Distillery District."
119 McKay, *Shell of the Tortoise*, 11.
120 Ibid., 24.
121 Ibid., 39.
122 Ibid., 50.
123 Ibid.
124 Ibid., 98.
125 Ibid., 137.
126 Ibid., 142.
127 Ibid., 147.
128 McKay, 13 November 2015.
129 McKay, *Angular Unconformity*, 520.
130 Ibid., 522.
131 McKay, "Six Poems," 87.
132 McKay, 9 August 2015.
133 Ibid.
134 McKay, *Angular Unconformity*, 566.
135 Ibid., 529.
136 Ibid., 518.
137 Ibid., 511.
138 Ibid., 525.
139 McKay, *Larix*, 8.
140 Ibid., 17.
141 Ibid., 13.
142 Ibid.
143 Hoffmeyer, *Signs of Meaning*, 2.
144 McKay, 29 June 2012.
145 McKay, 9 August 2015.
146 McKay, 3 December 2018.
147 McKay, 4 January 2017.
148 Ibid.
149 McKay, 3 December 2018.

CHAPTER THREE

1 Bringhurst, *Pieces of Map*, 103.
2 Bringhurst, *Palatino*, 7.
3 Bringhurst, *Selected Poems*, 35.
4 Ibid., 130.
5 Loy, *Nonduality*, 25.
6 Snyder, e-mail to the author, 3 February 2014.
7 Bringhurst, e-mail to the author, 7 August 2012.
8 Bringhurst, interview with the author, 10 August 2008.
9 Bringhurst, 7 August 2012.
10 Bringhurst, 10 August 2008.
11 Bringhurst, e-mail to the author, 12 September 2012.
12 Bringhurst, e-mail to the author, 7 May 2006.
13 Peglau, interview with the author, 1 September 2013.
14 Bringhurst, 7 May 2006.
15 Bringhurst, e-mail to the author, 6 March 2013.
16 Bringhurst, e-mail to the author, 5 March 2013.
17 Bringhurst, 6 March 2013.
18 Ibid.
19 Bringhurst, e-mail to the author, 2 March 2013.
20 Ibid.
21 Ibid.
22 Ibid.
23 Bringhurst, *Shipwright's Log*, 6.
24 Ibid., 12.
25 Ibid., 35.
26 Bringhurst, *Book of Silences*, unpaginated.
27 Aristotle, quoted in Bringhurst, *Beauty of the Weapons*, 48.
28 Bringhurst, 10 August 2008.
29 Kahn, *Art and Thought of Heraclitus*, 71.
30 Bringhurst, *Selected Poems*, 38.
31 Bringhurst, *Nine Tables*, 89.
32 Bringhurst, e-mail to the author, 28 May 2012.
33 Bringhurst, *Selected Poems*, 33.
34 Bringhurst, interview with the author, 11 August 2008.
35 Bringhurst, quoted in Munro, "Bringhurst's Range," 38.
36 Bringhurst, *Selected Poems*, 17.
37 Ibid., 20.
38 Bringhurst, quoted in Dickinson, "Heart of Consciousness," 104.

39 Bringhurst, *Nine Tables*, 85.
40 Reck, *Ezra Pound: A Close-Up*, 36.
41 Pound, *Selected Prose*, 24.
42 Reck, *Ezra Pound*, 171.
43 Bringhurst, *Nine Tables*, 141.
44 Bringhurst, *Palatino*, 8.
45 McIntyre, "Bringhurst in West Coast Book Design and Publishing," 176.
46 Bringhurst, quoted in Munro, "Bringhurst's Range," 40.
47 Bringhurst, quoted in Dickinson, "Heart of Consciousness," 103.
48 Bringhurst, interview with the author, 7 August 2012.
49 Ibid.
50 Bringhurst, *Selected Poems*, 75.
51 Bringhurst, interview with the author, 21 June 2005.
52 Elsted, e-mail to the author, 21 December 2004.
53 Bringhurst, 28 May 2012.
54 Ibid.
55 Ibid.
56 Bringhurst, *Solitary Raven*, 10.
57 Ibid., 5.
58 Ibid.
59 Bringhurst, "Crooked Knife, Straight Goods," 10 August 2002.
60 Reid, *Solitary Raven*, 17.
61 Bringhurst, e-mail to the author, 16 April 2006.
62 Ibid.
63 Bringhurst, quoted in Dickinson, "Heart of Consciousness," 109.
64 Bringhurst, *A Story as Sharp as a Knife*, 317.
65 Swanton, *Haida Myths and Texts*, 100.
66 Bringhurst, *Pieces of Map*, 104.
67 Bringhurst, *Nine Tables*, 82.
68 Ibid.
69 Ibid., 66.
70 Ibid., 69.
71 Ibid., 75.
72 Bringhurst, quoted in Dickinson, "Heart of Consciousness," 105.
73 Bringhurst, 10 September 2012.
74 Bringhurst, 30 August 2012.
75 Bringhurst, 10 September 2012.
76 Bringhurst, *Selected Poems*, 177.
77 Bringhurst, *Everywhere Being is Dancing*, 201.
78 Bringhurst, *Selected Poems*, 173.

79 Ibid., 176.
80 Ibid., 182.
81 Bringhurst, interview with the author, 18 July 2016.
82 Bringhurst, 16 April 2006.
83 Bringhurst, *Nine Tables*, 88.
84 Ibid., 122.
85 Bringhurst, *Everywhere Being is Dancing*, 29.
86 Bringhurst, *Nine Tables*, 74, 71.
87 Bringhurst, e-mail to the author, 29 March 2020.
88 Bringhurst, *Everywhere Being is Dancing*, 37.
89 Bringhurst, e-mail to the author, 3 December 2013.
90 Ibid.
91 Bringhurst, *Everywhere Being is Dancing*, 37.
92 Bringhurst, *Black Canoe*, 78.
93 Both phrases accompany installations of Reid's work at the Bill Reid
    Gallery of Northwest Coast Art, which I visited on 8 January 2010.
94 Bringhurst, *Black Canoe*, 26.
95 Bringhurst, e-mail to the author, 5 August 2011.
96 Bringhurst, e-mail to the author, 1 August 2011.
97 Bringhurst, e-mail to the author, 7 July 2006.
98 Ibid.
99 Bringhurst, *Selected Poems*, 204.
100 Ibid., 228.
101 Ibid., 230–1.
102 Bringhurst, e-mail to the author, 21 December 2008.
103 Bringhurst, *Selected Poems*, 207.
104 Sarah, *Little Eurekas*, 222.
105 Bringhurst, "That Also Is You," 32
106 Ibid.
107 Ibid.
108 Bringhurst, *Story as Sharp as a Knife*, 255
109 Bringhurst, "That Is Also You," 44.
110 Bringhurst, *Tree of Meaning*, 34.
111 Bringhurst, "Off the Road," 186–7.
112 Bringhurst, quoted in Dickinson, "Heart of Consciousness," 101.
113 Ibid., 118.
114 Ibid., 117.
115 Bringhurst, *Everywhere Being is Dancing*, 234.
116 Bringhurst, quoted in Dickinson, "Heart of Consciousness," 119.
117 Bringhurst, *The Calling*, 13.

118 Ibid., 26.
119 Bringhurst, 6 May 2013.
120 Bringhurst, quoted in Dickinson, "Heart of Consciousness," 112.
121 Bringhurst, *Everywhere Being is Dancing*, 37.
122 Evernden, *Natural Alien*, 152.
123 Bringhurst, *Everywhere Being is Dancing*, 61.
124 Bringhurst, 12 April 2015.
125 Bringhurst, *Nine Tables*, 143.
126 McIntyre, quoted in Bradley, "At Land's End,"194.
127 Hodgson, "Letters to the Editor," 4.
128 Hope, "Reincarnation of Stories," 229.
129 Yahgulanaas, e-mail to the author, 7 April 2015.
130 Bringhurst, *Nine Tables*, 16.
131 Snyder, personal correspondence, 2002.
132 Bringhurst, quoted in Dickinson, "Heart of Consciousness," 112.
133 Bringhurst, *A Story as Sharp as a Knife*, 197–9.
134 Ibid., 199.
135 Skaay, *Being in Being*, 148.
136 Ibid., 226.
137 Bringhurst, *Nine Tables*, 75.
138 Bringhurst, *Ursa Major*, 28.
139 Bringhurst, 13 August 2012.
140 Bringhurst, 1 August 2015.
141 Bringhurst, 7 August 2012.
142 Ibid.
143 Ibid.
144 Bringhurst, *Nine Tables*, 101.
145 Bringhurst, "Mind of the Wild," 31.
146 Ibid., 102.

CHAPTER FOUR

1 Zwicky, e-mail to the author, 18 July 2012.
2 Rilke, translated by Mitchell, *Paris Review*, 1981.
3 Zwicky, *Alkibiades' Love*, 263.
4 Zwicky, *New Room*, 39.
5 Zwicky, e-mail to the author, 20 July 2012.
6 Zwicky, *Songs for Relinquishing the Earth*, 81.
7 Zwicky, 20 July 2012.
8 Zwicky, e-mail to the author, 18 July 2012.

9 Zwicky quoted in Pinkmountain, "Perfect Fluency," 138.
10 Zwicky, e-mail to the author, 11 September 2013.
11 Zwicky, e-mail to the author, 13 September 2012.
12 Zwicky, 11 September 2013.
13 Zwicky, letter to the author, 1 August 2012.
14 Zwicky quoted in Simpson, "There Is No Place that Does Not See You," 117.
15 Zwicky, letter to the author, 4 August 2010.
16 Zwicky, 13 September 2012.
17 Zwicky, interview with the author, 8 July 2005.
18 Zwicky, 1 August 2012.
19 Zwicky, 8 July 2005.
20 Zwicky, *Wittgenstein Elegies*, 72.
21 Zwicky, 1 August 2012.
22 Russell, quoted in Monk, *Ludwig Wittgenstein*, 41.
23 Wittgenstein, quoted in Monk, *Ludwig Wittgenstein*, 151.
24 Zwicky, *Wittgenstein Elegies*, 72.
25 Wittgenstein, *Tractatus Logico-Philosophicus*, 110.
26 Zwicky, *Wittgenstein Elegies*, 72.
27 Zwicky, letter to the author, 1 November 2013.
28 Zwicky, 1 August 2012.
29 Ibid.
30 Zwicky, e-mail to the author, 21 July 2014.
31 Zwicky, 8 July 2005.
32 Zwicky, letter to the author, 1 September 2013.
33 Zwicky, e-mail to the author, 28 October 2012.
34 Zwicky, e-mail to the author, 18 July 2012.
35 Young, interview with the author, 1 September 2012.
36 Zwicky, *A Theory of Ineffability*, iii.
37 Zwicky, *Alkibiades' Love*, 244.
38 Zwicky, *Where Have We Been*, 45.
39 Zwicky, 1 August 2012.
40 Ibid.
41 Ibid.
42 Zwicky, 1 November 2013.
43 Ibid.
44 Zwicky, 1 August 2012.
45 Zwicky, *Wittgenstein Elegies*, 72.
46 Ibid., 71–2.
47 Ibid., 73.

48 Wittgenstein, quoted in Monk, *Ludwig Wittgenstein*, 291.
49 Sinclair, "Poem as Ally," 11.
50 Wittgenstein, quoted in Willard, Review of *Wittgenstein Elegies*, 109.
51 Zwicky, *Wittgenstein Elegies*, 27.
52 Ibid., 28.
53 Ibid., 68.
54 Ibid., 40.
55 Ibid., 46.
56 Sinclair, "Poem as Ally," 17.
57 Zwicky quoted in Simpson, "There Is No Place that Does Not See You," 119.
58 Zwicky, 1 August 2012.
59 Ibid.
60 Ibid.
61 Zwicky, *Lyric Philosophy*, unpaginated.
62 Lee, "Music of Thinking," 28.
63 Ibid.
64 Ibid., 31.
65 Zwicky, 1 August 2012.
66 Ibid.
67 Zwicky, letter to the author, 11 January 2009.
68 Zwicky, 1 August 2012.
69 Zwicky, *Lyric Philosophy*, LH69.
70 Ibid., LH68.
71 Ibid., LH127.
72 Ibid., LH299.
73 Zwicky, 1 August 2012.
74 Ibid.
75 Ibid.
76 Ibid.
77 Zwicky, *New Room*, 31.
78 Ibid., 65.
79 Barbour, "Echoes of the Ardent Voice," 248.
80 Zwicky, 1 August 2012.
81 Ibid.
82 Ibid.
83 Zwicky, 1 November 2013.
84 Ibid.
85 Ibid.
86 Zwicky, *Alkibiades' Love*, 8.

87 Zwicky, 19 July 2012.

88 Zwicky, 7 November 2013.

89 Zwicky, *Alkibiades' Love*, 8.

90 Heidegger, *Discourse on Thinking*, 55.

91 Zwicky, 10 April 2018.

92 Zwicky, e-mail to the author, 25 May 2018.

93 Ibid.

94 Zwicky, 6 September 2012.

95 Zwicky, 18 August 2018.

96 Zwicky, letter to the author, 9 February 2008.

97 Vogt, interview with the author, 7 October 2012.

98 Leckie, "Jan Zwicky's 'Brahms' Clarinet Quintet in B Minor, Op. 115,'" 70.

99 Zwicky, *Songs for Relinquishing the Earth*, 10.

100 Ibid., 56.

101 Ibid., 85.

102 Ibid., 12.

103 Zwicky, 1 November 2013.

104 Ibid.

105 McKay, *Speaker's Chair*, 15–16.

106 Ibid., 16.

107 Zwicky, 18 July 2013.

108 Pound, quoted in Zwicky, *Wisdom & Metaphor*, LH4.

109 Zwicky, *Wisdom & Metaphor*, LH52.

110 Ibid.

111 Zwicky, *Lyric Philosophy*, LH302.

112 Bifford and Heiti, "An Abridgement of a Conversation with Jan Zwicky," 72, 75, 76.

113 Zwicky, 1 November 2013.

114 Ibid.

115 Ibid.

116 Zwicky, *Robinson's Crossing*, 11.

117 Ibid., 39.

118 Ibid., 84.

119 Zwicky, "Introduction," 2.

120 Zwicky, 1 November 2013.

121 I am in debt to Darren Bifford for this phrasing.

122 Zwicky, 1 November 2013.

123 Zwicky, *Robinson's Crossing*, 37.

124 Ibid., 40.

125 Zwicky, 18 July 2015.

126 Zwicky, *Robinson's Crossing*, 16.
127 Zwicky, 18 July 2015.
128 Zwicky, *Robinson's Crossing*, 17.
129 Zwicky, 18 July 2015.
130 Zwicky, 16 July 2012.
131 Zwicky, 18 July 2015.
132 Zwicky, *Thirty-seven Small Songs*, 18.
133 Ibid., 24.
134 Ibid., 34.
135 Bifford and Heiti, "Introduction," xv.
136 Zwicky, *Thirty-seven Small Songs*, 45.
137 Zwicky, 1 November 2013.
138 Ibid.
139 Ibid.
140 Zwicky, *Alkibiades' Love*, 263.
141 Zwicky, 28 October 2012.
142 Zwicky, 1 August 2012.
143 Ibid.
144 Zwicky, 1 November 2013.
145 Ibid.
146 Zwicky, *Plato as Artist*, 84.
147 Ibid., 31.
148 Ibid., 77.
149 Zwicky, *Forge*, 21.
150 Ibid., 60.
151 Ibid., 38.
152 Zwicky, *Alkibiades' Love*, 3.
153 Ibid., 4.
154 Ibid., 5.
155 Ibid.
156 Ibid., 8.
157 Ibid., 9.
158 Ibid., 10.
159 Ibid., 18.
160 Ibid., 236.
161 Ibid., 227.
162 Ibid., 275.
163 Ibid., 176.
164 Ibid., 286.
165 Ibid., 290–1.

166 Ibid., 291.

167 Ibid., 292.

168 Ibid., 295 .

169 Zwicky, *Long Walk*, 7.

170 Ibid., 39.

171 Ibid., 72.

172 Zwicky, 1 April 2018.

173 Young, 1 September 2012.

174 Ibid.

175 Zwicky, "Ship from Delos," 43.

176 Ibid., 51.

177 Ibid., 66.

178 Zwicky, 1 November 2013.

CHAPTER FIVE

1 Here I am responding directly to a question critic Carmine Starnino raised
   concerning Lilburn's work in a 2003 review essay. Among other things,
   Starnino discerns a shift in Lilburn's poetry away from the spontaneous to
   a more forced, manufactured voice with the publication of *Moosewood
   Sandhills* in 1993. While my vision clearly differs from Starnino's, his
   essay on Lilburn is engaging and thought-provoking.

2 Lilburn, "Walking Out of Silence," 42.

3 Lilburn, interview with the author, 10 July 2012.

4 Lilburn, interview with the author, 11 August 2016.

5 Ibid.

6 Lilburn, 10 July 2012.

7 Lilburn, 11 August 2016.

8 Ibid.

9 Ibid.

10 Lilburn, *Larger Conversation*, 17.

11 Lilburn, 10 July 2012.

12 Ibid.

13 Ibid.

14 Ibid.

15 Lilburn, *Larger Conversation*, 20.

16 Lilburn, interview with the author, 13 August 2011.

17 Lilburn, interview with the author, 8 August 2012.

18 Lilburn, *Larger Conversation*, 21.

19 Lilburn, interview with the author, 13 April 2008.

20 Lilburn, interview with the author, 12 November 2015.
21 Lilburn, 8 August 2012.
22 Okigbo, *Labyrinths*, 3.
23 Lilburn, 8 August 2012.
24 Lilburn, interview with the author, 8 October 2012.
25 Lilburn, interview with the author, 9 August 2012.
26 Lilburn, 8 August 2012.
27 Ibid.
28 Lilburn, *Names of God*, 42.
29 Lilburn, 8 August 2012.
30 Lilburn, "Breakdown as School," 85.
31 Ibid. 86.
32 Ibid., 94.
33 Ibid.
34 Ibid.
35 Lilburn, interview with the author, 4 October 2012.
36 Lilburn, "thoughts towards a christian poetics," 34.
37 Lilburn, "A Discipline of Looking," unpaginated.
38 Lilburn, "thoughts towards a christian poetics," 35.
39 Ibid.
40 Lilburn, *Names of God*, 11.
41 Ibid., 30.
42 Ibid., 19.
43 Ibid., 63.
44 Lilburn, interview with the author, 1 June 2008.
45 Ibid.
46 McKay, *Angular Unconformity*, 264.
47 Lilburn, interview with the author, 19 December 2014.
48 Lilburn, 13 August 2011.
49 Lilburn, 19 December 2014.
50 Ibid.
51 Lilburn, *Larger Conversation*, 174.
52 Lilburn, 4 October 2012.
53 Lilburn, 13 April 2008.
54 Lilburn, 8 August 2012.
55 Lilburn, "Discipline of Looking," unpaginated.
56 Lilburn, *Living in the World as if It Were Home*, 28.
57 Ibid., 37.
58 Ibid., 30.
59 Lilburn, 9 August 2012.

60 Lilburn, *Living in the World as if It Were Home*, 30–1.
61 Lilburn, *Going Home*, 171.
62 Lilburn, 4 October 2012.
63 Ibid.
64 Lilburn, quoted in Tim Wilson, *Being Here as if It Were Home*.
65 Ibid.
66 Lilburn, 4 October 2012.
67 Lilburn, quoted in Tim Wilson, *Being Here as if It Were Home*.
68 Ibid.
69 Lilburn, 9 August 2012.
70 Zwicky, "Just the World," unpaginated manuscript.
71 Lilburn, quoted in Tim Wilson, *Being Here as if It Were Home*.
72 Lilburn, 4 October 2012.
73 Lilburn, *Going Home*, 178.
74 Lilburn, 4 October 2012.
75 Ibid.
76 Lilburn, *Moosewood Sandhills*, 15.
77 Ibid.
78 Lilburn, 4 October 2012.
79 Lilburn, *Moosewood Sandhills*, 15.
80 Ibid., 16.
81 Ibid.
82 Ibid.
83 Lilburn, 8 August 2012.
84 Planinc, e-mail to the author, 4 February 2015.
85 Ibid.
86 Lilburn, 4 October 2012.
87 Bringhurst, e-mail to the author, 7 November 2005.
88 Lilburn, 9 August 2012.
89 Ibid.
90 Zwicky, e-mail to the author, 6 May 2013.
91 Lilburn, 9 August 2012.
92 Lilburn, interview with the author, 28 July 2005.
93 Lilburn, *Poetry and Knowing*, 8.
94 Lilburn, *Living in the World as if It Were Home*, 3.
95 Ibid., 15.
96 Ibid., 17.
97 Ibid., 22.
98 Lilburn, 10 July 2012.
99 Lilburn, 4 October 2012.

100 Ibid.
101 Ibid.
102 Ibid.
103 Lilburn, interview with the author, 31 May 2013.
104 Ibid.
105 Lilburn, *Larger Conversation*, 93.
106 Lilburn, 31 May 2013.
107 Lilburn, *Larger Conversation*, 94.
108 Ibid., 94.
109 Lilburn, *To the River*, 18, 45, 62, 64, 68, 70.
110 Hinton, *Mountain Home*, xv.
111 Ibid., xv.
112 Lilburn, *To the River*, 45.
113 Lilburn, 31 May 2013.
114 Dickinson, e-mail to the author, 3 March 2019.
115 Harris, interview with the author, 30 July 2013.
116 Lilburn, 1 June 2008.
117 Zwicky, e-mail to the author, 16 July 2012.
118 Lilburn, "Discipline of Looking," unpaginated manuscript.
119 Lilburn, *Thinking and Singing*, 2.
120 Lilburn, *Thinking and Singing*, 3.
121 Lilburn, interview with the author, 28 July 2005.
122 Lilburn, e-mail to the author, 25 July 2015.
123 Bateson, *Small Arcs of Larger Circles*, 169.
124 Ibid.
125 Lilburn, *Larger Conversation*, 234.
126 Ibid.
127 Ibid.
128 I am indebted to Ross Hoffman for my understanding of Joe Cardinal, his biography, and his teachings.
129 Lilburn, *Larger Conversation*, 174.
130 Lilburn, 13 August 2011.
131 Lilburn, *Larger Conversation*, 174.
132 Lilburn, 10 July 2012.
133 Ibid.
134 Lilburn, *Kill-site*, 3.
135 Ibid., 63.
136 Lilburn, 11 August 2016.
137 Ibid.
138 Lilburn, 31 May 2013.

139 Lilburn, e-mail to the author, 16 November 2015.

140 Lilburn, 30 July 2013.

141 Lilburn, 9 August 2012.

142 Ibid.

143 Lilburn, 28 July 2005.

144 Lilburn, *Larger Conversation*, 8.

145 Ibid., 59.

146 Lilburn, *Orphic Politics*, 3.

147 Heiti, "Sickness, Catharsis, and the City Inside the Skin," 127.

148 Lilburn, *Going Home*, 2.

149 Ibid., 14.

150 Brankley, e-mail to the author, 3 April 2010.

151 Lilburn, *Going Home*, 78–9.

152 Ibid., 101.

153 Ibid., 190.

154 Ibid., 191.

155 Ibid.

156 Lilburn, *Larger Conversation*, 193

157 Lilburn, *Assiniboia*, ix.

158 Lilburn, *Larger Conversation*, xiv.

159 Lilburn, *Assiniboia*, 27.

160 Ibid., 14.

161 Lilburn, *Larger Conversation*, 188.

162 Lilburn, 9 August 2012.

163 Lilburn, *Assiniboia*, 84.

164 Lilburn, *Larger Conversation*, x.

165 Ibid., xii.

166 Lilburn, "Walking Out of Silence," 48.

167 Ibid.

168 Simpson, "Looking after Gdoo-naaganinaa," 35.

169 Lilburn, *Larger Conversation*, xiv.

170 Ibid., xii.

171 Ibid., 13.

172 Lilburn, 9 July 2013.

173 Lilburn, *Larger Conversation*, 15.

174 Lilburn, *Larger Conversation*, 6.

175 Ibid., 232

176 Ibid.

177 Ibid., 232–3.

178 Lilburn, 9 August 2012.

179 Ibid.

PERSONAL CODA

1   Buhner, *Ensouling Language*, 93.
2   Kane, letter to the author, 15 June 2003.
3   Zwicky, letter to the author, 15 July 2003.
4   Bringhurst, letter to the author, 30 June 2003.
5   Bringhurst, interview with the author, 3 July 2005
6   Lilburn, interview with the author, 28 July 2005.
7   Lee, interview with the author, 25 February 2006.
8   Lee, personal communication, 19 July 2007.
9   Lee, *Heart Residence*, 126.
10 Lee, personal communication, 5 April 2007.
11 Lilburn, *Assiniboia*, 42.
12 Zwicky, personal communication, 10 August 2012.
13 Zwicky, interview with the author, 23 July 2013.
14 Zwicky, *Lyric Philosophy*, LH89.
15 Zwicky, *The Long Walk*, 68.
16 Zwicky, personal communication, 18 July 2012.
17 Kimmerer, *Braiding Sweetgrass*, 125.
18 Zwicky, *Wisdom & Metaphor*, LH92.

Bibliography

Abram, David. *The Spell of the Sensuous*. New York: Vintage, 1996.

Ackerman, John. *A Dylan Thomas Companion: Life, Poetry and Prose*. London: Macmillan, 1991.

Atwood, Margaret. "Introduction." In Robert Bringhurst, *A Story as Sharp as a Knife*, xv–xx. London: Folio Society, 2015.

– *Moving Targets: Writing with Intent 1982–2004*. Toronto: House of Anansi, 2005.

– *Survival: A Thematic Guide to Canadian Literature*. Toronto: House of Anansi, 1972.

– "Uncovered: An American Iliad." In *Listening for the Heartbeat of Being: The Arts of Robert Bringhurst*, edited by Brent Wood and Mark Dickinson, 188–93. Montreal and Kingston: McGill-Queen's University Press, 2015.

Avison, Margaret. *I Am Here and Not Not-There: An Autobiography*. Erin, ON: Porcupine's Quill, 2009.

– "Snow." In *Open Wide a Wilderness: Nature Poems*, edited by Nancy Holmes, 187. Waterloo: Wilfrid Laurier University Press, 2009.

Babstock, Ken. "The Appropriate Gesture, or Regular Dumb-Ass Guy Looks at Bird." In *Don McKay: Essays on His Works*, edited by Brian Bartlett, 167–87. Toronto: Guernica Editions, 2006.

Baggett, Marybeth. "An Experiment in Poetry: Margaret Avison Invites Us to Wonder." *Moral Apologetics*, 7 January 2019.

Barbour, Charles. "Echoes of the Ardent Voice." In *Lyric Ecology: An Appreciation of the Work of Jan Zwicky*, edited by Mark Dickinson and Clare Goulet, 248–53. Toronto: Cormorant Books, 2010.

Barton, John. *Seminal: The Anthology of Canada's Gay Male Poets*. Vancouver: Arsenal Pulp Press, 2007.

Bateson, Gregory. *Mind and Nature: The Necessary Unity*. London: Dutton, 1979.

Bateson, Nora. *Ecology of Mind*. Bullfrog Films, 2011. 60 mins.

– *Small Arcs of Larger Circles: Framing through Other Patterns*. Axminster: Triarchy Press, 2016.

Beattie, Steven. "'Modernism Has Come to Canada': The Enduring Legacy of Dave Godfrey." *Quill & Quire*, 25 June 2015.

Bifford, Darren, and Warren Heiti. "An Abridgement of a Conversation with Jan Zwicky." In Jan Zwicky, *Chamber Music: The Poetry of Jan Zwicky*, 69–78. Waterloo: Wilfrid Laurier University Press, 2015.

– "Introduction." In Jan Zwicky, *Chamber Music: The Poetry of Jan Zwicky*, xi–xx. Waterloo: Wilfrid Laurier University Press, 2015.

Bjornerud, Monica. *Reading the Rocks: The Autobiography of the Earth*. New York: Basic Books, 2006.

Bondar, Alanna F. "'that every feather is a pen, but living, // flying' Desire: The Metapoetics of Don McKay's *Birding, or desire*." *Studies in Canadian Literature* 19, 2 (1990): 14–29.

Bradley, Nicholas. "At Land's End: Masterworks of the Classical Haida Mythtellers." In *Listening for the Heartbeat of Being: The Arts of Robert Bringhurst*, edited by Brent Wood and Mark Dickinson, 194–223. Montreal and Kingston: McGill-Queen's University Press, 2015.

Bringhurst, Robert. "At Home in the Difficult World." In *Tasks of Passion: Dennis Lee at Mid-Career*, edited by Karen Mulhallen, Donna Bennett, and Russell Brown, 57–81. Toronto: Descant Books, 1982.

– *The Beauty of the Weapons*. Port Townsend: Copper Canyon Press, 1982.

– *The Black Canoe*. Vancouver: Douglas & McIntyre, 1991.

– *The Book of Silences*. Los Angeles: Ninja Press, 2000.

– *The Calling: Selected Poems 1970–1995*. Toronto: McClelland & Stewart, 1995.

– "Crooked Knife, Straight Goods." *The Globe and Mail*, 10 August 2002.

– "Editor's Foreword." In Dennis Lee, *Heart Residence: Collected Poems 1967–2017*, 3–6. Toronto: House of Anansi, 2017.

– *Everywhere Being is Dancing: Twenty Pieces of Thinking*. Kentville, NS: Gaspereau Press, 2007.

– "Introduction." In Bill Reid, *Solitary Raven: The Selected Writings of Bill Reid*. Vancouver: Douglas & McIntyre, 2000.

– "The Mind of the Wild." In Robert Bringhurst and Jan Zwicky, *Learning to Die: Wisdom in the Age of Climate Crisis*, 7–40. Regina: University of Regina Press, 2018.

– *Nine Tables, Two Chairs*. Unpublished manuscript.
– "Off the Road: Journeys in the Past, Present and Future of Canadian Literature." In *Best Canadian Essays 1989*, edited by Douglas Fetherling, 185–94. Saskatoon: Fifth House, 1989.
– *Palatino: The Natural History of a Typeface*. Boston: David Godine, 2016.
– *Pieces of Map, Pieces of Music*. Port Townsend: Copper Canyon Press, 1987.
– "Reflections on the Stone Age." In *The Second Macmillan Anthology*, edited by John Metcalfe and Leon Rooke, 212–14. Toronto: Macmillan, 1989.
– *The Ridge Part VIII*. Vancouver: In Finibus Mundi, 2018.
– *Selected Poems*. Kentville, NS: Gaspereau Press, 2009.
– *The Shipwright's Log*. Bloomington: Kanchenjunga Press, 1972.
– *A Story as Sharp as a Knife: The Classical Haida Mythtellers and Their World*. Vancouver: Douglas & McIntyre, 2011.
– "That Is Also You: Some Classics of Native Canadian Literature." *Canadian Literature* 124–5 (Spring 1990): 32–47.
– *The Tree of Meaning: Thirteen Talks*. Kentville, NS: Gaspereau Press, 2006.
– *Ursa Major: A Polyphonic Masque for Speakers & Dancers*. Kentville, NS: Gaspereau Press, 2003/2009.
Buhner, Stephen Harrod. *Ensouling Language: On the Art of Nonfiction and the Writer's Life*. Rochester, VT: Inner Traditions, 2010.
– *Plant Intelligence and the Imaginal Realm*. Toronto: Bear and Company, 2014.
Capra, Fritjof. *The Web of Life: A New Scientific Understanding of Living Systems*. New York: Anchor Books, 1996.
Chan, Wing-Tsit. *A Source Book in Chinese Philosophy*. Princeton: Princeton University Press, 1963.
Christian, William. *George Grant: A Biography*. Toronto: University of Toronto Press, 1993.
Deloria, Vine. *God Is Red: A Native View of Religion*. New York: Putnam Publishing Company, 1973.
Dickinson, Mark, and Robert Bringhurst. "The Heart of Consciousness." *Philosophy, Activism, Nature* (2019): 14.
Dragland, Stan. "Who Is Don McKay?" *Applegarth's Folly* 2 (1975): r2–r8.
Everndon, Neil. *The Natural Alien*. Toronto: University of Toronto Press, 1985.

Fox, Matthew. *Meditations with Meister Eckhart*. Rochester: Bear & Company, 1983.

Frye, Northrop. *The Bush Garden*. Toronto: House of Anansi, 1971.

Graham, A.C. *Disputers of the Tao: Philosophical Argument in Ancient China*. La Salle, IL: Open Court, 1989.

Grant, George. *Philosophy in the Mass Age*. Toronto: University of Toronto Press, 1995.

– *Technology and Empire*. Toronto: House of Anansi, 1969.

Grant, Robert Stuart. "Negative Nationalism and the Poetry of Dennis Lee." Unpublished master's thesis, University of Windsor, 1971.

Harold, Ellen. "Edmund Carpenter." Association for Cultural Equity. www.culturalequity.org/alan-lomax/friends/carpenter.

Harris, Sharon. "Dancing in the Distillery District." *Torontoist*, 8 June 2007.

Heidegger, Martin. *Discourse on Thinking*. New York: Harper and Row, 1966.

– *Poetry, Language, Thought*. New York: HarperCollins, 1971.

Heiti, Warren. "Sickness, Catharsis, and the City Inside the Skin." *The Fiddlehead* 241 (Autumn 2009): 124–9.

Hinton, David. *Mountain Home: The Wilderness Poetry of Ancient China*. New York: New Directions, 2002.

Hodgson, C.W. "Letters to the Editor: Sharp Knives." *Books in Canada* 29, 1 (2000): 4.

Hoffman, Michael. "The Unquenchable Spirit." *The Guardian*. 20 November 2004.

Hoffmeyer, Jesper. *Signs of Meaning in the Universe*. Bloomington: Indiana University Press, 1997.

Holmes, Nancy. *Open Wide a Wilderness: Canadian Nature Poems*. Waterloo: Wilfrid Laurier University Press, 2009.

Hope, Ishmael. "The Reincarnation of Stories." In *Listening for the Heartbeat of Being: Perspectives on the Arts of Robert Bringhurst*, edited by Brent Wood and Mark Dickinson, 227–30. Montreal and Kingston: McGill-Queen's University Press, 2015.

Jasen, Patricia. *Wild Things: Nature, Culture and Tourism in Ontario, 1790–1914*. Toronto: University of Toronto Press, 1995.

Kahn, Charles. *The Art and Thought of Herakleitos*. Cambridge: Cambridge University Press, 1981.

Kennedy, Kate. Catalogue description of *Thirty-seven Small Songs and Thirteen Silences*. Kentville, NS: Gaspereau Press, 2005. www.gaspereau.com/thirtyseven.html.

Kimmerer, Robin Wall. *Braiding Sweetgrass: Indigenous Wisdom, Scientific Knowledge and the Teaching of Plants*. Minneapolis: Milkweed Editions, 2013.

Lang, Nancy, and Peter Raymont. *Where the Universe Sings: The Spiritual Journey of Lawren Harris*. White Pine Productions, 2016. 90 mins.

Lecker, Robert. *The Cadence of Civil Elegies*. Toronto: Cormorant Books, 2006.

Leckie, Ross. "Jan Zwicky's 'Brahms' Clarinet Quintet in B Minor, Op. 115.'" In *Lyric Ecology: An Appreciation of the Work of Jan Zwicky*, edited by Mark Dickinson and Clare Goulet, 69–75. Toronto: Cormorant Books, 2010.

Leduc, Timothy B. *A Canadian Climate of Mind: Passages from Fur to Energy and Beyond*. Montreal and Kingston: McGill-Queen's University Press, 2016.

Lee, Dennis. *Alligator Pie*. Toronto: Macmillan, 1974.

– *Body Music: Essays*. Toronto: House of Anansi, 1998.

– *Heart Residence: Collected Poems 1967–2017*. Toronto: House of Anansi, 2017.

– *Kingdom of Absence*. Toronto: House of Anansi, 1968.

– *Labyrinth*. Unpublished film treatment, 1983.

– "The Music of Thinking: The Structural Logic of *Lyric Philosophy*." In *Lyric Ecology: An Appreciation of the Work of Jan Zwicky*, edited by Mark Dickinson and Clare Goulet, 19–39. Toronto: Cormorant Books, 2010.

– *The New Canadian Poets 1970–1985*. Toronto: McClelland & Stewart, 1985.

– "Principles of Ekstatic Form." Master's thesis, University of Toronto, 1965.

– *Regreening the Undermusic*. Nanaimo, BC: Institute for Coastal Research, 2016.

– *Savage Fields: An Essay in Literature and Cosmology*. Toronto: House of Anansi, 1977.

– *SoCool*. Toronto: Key Porter, 2004.

Levinas, Emmanuel. *Entre Nous: On Thinking-of-the-Other*. New York: Columbia University Press, 1998.

– "From Being to the Other: Paul Celan." *Descant* 59, 18, 4 (1987): 99–105.

Lilburn, Tim. *Assiniboia*. Toronto: McClelland & Stewart, 2012.

– "Breakdown as School" *Grail* 6, 3 (1990): 82–102.

– "A Discipline of Looking." Unpublished manuscript.

– *Going Home: Essays.* Toronto: House of Anansi, 2008.
– *Kill-site.* Toronto: McClelland & Stewart, 2003.
– *The Larger Conversation: Contemplation and Place.* Edmonton:
   University of Alberta Press, 2017.
– *Living In The World As If It Were* Home. Toronto: Cormorant Books,
   1999.
– *Moosewood Sandhills.* Toronto: McClelland & Stewart, 1993.
– *The Names.* Toronto: McClelland & Stewart, 2016.
– *Names of God.* Lantzville: Oolichan Books, 1986.
– *Orphic Politics.* Toronto: McClelland & Stewart, 2008.
– *Poetry and Knowing: Speculative Essays and Interviews.*
   Kingston: Quarry Press, 1995.
– "Summoning the Land" In *Home and Animal.* Swift Current,
   SK: Art Gallery of Swift Current, 1999.
– *Thinking and Singing: Poetry and the Practice of Philosophy.* Toronto:
   Cormorant Books, 2002.
– "thoughts towards a christian poetics." *Brick* 29 (Winter 1987): 34–6.
– *To The River.* Toronto: McClelland & Stewart, 1999.
– "Walking Out of Silence." In *Desire Never Leaves: The Poetry of Tim
   Lilburn*, edited by Alison Calder, 41–8. Waterloo: Wilfrid Laurier
   University Press, 2007.
Lilburn, Tim, and Kevin Paul. "Notes on Language: At the Foot of
   Wmieten." *Artseverywhere.* 26 March 2017. https://artseverywhere.ca.
Loy, David. *Nonduality: A Study in Comparative Philosophy.* Amherst,
   NY: Humanity Books, 1998.
Malka, Salomon. *Emmanuel Levinas: His Life and Legacy.* Pittsburgh:
   Duquesne University Press, 2006.
McIntyre, Scott. "Bringhurst in West Coast Book Design and Publishing."
   In *Listening for the Heartbeat of Being,* edited by Brent Wood and
   Mark Dickinson, 175–82. Montreal and Kingston: McGill-Queen's
   University Press, 2015.
McKay, Don. *Air Occupies Space.* Windsor: Sesame Press, 1973.
– *Angular Unconformity: Collected Poems 1970–2014.* Fredericton, NB:
   Goose Lane, 2014.
– "Common Sense and Magic." *The Fiddlehead* 185 (1995): 233–8.
– *Deactivated West 100.* Kentville, NS: Gaspereau Press, 2005.
– "The Holy Ground of Plate Tectonics." *The New Quarterly* 119.
– "The Impulse to Epic in Goderich, Ontario." *Brick* 2 (1978): 28–32.
– "It Won't Work." Remarks prepared for the 25th anniversary of Brick
   Books. Toronto: Harbourfront Centre, 2001.

– *Larix*. Montreal: Vallum, 2015.
– "Local Wilderness." *The Fiddlehead* 169 (Autumn 1991): 5–6.
– "Reflection on Sleeping Places." In *Marlene Creates: Places, Paths, and Pauses*, edited by Susan Gibson Garvey and Andrea Kunard, 49. Fredericton, NB: Goose Lane, 2017.
– *The Shell of the Tortoise*. Kentville, NS: Gaspereau Press, 2011.
– "Six Poems." *The Fiddlehead* 244 (Summer 2010): 76–88.
– "Some Remarks on Poetry and Poetic Attention." In *The Second MacMillan Anthology*, edited by John Metcalfe and Leon Rooke, 206–8. Toronto: MacMillan, 1989.
– *The Speaker's Chair: Field Notes on Betweenity*. Tors Cove, NL: Running the Goat Books and Broadsides, 2013.
– *Vis à Vis: Field Notes on Poetry and Wilderness*. Kentville, NS: Gaspereau Press, 2001.
– "Why Poetry?" Presentation at Reykjavik International Literary Festival, 12 September 2009. www.griffinpoetryprize.com/awards-and-poets/speeches/don-mckay-2009-reykjavik/.
McKay, Donald. *Moccasins on Concrete*. Montreal: privately printed, 1972.
mclennan, rob. "Boiling Down to Stone: Recent Don McKay." rob mclennan's blog. 14 April 2006.
Merleau-Ponty, Maurice. *Sense and Non-Sense*. Evanston, IL: Northwestern University Press, 1964.
Middleton, Christopher. *Friedrich Hölderlin: Selected Poems*. Chicago: University of Chicago Press, 1972.
Miller, Eric. Review of *Ornithologies of Desire*. *The Malahat Review* 185 (Winter 2013): 105–7.
Monk, Ray. *Ludwig Wittgenstein: The Duty of Genius*. New York: Penguin Books, 1990.
Mount, Nick. *The Arrival: The Story of CanLit*. Toronto: House of Anansi Press, 2017.
Munro, Jane. "Bringhurst's Range: Essential Information." *CV II* 5, 2 (Winter 1980–81): 10–17.
Neruda, Pablo. "Ode To My Socks." In Jan Zwicky, *Lyric Philosophy*, RH136. Kentville, NS: Gaspereau Press, 2011.
Nwakanma, Obi. *Christopher Okigbo 1930–1967: Thirsting for Sunlight*. Martlesham, UK: James Currey, 2010.
Okigbo, Christopher. *Labyrinths and Path of Thunder*. New York: Holmes & Meier Publishing, 1971.
Ondaatje, Michael. *The Long Poem Anthology*. Toronto: Coach House Press, 1979.

– "TBA." In *Tasks of Passion: Dennis Lee at Mid-Career*, edited by Karen Mulhallen, Donna Bennett, and Russell Brown, 57–81. Toronto: Descant Books, 1982.

Oughton, John. "The Lord of the Wings." In *Don McKay: Essays on His Works*, edited by Brian Bartlett, 35–8. Toronto: Guernica, 2006.

Pinkmountain, Scott. "Perfect Fluency: An Interview with Jan Zwicky." *Owen Wister Review* (2011): 134–45.

Pound, Ezra. *Selected Poems of Ezra Pound*. New York: New Directions, 1957.

– *Selected Prose: 1909–1965*. New York: New Directions, 1975.

Reck, Michael. *Ezra Pound: A Close-Up*. New York: McGraw-Hill, 1967.

Reid, Bill. *Solitary Raven: The Selected Writings of Bill Reid*. Edited by Robert Bringhurst. Vancouver: Douglas & McIntyre, 2000.

Rilke, Rainer Maria. "There Stands Death." Translated by Stephen Mitchell. *The Paris Review* 82 (Winter 1981). https://www.theparisreview.org/poetry/6855/death-rainer-maria-rilke.

Sarah, Robyn. *Little Eurekas: A Decade's Thoughts on Poetry*. Windsor: Biblioasis, 2008.

Simpson, Anne. "There Is No Place That Does Not See You." In *Where the Words Come From: Canadian Poets in Conversation*, edited by Tim Bowling, 115–22. Roberts Creek, BC: Nightwood Editions, 2002.

Simpson, Leanne. "Looking after Gdoo-naaganinaa: Precolonial Nishnaabeg Diplomatic and Treaty Relationships." *Wicazo Sa Review* 23 (Fall 2008): 29–42.

– "Foreword." In Doug Williams, *Michi Saagiig Nishnaabeg: This Is Our Territory*, 7–9. Winnipeg: ARP Books, 2018.

Sinclair, Sue. "Introduction." In Jan Zwicky, *Wittgenstein Elegies*, 9–20. London: Brick Books, 2015.

Sioui, Georges. *Histories of Kanatha: Seen and Told. Essays and Discourses 1991–2008*. Ottawa: University of Ottawa Press, 2008.

Skaay of the Qquuna Qiighawaay. *Being in Being: The Collected Works of a Master Haida Mythteller*. Vancouver: Douglas & McIntyre, 2001.

Starnino, Carmen. *A Lover's Quarrel: Essays and Reviews*. Erin, ON: Porcupine's Quill, 2004.

Sullivan, Rosemary. "Writing Lives." In *Writing Life: Celebrated Canadian and International Authors on Writing and Life*, edited by Constance Rooke, 367–80. Toronto: McClelland & Stewart, 2006.

Swanton, John. *Haida Myths and Texts: Skidegate Dialect*. Washington, DC: Bureau of American Ethnology Bulletin 29 (1905).

Thunberg, Lars. *Man and the Cosmos: The Vision of St Maximus the Confessor*. Crestwood, NY: St Vladimir's Seminary Press, 1985.

Vermeersch, Paul. "That Funny Ping." In Dennis Lee, *Riffs*, 13–19. London: Brick Books, 2015.

Weber, Andreas. *The Biology of Wonder: Aliveness, Feeling and the Metamorphosis of Science*. Gabriola Island: New Society Publishers, 2016.

Willard, Thomas. Review of *Wittgenstein Elegies*. *Journal of Canadian Poetry* 3 (1988).

Wilson, Tim. *Being Here as if It Were Home: Tim Lilburn*. 1994; Muenster, SK: Vision TV. 16 mins.

Wittgenstein, Ludwig. *Tractatus Logico-Philosophicus*, translated by D.F. Pears and B.F. McGuinness. London: Routledge & Kegan Paul, 1921 [1961].

Yeats, W.B. *The Winding Stair and Other Poems*. London: Macmillan, 1932.

Zwicky, Jan. *Alkibiades' Love*. Montreal and Kingston: McGill-Queen's University Press, 2015.

– "Being, Polyphony, Lyric: An Open Letter to Robert Bringhurst." *Canadian Literature* 156 (Spring 1998): 181–4.

– "Dream Logic and the Politics of Interpretation." In *Thinking and Singing: Poetry and the Practice of Philosophy*, edited by Tim Lilburn, 121–51. Toronto: Cormorant Books, 2002.

– *The Experience of Meaning*. Montreal and Kingston: McGill-Queen's University Press, 2019.

– *Forge*. Kentville, NS: Gaspereau Press, 2011.

– "Introduction." In *Hard Choices: Climate Change in Canada*, edited by Harold Coward and Andrew J. Weaver, 1–9. Waterloo: Wilfrid Laurier University Press, 2004.

– "Just the World." In *Bush Dweller: Essays in Memory of Father James Gray, OSB*, edited by Donald Ward. Muenster, SK: St Peter's Abbey, 2010.

– *The Long Walk*. Regina: University of Regina Press, 2016.

– *Lyric Philosophy*. rev. 2nd edition. Kentville, NS: Gaspereau Press, 2011.

– "Lyric Realism: Nature Poetry, Silence, and Ontology." *The Malahat Review* 165 (Winter 2008): 85–91.

– *The New Room*. Toronto: Coach House Press, 1989.

– *Plato as Artist*. Kentville, NS: Gaspereau Press, 2009.

– *Robinson's Crossing*. London: Brick Books, 2004.

– "A Ship from Delos." In Robert Bringhurst and Jan Zwicky, *Learning to*

    Die: Wisdom in the Age of Climate Crisis, 41–72. Regina: University of
    Regina Press, 2018.
– *Songs for Relinquishing the Earth*. London: Brick Books, 1998.
– *A Theory of Ineffability*. PhD dissertation, University of Toronto, 1981.
– *Thirty-seven Small Songs and Thirteen Silences*. Kentville, NS: Gaspereau
    Press, 2005.
– *Where Have We Been*. Coldstream: Brick Books, 1982.
– *Wisdom & Metaphor*. Kentville, NS: Gaspereau Press, 2003.
– *Wittgenstein Elegies*. London: Brick Books, 1986/2015.

Index

Gray, James, 204–5, 216, 221
Griffin, Scott, 51
Griffin Poetry Prize, 51, 84–5, 128

Harris, Lawren, xii
Harris, Maureen Scott, 85, 215,
    216, 221
Harris, Raymond, 218
Heidegger, Martin, 8, 15, 19, 22,
    36–7, 43, 79–80, 101, 144, 164,
    196
Heiti, Warren, 170, 174, 223
Hensen, Jim, 4, 41
Herakleitos, 92, 101–2, 161
Heriot Ridge, 132, 175, 183
Hölderlin, Friedrich, 10–11, 14
honkabeest, silver, 32–4, 241
House of Anansi Press, xiv, 4,
    19–20, 22, 24–5, 34, 51

incunabula, 77
Indonesia, 117, 119, 132, 230, 232,
    236
Israel Defense Forces, 98–9

Jung, Carl, 158

Kâ-kîsikâw-pîhtokêw (Coming
    Day), 130–1
Kanchenjunga Press, 29, 34, 37,
    100
Kane, Sean, 231

labradorite, 88
Lascaux, 42; dog falls into and dis-
    covers, 42
Lee, Dennis
    ancestry, 5
    Barcelona, 48–9
    breaks through as poet, 17

childhood fascination with
    magic, 7
co-founds House of Anansi Press,
    16
critique of colonialism, 16, 19,
    26–9, 32–4, 46–8
early poems, 11, 13, 14–15
ecological concerns, 48–50
editorial philosophy, 24, 107,
    235–6
Einsteinian space–time, 4, 9, 11,
    13, 40
enrols at Victoria College, 8
helps salvage *The Dark Crystal*,
    41
in high school, 7–8
hired as lecturer at Victoria
    College, 11
joins Rochdale, 15
Labyrinth, 4, 41–2
master's thesis, 11–12
meets Dave Godfrey, 16
meets George Grant, 19
meets Jim Hensen, 41
as playwright, 10
publication of *Alligator Pie*,
    31–2
purchases house in Costa Rica,
    43
Toronto Legacy Project, 50–1
Levinas, Emmanuel, 54, 75, 79,
    80–1, 217
Lévi-Strauss, Claude, 109
lichen, 81, 90, 107
Lilburn, Tim
    ancestors, 186
    childhood, 186–7
    Cree ceremony, 217–21
    digs root cellar, 205
    goat herding, 198

Deeper

by Dennis Lee

Often at night, sometimes
out in the snow or going into the music, the voice says,
"Deeper."
I don't know what it means.
Just, "Push it. Go further. Go deeper."
And when they come talking at me I get
antsy at times, but always the voice keeps saying:
"That is not it. Go deeper."
There is danger in this, also
breakaway hunches and I believe it can issue in
flickers of homing; but I
cannot control it, all I know is the one thing –
"Deeper. You must go further. You must go deeper."

If you are, as I am, a descendant of white settlers, you may be struck by the apparent anomaly of living on land that has been thoroughly colonized, exploited, and mapped, but not yet truly perceived by our forebears or ourselves. The perceptual lenses have been those of colonialism, Romanticism, technology, and Tourism, all of them distortions. The question concerning hereness, or place, remains a live issue. We live in a country we have barely begun to perceive.

Don McKay

From "Know Not"

by Robert Bringhurst

Am I my planet's keeper?
The planet is a creature too –
a giant being dancing on its axis
as it glides around the sun, a kind of
mammoth coral reef of trees and grasses,
dragonflies and chickadees,
creating its own ocean of sweet air.
And she can keep herself just fine,
that dancing planet.
She can keep herself
just fine when no one
pushes her too long, too hard, too far.

But if you've damaged someone badly,
are you not that person's keeper,
nurse, or helper for a time?

Rocky Shore

by Jan Zwicky

Sharp sun and a big northwest wind,
the world a breathless rumpus
underneath. Gulls up,
wheeling high against the light, tide
running fast out in the strait.
Earth with its arms wide open:
uncountable its loves.
Even you. Even me.

Why do people change? People can change because they've been disarmed or caught by the beauty of something. Being in the thrall of beauty is probably the most efficient means of transformation.

Tim Lilburn